CREATING
"GREATER MALAYSIA"

CREATING "GREATER MALAYSIA"

Decolonization and the Politics of Merger

TAN TAI YONG

LSEAS

INSTITUTE OF SOUTHEAST ASIAN STUDIES

Singapore

First published in Singapore in 2008 by
Institute of Southeast Asian Studies
30 Heng Mui Keng Terrace
Pasir Panjang
Singapore 119614
<http://www.bookshop.iseas.edu.sg>

© 2008 Tan Tai Yong

The responsibility for facts and opinions in this publication rests exclusively with the author and his interpretations do not necessarily reflect the views or the policy of the Institute or its supporters.

ISEAS Library Cataloguing-in-Publication Data

Tan Tai Yong.
   Creating "Greater Malaysia" : decolonization and the politics of merger.
   1. Decolonization—Southeast Asia—History.
   2. Malaysia—Politics and government—1963–
   3. Singapore—Politics and government—1963–1965.
   4. Malaysia—Foreign relations—Singapore.
   5. Singapore—Foreign relations—Malaysia.
   I. Title
DS597.2 T77   2008

ISBN 978-981-230-743-9 (soft cover)
ISBN 978-981-230-747-7 (hard cover)

COVER PHOTO: Malaysia Day Celebrations in Singapore, 1963. Reproduced from the MICA collection with kind permission of the National Archives of Singapore.

Typeset by Superskill Graphics Pte Ltd
Printed in Singapore by Utopia Press Pte Ltd

Contents

Preface   vii

Map of British Colonies in Southeast Asia (1946)   x

Map of Malaysia (1963)   xi

Introduction   1

Chapter One   Decolonization and the "Grand Design":
                   Aspects of British Policy in Post-War
                   Southeast Asia   13

Chapter Two   Merger and Greater Malaysia:
                   Political Attitudes towards Union between
                   Singapore and the Federation   29

Chapter Three   Setting the Stage: Tunku's Ulster-type
                   Merger and Singapore's White Paper
                   Proposals   67

Chapter Four   The Citizenship Issue   91

Chapter Five   Financial Arrangements and the
                   Common Market   123

Chapter Six   The Borneo Territories and Brunei   151

Conclusion   189

Bibliography   199

Chronology of Key Events Leading to the Formation of Malaysia   205

Dramatis Personae   209

Index   213

About the Author   224

Preface

This study of the politics of merger between Singapore and Malaysia stems from my on-going interest in the emergence of post-colonial states in the aftermath of empire in Asia. While the formation of Malaysia has attracted the attention of scholars since the late 1960s, the contexts and processes have not been subjected to deep historical analysis that could illuminate the critical decisions that were taken during that episode in the history of Singapore and Malaysia. Although there has been a spate of books dedicated to Singapore's association with Malaysia, none has examined, in detail, the manner in which the deal was constructed by the major parties concerned — British officials on the ground and in Whitehall, the People's Action Party (PAP) government in Singapore and the Alliance leaders at Kuala Lumpur. With the de-classification of official records of the 1960s in the British archives in the past few years, the opportunity has presented itself for historians to dig deeper and to provide a fuller picture of the events of that momentous period — the transition between the end of British rule and Singapore's independence through Malaysia.

My interest in the history of Singapore's independence through merger was further piqued by the publication of the memoirs of Singapore's founding Prime Minister, Lee Kuan Yew in 1998. In volume 1, *The Singapore Story*, Lee recounted Singapore's tumultuous years in Malaysia, culminating in separation in 1965. The story of the failed merger between Singapore and Malaysia has generated excitement from both sides of the causeway, especially on the personalities and issues that had contributed to the break-up. Analysing the contentious and acrimonious relationship between Singapore and Kuala Lumpur between 1963 and 1965, it became apparent that the seeds of dissension had indeed been sown earlier, when the deal was being worked out that would bring Singapore, the Federation of Malaya and the Borneo Territories of North Borneo and Sarawak together to form Malaysia. To understand the difficulties that emerged between 1963 and 1965, it is therefore necessary to take a few steps back — to look into the history of the making of Malaysia — to understand why the new Federation that was constructed in 1963 was fraught with so many innate problems. This study is intended as an analysis in the making of a flawed federation, the important prequel to the story of separation.

In the course of the research and writing of this book, I have benefited from the guidance and support from several colleagues and friends. It was Edwin Lee, former Head of the History Department, who set me on the path by suggesting that I venture beyond my preoccupation with South Asia to explore Singapore's own historical transition from colonial to post-colonial state. As Head, he generously provided me with time to research and write, and it was with his support that I was able to secure a research grant from the National University of Singapore to undertake research in London and Australia. I would like to acknowledge the university's support in this regard. Ernest Chew and Albert Lau, my colleagues in the History Department, encouraged and guided me in the early stages of my research.

I would like to express my gratitude to Mr Pitt Kuan Wah, Director of the National Archives, and his colleagues for facilitating my research through ready access to their archival and oral history collections. Tim Yap Fuan from the Central Library at the National University of Singapore (NUS) has offered constant support by keeping me updated with new publications on Singapore and Malaysia. I am grateful to the Singapore Press Holdings for allowing me use of a number of images from their photograph collections.

In the course of my research I have received timely help from a number of research assistants. I would like to express my thanks to Gabriel Thomas, Claudine Ang and Irene Lim. To Irene, I am especially grateful for her tremendous effort during the final stages of this book. She was able to multi-task admirably, helping with research, bibliographic compilations, proof-reading, and pulling all the loose ends together.

I would like to thank Mr Kesavapany, Director of the Institute of Southeast Asian Studies, for encouraging me to publish this manuscript, and Mrs Triena Ong, for being such a supportive and efficient editor. I am grateful to the three anonymous reviewers, whose constructive comments have helped improve my manuscript. While many people have helped in one way or another to improve this book, the shortcomings in this book remain my sole responsibility.

As always, this book is dedicated to Sylvia, Cheryl and Benjamin.

Tan Tai Yong
August 2007

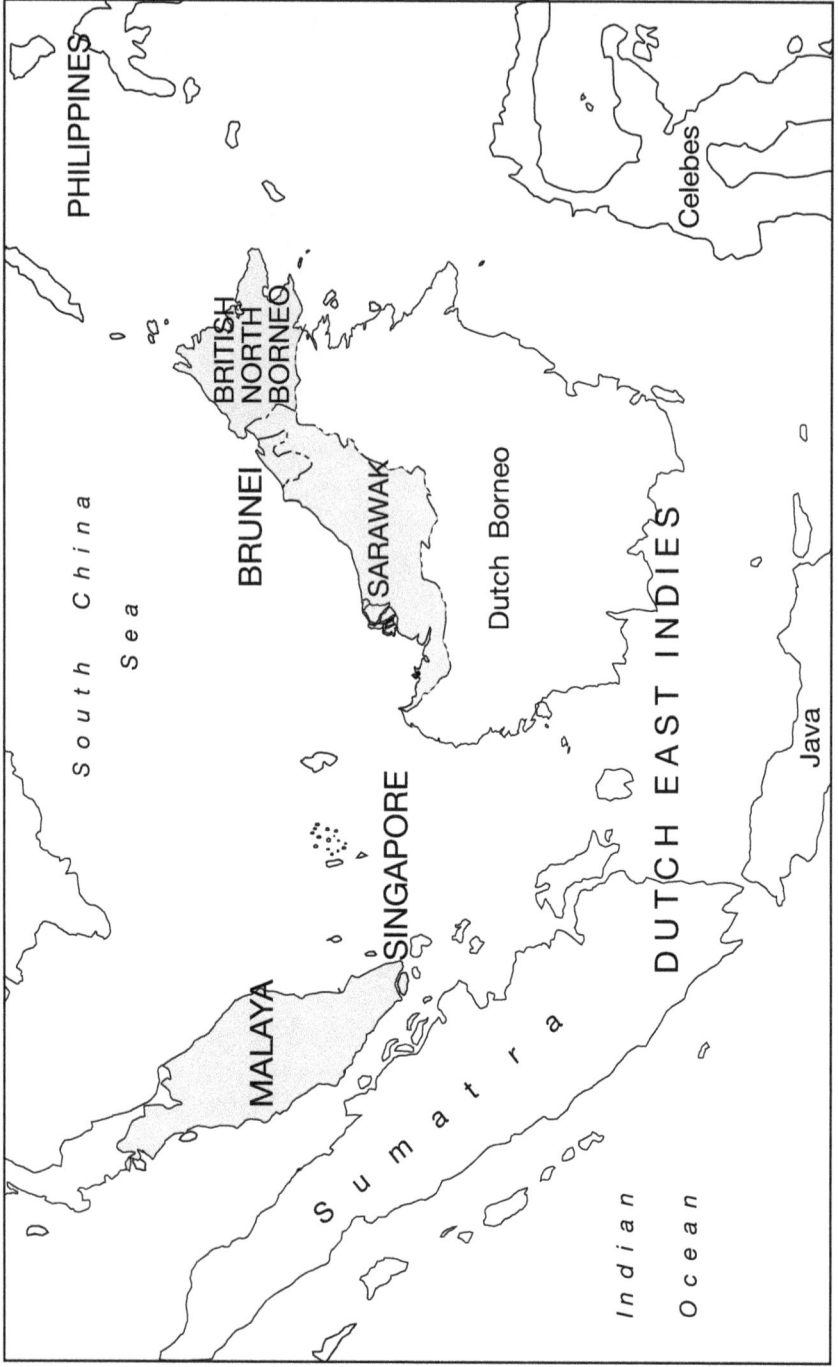

British Colonies in Southeast Asia (1946) (Shaded portions)

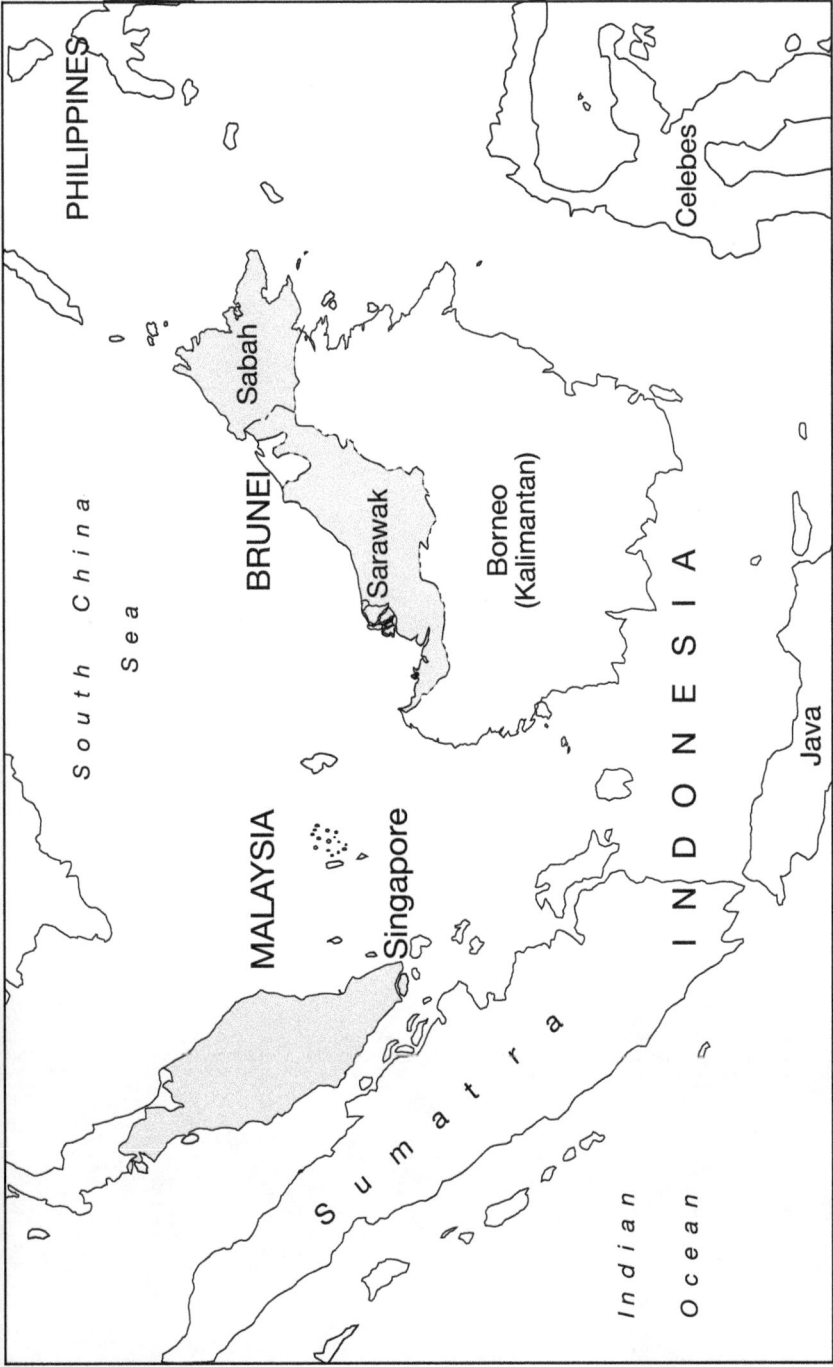

Malaysia (1963) (Shaded portions)

1) Malayan Prime Minister, Tunku Abdul Rahman, addressing the Foreign Correspondents Association of South-East Asia, where he broached the "possibility of bringing the territories of Singapore, North Borneo, Brunei and Sarawak and the Federation of Malaya closer together in political and economic co-operation". [*Courtesy of Singapore Press Holdings*]

2) Delegates from the Federation, North Borneo, Sarawak and Singapore coming together for the first meeting of the Malaysia Solidarity

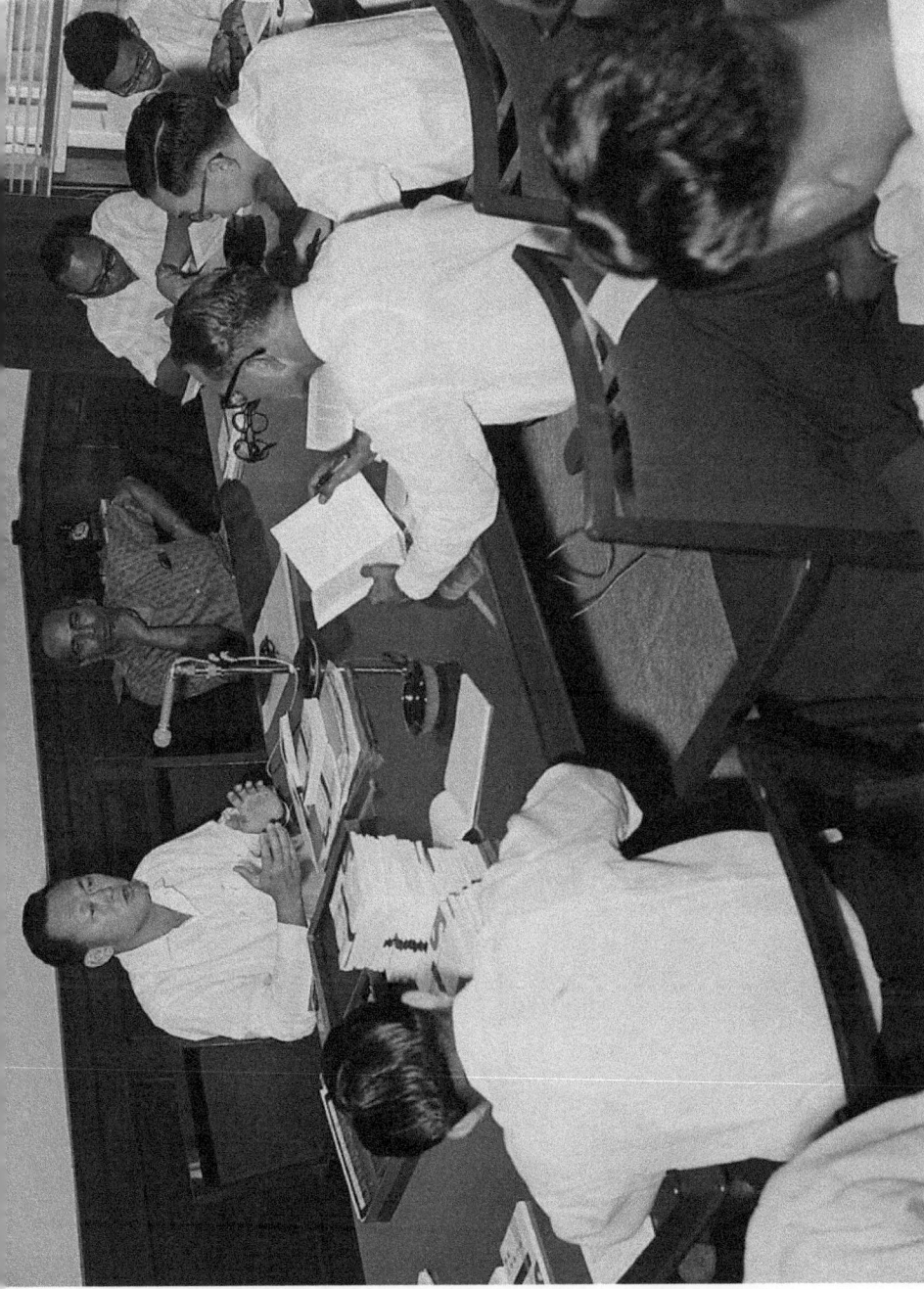

3) Lee Kuan Yew addressing a press conference on Singapore–Malaya merger. On his left is S. Rajaratnam. [*Courtesy of Singapore Press Holdings*]

4) Donald Stephens speaking at the opening meeting of the Malaysia Solidarity Consultative Committee. On his

5) Chairman of the Malaysia Commission of Enquiry, Lord Cobbold arriving in Singapore before leaving for the Borneo Territories (February 1962). [*Courtesy of Singapore Press Holdings*]

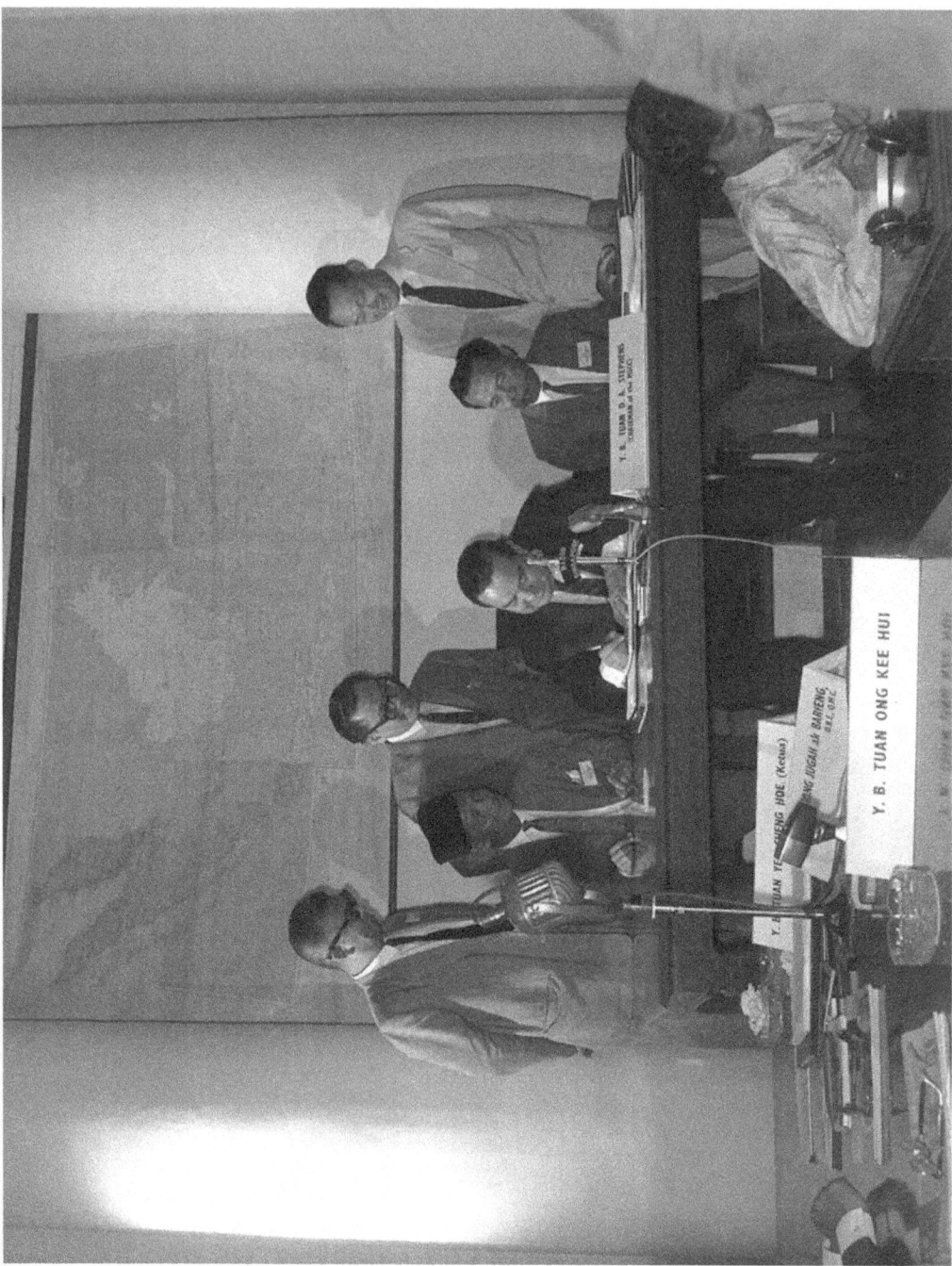

6) Chief delegates from Sarawak, North Borneo, Brunei, Singapore and Malaya signing the Memorandum for Malaysia in

7) Lord Cobbold and other members of the Commission of Enquiry at the Singapore Airport after flying in from Kuching. [*Courtesy of Singapore Press Holdings*]

8) Delegates from North Borneo and Sarawak arriving in Singapore to see Tunku Abdul Rahman off for

9) Tunku Abdul Rahman and Lee Kuan Yew being welcomed at the airport on their return from talks in London (August 1962). [*Courtesy of Singapore Press Holdings*]

11) Lee Siew Choh addressing a Barisan Sosialis rally on the Singapore-Malaysia merger. [*Courtesy of Singapore Press Holdings*]

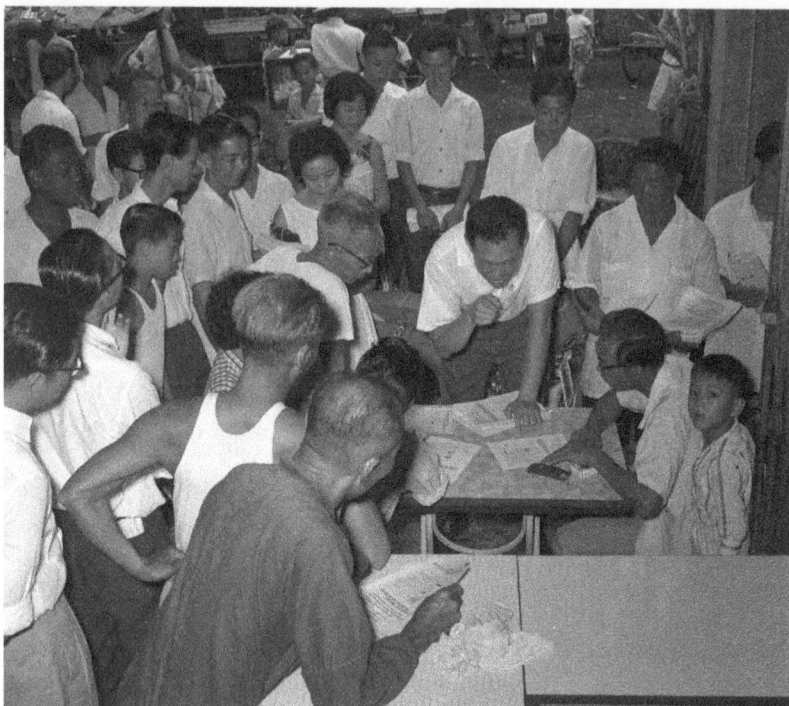

12) Lee Kuan Yew explaining options to voters during the National Referendum on the Singapore-Malaysia merger. [*Courtesy of Singapore Press Holdings*]

13) Lee Siew Choh and David Marshall at a Radio Singapore forum on the merger between Malaya and Singapore. [*Courtesy of Singapore Press Holdings*]

14) Lee Kuan Yew and Goh Keng Swee in a radio debate with members of opposition parties on Singapore–Malaya merger. [*Courtesy of Singapore Press Holdings*]

16) Lee Kuan Yew on a "Thank You" tour of his constituency after victory at the National Referendum polls. [*Courtesy of Singapore Press Holdings*]

17) Lord Selkirk, Commissioner-General for South-east Asia, in Singapore (February 1963). [*Courtesy of Singapore Press Holdings*]

18) The Malaysian flag being raised on 16 September 1963 at the proclamation ceremony in front of City Hall in Singapore. [*Courtesy of Singapore Press Holdings*]

Introduction

In September 1963 Britain ended colonial rule in Singapore, Sarawak and Sabah (North Borneo) by integrating these ethnically distinct states with independent Malaya to form an expanded federation known as Malaysia. The making of Malaysia was an important watershed in the post-war history of Southeast Asia. It marked the formal end of the British Empire in Southeast Asia: Singapore and the Borneo territories of Sarawak and North Borneo (later renamed Sabah) achieved their political independence through merger with Malaya, having been independent since 1957, to constitute the new state of Malaysia. Brunei decided, just before the signing of the Malaysia Agreement, to stay out of the Federation and eventually became a sovereign state on its own. The transfer of sovereignty of the erstwhile British dependencies to the new Federation of Malaysia marked the successful attainment of British policy in post-war Southeast Asia. The British had been able to relinquish their formal empire in Southeast Asia without a major political fall-out in the region, and de-colonization had taken the wind out of the sails of their critics, among them international opinion against imperialism, domestic detractors who complained of the cost, burden and immorality of empire, indigenous nationalists advocating self-determination, as well as anti-imperialist communists. The outcome was indeed a happy one for Britain; its former empire in Southeast Asia had been replaced by a centrally positioned Commonwealth bastion, linking an extensive British strategic and military belt stretching from Aden to New Zealand.

The making of Malaysia, although a relatively small state compared to Indonesia, Thailand and the Philippines in Southeast Asia, represented federation-formation on quite an ambitious scale for it entailed the attempted integration of four very different and disconnected territorial entities — in terms of historical development, ethnic make-up and stages of political and economic development — into a single unified state. The parts that came together "lacked an integrating, pre-colonial core" and the only common experience that they shared was that they had all been subjected to "various forms of British rule".[1] Yet, this was not an attempt at building an expanded nation-state. The Malaysia that came into being in 1963 was a political creation whose only rationale was that it served a convergence of political and economic expediency for the departing colonial power, the Malayan leadership and the ruling party of self-governing Singapore. The new state that was created within a relatively short period was the outcome of a series of decisions taken by British policy-makers and local political leaders from 1960 to 1963 and effectively entailed the attempt at politically grafting Singapore and the Borneo Territories onto the Federation of Malaya. Although the idea of integrating all the British dependencies in Southeast Asia into a super-federation had been talked about in British official circles since the late 1940s, the subject of which came to be known as the "Grand Design", official negotiations on the formation of Malaysia only began in earnest in the middle of 1961. Two years later, in September 1963, the Malaysian Federation, or Greater Malaysia, came into being. The new state was fragmented geographically, and the multi-ethnic diversity of its population made economic, social and political integration a tricky proposition.[2]

The problems of such a contrived and complex exercise in state-building were evident no more than two years after its formation, when Singapore separated from Malaysia in August 1965 under rather acrimonious circumstances. For Singapore, at least, this break-up has been emphasized in school textbooks and political biographies as a major turning point in the narrative of its national history. In his memoirs, Lee Kuan Yew, who probably did more than anyone else in Singapore to secure merger with the Federation of Malaya in 1963, recalls the painful memory of his "moment of anguish" when Singapore separated from Malaysia two years later. Singapore's failure in its quest to be part of a wider Malayan nationalism has ironically become a critical feature underpinning its post-1965 definition of a Singaporean identity. On occasions, the historical interpretations of the reasons and circumstances leading to separation have contributed to the on-and-off relations between Singapore and Malaysia for the past forty years.[3] Fortunately for the rest of Malaysia, Singapore's departure did not trigger a similar reaction from the Sarawak and Sabah components of the Federation, but tensions in the relationship between East Malaysia and Kuala Lumpur were common features of Malaysian political life after 1963.[4]

Malaysia was thus an artificial political creation, the outcome of a concatenation of interests and motives of a number of political actors in Southeast Asia in the early 1960s. This study seeks to examine the various factors and motives that came together to result in the formation of Malaysia. Geo-politics, in the form of post-war international pressures to decolonize, Cold War calculations and security considerations certainly played a part in pushing the impetus for the formation of Malaysia. It has been suggested that the formation of Malaysia was a masterstroke orchestrated by London and its successful outcome had allowed the British to perpetuate their hold (albeit in an indirect manner) on the region. This view argued that the transformation of the erstwhile British colonies in Southeast Asia into a new Commonwealth state was indeed a remarkable feat of British de-colonization in the 1960s. In Malaya the British were able to conspire with the local élite that they had created to establish a post-colonial entity in Southeast Asia that would continue to maintain British commercial and strategic interests in the region. To this, the British attached the tiny island-colony of Singapore, solving the security issue of an island about to go 'red' by rescuing the non-communist People's Action Party (PAP) government through merger with Malaya. In the process the British were able to preserve the important strategic bases in Singapore well into the 1970s. At the same time, the British, in a single stroke, managed to solve the problems of the politically "under-developed" territories in North Borneo by allowing them to de-colonize as part of the Malaysian state, preventing them from falling into the hands of Indonesia and the Philippines which had long laid claims to them. Indeed, Malaysia worked so well that it came to be argued that the new state represented a very successful attempt by the British to impose a form of neo-colonialism in Southeast Asia.[5]

This view has since been challenged. While the idea of Malaysia appeared to be the culmination of an expressed British objective of regional consolidation, A.J. Stockwell and others have pointed out that in reality, "Britain lacked the power locally to secure control over its continuing interests in the post-colonial period".[6] The inspiration and initiative for Malaysia, Stockwell maintains, came from the Federation and Singapore, and that Britain merely "followed their lead, but never commanded the heights from which it might assert mastery over the planning and execution of the 'Grand Design'".[7] Karl Hack asserts that "the reason for federation ... had much to do with local developments, little to do with British plotting".[8] Reflecting on events when he was the United Kingdom High Commissioner of Singapore and British Commissioner in Southeast Asia, Lord Selkirk recounted that:

> Whitehall in fact took no initiative until the Federation had been proposed, first in private and then in public, by the Prime Minister of Malaya and immediately supported by the Prime Minister of Singapore....It was only after the proposals had been endorsed by all the territories concerned that Whitehall gave its full cooperation to the establishment of the Federation and sought to make it a success.[9]

The British 'Grand Design' notwithstanding, regional and local developments were instrumental in bringing about Malaysia. The role of the Malayan Prime Minister, Tunku Abdul Rahman, in this enterprise was fundamental. On 27 May 1961, at a luncheon meeting at the Adelphi Hotel in Singapore, the Tunku, who had previously objected to the idea of taking the Chinese majority state of Singapore into the Federation, sounded the possibility of bringing the territories of Singapore, Borneo, Brunei and Sarawak and the Federation of Malaya "closer together in political and economic co-operation". Although the idea of a union between Malaya and the Borneo states had been current in UMNO circles from about 1956, and was already well-established by 1960,[10] this public announcement by the Malayan Prime Minister has often been taken as the genesis of the Malaysia idea, which saw its fruition two years later, in September 1963. The main reason for the Tunku's initiative was essentially political: he had to overcome his earlier reluctance for merger with Singapore in an attempt to avoid the risk of having a "Cuba in his Malayan backyard".[11] He had come to accept that an independent Chinese-dominated Singapore, which might become increasingly oriented towards Peking, would be a greater danger to Malaya than a Singapore, which, if brought into the Federation, he could exercise some control over. Years after the event, the Tunku admitted that he had also harboured the romantic notion of his newly independent Malayan Federation offering a natural beacon of freedom, attracting the other still colonized states in the region to come into association with it as the way towards freedom. As he recalled in 1975

> Merdeka brought such happy years to Malaya, such peace, progress and prosperity, that it was only natural that other States in the region, which were still 'British' should look towards Kuala Lumpur, the glint of freedom in their eyes, thinking of ways to come into closer association.[12]

Such a view may have been indicative of an elder statesman reminiscing personal glories in the twilight of his political career, but it does generate the impression that Greater Malaysia was borne out of the initiative and will of the Tunku. Yet the Tunku was never an advocate of merger with Singapore and had resisted the move until 1961, when he was finally convinced that unless he acted, Singapore would turn communist and the contamination would spread both to the Malayan peninsula and through Indonesia to the Borneo Territories. And even after his momentous announcement in May 1961, he had changed his mind several times, and on many occasions during the difficult negotiations leading to the agreement, he threatened to pull off the deal. If the Tunku believed that Britain could remain in charge of Singapore as long as the communist threat remained, he would never have agreed to merger with Singapore. But he understood that the British Government would not be able, or willing, to resist for long Singapore's demand for independence. The Tunku was therefore clearly not interested in having Singapore; the real prize he was after was the Borneo Territories, and Singapore was the price he had to pay to secure it.

The inclusion of Singapore was essentially motivated by security considerations, and its 'special' place and position in the new state of Malaysia was to reflect the circumstances in which the Tunku had agreed to take Singapore into the Federation. It also informed the urgency and imperative of a Greater Malaysia that would incorporate the Borneo Territories. Cheah Boon Kheng has argued that the most significant consideration for Malaysia from the Tunku's point of view was the ethnic factor. An enlarged federation of Malaysia, incorporating the Borneo Territories, would ensure that Malays and "natives of Malaya would always outnumber the Chinese, Indians and 'non-natives', 'non-Malay' population".[13] The Tunku's real design was to secure the integration of the Borneo Territories (more specifically Sarawak and Brunei) into the Malayan Federation.[14] The motivation may have been political and economic, an expanded Federation that would have a huge reserve of natural resources, but it also stemmed from the Malayan leader's desire to ensure that the Malaysian Federation would stay a Malay or indigenous majority state. It did not matter that the indigenous races in the Borneo Territories did not consider themselves akin to the Malays of the Federation; as far as the Tunku was concerned, they would assimilate more easily than the Chinese. There was clearly no cultural or social basis for the state; Malaysia was strictly a product of political expediencies.

The period leading up to merger was a fundamental turning point in the political history of Singapore. This was also a period of political plurality in which several different visions of Singapore's political future contested one another in the political arena. The political awakening, in many ways triggered by the prospects of 'independence through merger', saw the rise of the People's Action Party (PAP), whose leader, Lee Kuan Yew, was a tireless champion for merger with Malaya. In the first volume of his memoirs, *The Singapore Story,* Lee offers a fascinating account of the PAP's battles for merger. Lee's account, derived from memory as a key participant in the events that unfolded during that period as well as from contemporary documents, offers a version of the country's freedom struggle, and it emphasized his committed belief (and justified his actions) that independence through merger was the only means by which the political and security threat of communism could be defeated and the economic future of Singapore assured. Lee Kuan Yew and the PAP thus cut their political teeth during the political battles for merger, domestically with their bitter rivals the Barisan Socialis (Socialist Front, hereafter BS), and through persistent and often acrimonious negotiations with a reluctant government in Kuala Lumpur to effect merger. The battles for merger had to be fought on a number of fronts, for Lee not only had to defeat his domestic detractors, but had to contend with British anxiety and Malayan mistrust as well. The colony eventually obtained political independence from the British by joining the Malaysian Federation, in the process entrenching the power and position of the PAP as the dominant political party in Singapore. Some had thought, in 1965, that the short-lived Malaysia was but a pyrrhic victory for Lee and the PAP. These doubters were proved wrong. By 1963, the defeat of the political opponents of the ruling party had indeed been thorough, and the PAP's position, considerably strengthened as a consequence, was maintained despite separation from Malaysia two years later. In this respect, the story of Singapore's road to nationhood must therefore be understood in the context of its major detour through Malaysia.

Despite the Tunku's May 1961 announcement and the enthusiasm expressed in Singapore for a merger, the deal was, at that point in time, far from done. What followed from the announcement was a complex exercise involving complicated negotiations of the terms by which Singapore would merge with the Malayan Federation as well as the intricate manoeuvrings through which the Borneo Territories were cajoled into joining Malaysia. The detailed negotiations revealed that local politics, and locality specific interests — social, economic, political and ethnic — all of which were quite varied, complicated the progress towards and created problems for the constitutional agreement that would result in the formation of the Federation of Malaysia. In the upshot, Malaysia was ultimately an "uneasy agreement",[15] the outcome of a series of compromises among its constituent parts. In all this, without the role of an "honest broker", played admirably by key British ministers and officials in the region, the Malaysian enterprise, beset as it was by doubts, disagreements, and distrusts, would have been aborted at an early stage. Selkirk might thus have understated the role played by the British when he asserted that the initiative and driving force were mainly the Tunku's. British policy thus had to be considered alongside the local dynamics which contributed in no small measure to the form and content of the Malaysia that eventually emerged. This study intends to demonstrate the interplay between high policy (of decolonization) and the dynamics of local politics in the processes that led to the formation of Malaysia.

The broad storyline on the formation of Malaysia is relatively well-trodden ground. Many of the early accounts were written by political scientists and contemporary commentators fascinated by the emergence of a new political entity in Southeast Asia. Relying mainly on secondary sources and newspaper reports, these publications were but broad descriptions of the events that led to 1963, when the Federation of Malaysia was formed. The interest in the new state was eventually overshadowed by the greater absorption with the story of Singapore's separation from the Federation just two years after the new state was heralded.[16] In a similar manner, the national histories of Singapore and Malaysia carried the inevitable episode of merger and separation, but these accounts often treated the Greater Malaysia episode in a cursory manner, as a glitch in a dominant national narrative. Without the benefit of archival documents that could throw light on the thinking and actions of the major players as well as the wider context against which the events were unfolding during those critical years, these standard accounts of Malaysia's formation, most of them published in the 1960s, could not offer anything beyond a broad recounting of the main events and issues that led up to Malaysia.[17] In the 1980s, the story of merger was recounted in the autobiographies of key political actors who lived through that period. The memoirs of the Tunku, Ghazali Shafie and Lee Kuan Yew offered useful insights, but these personal recollections often reflected individual views and perspectives and were not always complete or comprehensive. In the 1990s, when archival records were gradually declassified in the London archives, historians have begun using these documents to construct more detailed accounts of the key events of the 1960s, and a number of useful analyses of aspects of the formation of Malaysia have since been written. In this regard, the works of Anthony Stockwell and Matthew Jones are especially noteworthy, although they focus mainly on the perspectives of British policy-makers.[18] Building on these earlier works, and utilizing recently de-classified documentary materials from London as well as oral interviews from some of the principal participants in Singapore and Malaysia, this study challenges the views that Malaysia was a done deal the moment the Tunku made his announcement in May 1961 by providing a detailed and in-depth analysis of the intricate processes involved in the making of Greater Malaysia. By moving beyond the simple expansionist-security explanations of the motives behind Malaysia, this study seeks to historicize the formation of Malaysia in the contexts of decolonization, domestic power struggles (especially in Singapore) and state-building. It addresses a fundamental question: how and why did merger take the shape and form that it did in 1963? The manner and timing in which the Federation of Malaysia came into being were instrumental in defining the character and content of the new state as well as creating the fault-lines that were inherent in its political structures. Subsumed under this larger question are a series of related questions: how did the Federation of Malaysia serve the purposes and interests of these disparate territories and the main political actors there — Malaya, Singapore, and the Borneo Territories — each with their own special conditions and interests? Did these diverse interests explain why the form of merger that was effected between Singapore and Malaya was substantially different from the arrangements that were made between the Borneo Territories and the Federation? How did one set of agreements and arrangements affect the other? In a way, the Federation was incomplete without Brunei. Why did it happen in that way? Did the terms of merger, especially between Singapore and Malaya, sow the seeds of subsequent dissension that led to the eventual failure of merger in less than two years? It is these questions, and the intricate processes of negotiations and positioning among the main actors, that this book is concerned about.

The opening chapter of this book will explore British policies in post-war Southeast Asia, with emphasis on the so called "Grand Design", the plan to integrate the disparate dependencies into a single political entity as a precursor to self-government and political independence for these colonies. British plans depended on local conditions and Chapter Two explains how local politics in Singapore and Malaysia dove-tailed with British interests to lead to a concrete expression of the intention to create Malaysia. However, divergent interests between the two countries necessitated the adoption of special conditions for merger — the Ulster Model — that was effected between Malaya and Singapore. Chapters Four and Five deal with the complicated negotiations revolving around two key issues — citizenship and financial arrangements — that threatened at different times to derail the Malaysia Plan. Chapter Six explores and explains how the Borneo Territories were brought into Malaysia. The ease with which this was facilitated stood in stark contrast to the tricky negotiations that plagued the negotiations between Singapore and the Federation. It also seeks to explain why and how Brunei managed to stay out of Malaysia at the final hour.

NOTES

1   Anthony J. Stockwell, "Forging Malaysia and Singapore: Colonialism, Decolonisation and Nation-Building", in Wang Gungwu, ed., *Nation-Building: Five Southeast Asian Histories* (Singapore: Institute of Southeast Asian Studies, 2005), pp. 192–93.

2   See Cheah Boon Kheng, *Malaysia: The Making of a Nation* (Singapore: Institute of Southeast Asian Studies, 2002), p. 93.

3   See, for instance, some Malaysian reactions to an account by Singapore historian, Albert Lau, on the circumstances leading to Singapore's separation from Malaysia in *A Moment of Anguish* (Singapore: Times Academic Press, 1998).

4   Cheah, *Malaysia*, p. 93.

5   See Anthony J. Stockwell, "Malaysia: The Making of a Neo-Colony?", *Journal of Imperial and Commonwealth History* 26, no. 2 (1998): 141.

6   Ibid., p. 152.

7   Stockwell, "Malaysia", p. 152.

8   Karl Hack, *Defence and Decolonisation in Southeast Asia: Britain, Malaya and Singapore, 1941–1968* (Richmond: Curzon, 2001), p. 275. See also Matthew Jones, "Creating Malaysia: Singapore Security, the Borneo Territories, and the Contours of British Policy, 1961–63", *Journal of Imperial and Commonwealth History* 28, no. 2 (2000): 85–109.

9   Cited from a letter written by Lord Selkirk to *The Times* (London) in 1965, as quoted by John Drysdale, *Singapore: Struggle for Success* (Singapore: Times Book International, 1984), p. 259.

10   Mohamed Noordin Sopiee, *From Malayan Union to Singapore Separation: Political*

Unification in the Malaysian Region, 1945–1965 (Kuala Lumpur: Universiti Malaya, 1974), p. 128.

11 See Mohammed Noordin Sopiee, "The Advocacy of Malaysia — Before 1961", *Modern Asian Studies* 7, no. 4 (1973): 717–32.

12 Tunku Abdul Rahman, "Formation of Malaysia: The Trend Towards Merger Cannot be Reversed", in *Looking Back: Monday Musings and Memories* (Kuala Lumpur: Pustaka Antara, 1977), p. 77.

13 Cheah, *Malaysia*, p. 93.

14 Noordin Sopiee refers to this explanation as the expansionist theory on the formation of Malaysia. See Sopiee, "The Advocacy of Malaysia — Before 1961", p. 719.

15 Stockwell, "Forging Malaysia and Singapore", p. 207.

16 See, for example, Michael Leifer, "Singapore in Malaysia: The Politics of Federation", *Journal of Southeast Asian History* 6, no. 2 (1965): 54–70, and R.S. Milne, "Singapore's Exit from Malaysia: The Consequences of Ambiguity", *Asian Survey* 6, no. 3 (1966): 175–84.

17 See, for instance, Willard A. Hanna, *The Formation of Malaysia: New Factor in World Politics: An analytical history and assessment of the prospects of the newest state in Southeast Asia, based on a series of reports written for the American Universities Field Staff* (New York: American Field Staff, 1964); and Milton E. Osborne, *Singapore and Malaysia* (New York: Cornell University, 1969).

18 See, for example, Anthony J. Stockwell, "Malaysia: The Making of a Grand Design", *Asian Affairs* 24, no. 3 (2003): 227–42; Anthony J. Stockwell, "Britain and Brunei 1945–63: Imperial retreat and royal ascendancy", *Modern Asian Studies* 38, no. 4 (2004): 785–820; Matthew Jones, "Creating Malaysia: Singapore's Security, the Borneo Territories and the Contours of British Policy, 1961–63", *Journal of Imperial and Commonwealth History* 28, no. 2 (2000): 61–86.

CHAPTER ONE

Decolonization and the "Grand Design": Aspects of British Policy in Post-War Southeast Asia

The process of decolonization that began in Asia in the aftermath of World War II was brought about by a combination of post-bellum political and economic fatigue in the European capitals, a dramatically altered post-war international landscape, and the rise of indigenous nationalisms across the region, in many instances spawned and spurred by the defeat of the European powers at the hands of Japan. The ease with which the European powers capitulated to a non-white, Asian power during the war effectively shattered the image of western superiority in the eyes of the subject peoples and unravelled the pre-war social and political order in the colonies. The ensuing social and economic disruption brought about by occupation left a deep political and psychological impression on the local populace in Asia. While the occupied populations often bore the brunt of Japanese brutality and resisted Japan's own imperial ambitions, the idea of Asian liberation from western imperialism caught the imagination of many nationalist groups in the region.[1] The ties which had bound Europe to its empire in the region had been swept away, and under Japanese sponsorship indigenous nationalist leaders found renewed energy and opportunities to attack and undermine the old colonial system to widen their own bases of support. This was to signal the beginning of the end of the European empires in Asia. When the European powers returned to their erstwhile colonies after the War, hoping to "rediscover the grandeur of an imperial past", they were faced with a very different reality.[2] The Dutch lost their empire in the East Indies in the wake of a revolutionary movement which started in 1945 and ended five years later with the declaration of an independent state of Indonesia in 1949. The French faced determined opposition from the revolutionary communist Viet Minh forces, and after a protracted struggle had to leave their empire in Indochina in 1954 under rather ignominious circumstances. British decolonization in South Asia was effected in a more peaceful and orderly manner; in 1947, power was transferred to the independent states of India and Pakistan with Sri Lanka and Burma following a year later.

Britain was quick to relinquish its hold on the Indian subcontinent because the Indian empire had seemingly lost its economic and strategic value, and holding on to it, with all its attendant political and social problems, would exact too heavy a political price while imposing an unbearable burden on the national treasury. At the end of World War II, Britain had come to accept that the jewel of the imperial crown had lost its lustre and Prime Minister Clement Attlee had made the liquidation of the Indian empire a key priority when his Labour party came to power in 1945. The retreat from India did not, however, suggest that Britain was about to relinquish its position as a world power and retire from empire. Indeed, in the Southeast Asian colonies, which were still critical for Britain's global interests and responsibilities, the plan was to stay on for an indefinite period of time. Malaya was especially valuable because it was the world's primary producer of rubber and tin, both critical dollar earners for the Sterling area[3] while Singapore's command of the vital sea-lanes of the Indian Ocean, South China Seas and the Southern Pacific made it a critical lynchpin of Britain's long-term security considerations and defence obligations in the region, especially in relation to Australia and New Zealand.[4] Self-government for these territories, if at all contemplated in the late 1940s, would have to take on a more gradual and drawn-out approach. When the British returned to their empire in Southeast Asia in 1945, their first aims were thus to re-establish security and stability in the region, to create the necessary conditions for rehabilitation and economic revival. In pursuing these objectives, British policy-makers attempted, for the purposes of policy-coordination, security pacts and economic collaboration, to adopt a regional approach.[5] While each colony presented its own problems and challenges, and had to be managed on its own terms, British policy sought to treat each part not in isolation but as they related to each other, and to wider regional considerations. It was understood that a collective, regional approach would best serve Britain's interests in Southeast Asia and beyond.

British post-war intentions in Southeast Asia thus revolved around a desire towards the consolidation of the disparate dependencies in the region, a long-held objective of the British Government. Indeed, when the British re-occupied their dependencies in the region after the War, a structure for regional cooperation was created in the office of the governor-general (later commissioner-general) of Southeast Asia. This aimed at setting the direction and creating the necessary conditions for the eventual establishment of a unified "British dominion of Southeast Asia".[6] This was not a plan that emerged only in the aftermath of the War, for as early as 1942 the Colonial Office and Foreign Office had agreed that once the War was over an eventual union of the Malay states, Straits Settlements and the Borneo Territories would be a desirable policy objective for the region. Throughout the 1940s and early 1950s, as the British contemplated the long-term future of the region the overall plan, it seemed, was that eventual self-government would not be apportioned to the territories individually, but in blocs.[7] In April 1955, Malcolm MacDonald, Britain's Commissioner-General of Southeast Asia, enunciated the approach:

> Our ultimate objective is a Confederation between the five present territories of the Federation of Malaya, Singapore, Sarawak, North Borneo and Brunei. We have already agreed that this should be achieved in two stages: first by a combination of (a) Singapore and the Federation and (b) the three Borneo Territories as separate entities; and second, by bring [sic] together these two groups under one appropriate constitutional government.[8]

Developments in the aftermath of the War and subsequent events slowed the momentum towards territorial consolidation. At times, it seemed that the idea of a "dominion of Southeast Asian territories", despite the best efforts of Malcolm MacDonald, was nothing more than a distant dream.

While the separation of Singapore from Malaya in 1946, a decision that was "deeply regretted in many quarters", was never regarded by policy-makers as permanent,[9] political developments in both colonies had made increasingly remote the future fusion of the two territories. The immediate British post-war plan for a Malayan Union in 1946, with its provisions of liberal citizenship for non-Malays and the intention to end the sovereignty of the Malay rulers, encountered vociferous opposition from the Malay political community. Malay nationalism was stirred, giving rise to the emergence of Malaya's first Malay political party, the United Malays National Organisation (UMNO). The British adroitly handled the crisis by replacing the ill-fated Malayan Union with the Malayan Federation in 1948. The political compromise that resulted in the Federation, which constitutionally re-asserted the special rights of the Malays, gave rise to a nascent "nation-state" that was based on the political primacy of the Malays over the other races, allowing the Malay leadership "to set the pace and agenda for the creation of a new Malay state".[10] The communal politics that emerged during that uproar against the Malayan Union Plan and its aftermath pushed Singapore, with its overwhelming Chinese population, further adrift from the Malayan hinterland. The outbreak of a communist-led insurrection in 1948 in Malaya, believed to be backed in large part by a discontented Chinese population, further deepened suspicion among Malay leaders of radical Chinese politics which was seen to be rife in Singapore. By the 1950s, as Malaya moved towards independence on its own, the idea of taking Singapore back into the Federation had become anathema to the conservative Malay leadership of UMNO. The growing influence of a pro-communist movement and the radicalization of labour and student politics in Singapore caused deep concern among the Malayan leaders. Witnessing the growing incidence of Chinese middle school riots and trade union protests in Singapore in the 1950s, the Malayan Government was convinced that embracing Singapore would only compound their political problems in the Federation.

The situation in the Borneo territories presented its own set of issues. There, political and economic backwardness of the territories, coupled with Brunei's intransigent stance against any form of integration with Sarawak and North Borneo, obstructed progress towards the amalgamation of these territories into a single bloc. North Borneo, which was governed by a chartered company since 1881, became a crown colony in 1946. In a similar way, Sarawak assumed colony status after the Brooke *rajahs*, who ruled the territory from 1841 to 1946, ceded power to the Crown after the Japanese War. Under their previous administrations, political organizations and activities in both North Borneo and Sarawak were virtually absent, although the latter did experience political agitation among Malay groups opposed to the cession in 1946. Local governments, political debates, political parties and elections were non-existent in either territory until the late 1950s. It was thought almost impossible that these territories, with small populations comprising different cultures and undeveloped political systems and economies, would make viable states. The local conditions thus encouraged the British to look to a federal arrangement, as was done in Central Africa and the West Indies, to ensure the security and economic viability to this group of small, disparate dependencies in North Borneo, an idea that had been canvassed since 1945 by officials in the Colonial Office and in the Borneo Territories. The intention notwithstanding, practical difficulties on the ground militated against a firm partnership of the Borneo territories. Limited administrative cooperation among the three territories (in geology survey, judiciary and aviation) were started by the British but political development towards forms of self-government and political organization was still at a nascent stage. To complicate matters, the Sultan of Brunei was especially reluctant to subject his kingdom to any form of political control from Sarawak, and was not about to agree to any arrangement that would lead to a distribution of his oil wealth with the neighbouring states. In 1956, he publicly rejected the idea of a Borneo federation.

Despite these developments and setbacks, the British did not abandon their eventual objective of regional consolidation. As the British pondered the future of their colonies in Southeast Asia, the idea of forming a wider federation of the colonial territories anchored on the Malayan Federation never lost its appeal. The idea became more salient as Southeast Asia became a hotbed of Cold War tensions and great power rivalry following the emergence of communist China in 1949. Political problems in Burma,

Vietnam and Indonesia further reinforced the belief that Southeast Asia was on the verge of turning communist, with frightening consequences for British (and western) interests in the region and the security of Australia and New Zealand. The logic behind territorial consolidation of its dependencies became increasingly compelling: a Southeast Asia that was facing such uncertainties could do well with a stable pro-British core on which British strategic and economic interests could be secured even after the formal decolonization of the region. Still, throughout the 1950s, the idea was bandied around without concrete progress.[11] In any case, no plans detailing the timing or manner of the withdrawal of the British from the region were ever laid out or submitted as a firm policy proposal to Whitehall. While British policy-makers spoke about the possibility of amalgamating their territories in conferences discussing the future of British territories in Southeast Asia, the plan that came to be known as the "Grand Design" never obtained focussed official consideration in London until the late 1950s.

The Grand Design gained an added degree of currency and urgency in British circles in the late 1950s, fuelled essentially by the concerns about the political future of Singapore, especially in the wake of Malaya's independence in 1957. Following the constitutional talks in London in 1957, Singapore was headed towards self-government but the issue of the security of the bases was still unresolved. British prognosis on the future of the Singapore base was relatively bleak. London had hoped that as Singapore progressed towards self-government and eventual independence, it would be governed by a moderate pro-British government that would ensure the security and accessibility of British bases there. However, if the communists were to gain political ground, as they were showing signs of doing in the 1950s, the British would lose their hold on this prized strategic asset in Southeast Asia, with possible dire consequences for the security of the region, as well as Australia and New Zealand. The only way to secure the bases, so the British reasoned, was to ensure that Singapore would not turn "red" and the best way of "guaranteeing" this was to make sure that Singapore became part of the staunchly anti-communist Malaya. The Defence establishment in London, however, had their doubts about such an arrangement and were concerned that Singapore's integration with Malaya would restrict British access to and use of the military base.[12] The Chiefs of Staff argued that the "run-down of British presence in Singapore would discourage friends and allies",[13] and that since Malaya was already an independent country there was no guarantee that the government in Kuala Lumpur, once they had secured Singapore, would continue to do the bidding of the British. Secretary of State for Air, Julian Amery, was of the view that "Singapore's integration within Malaysia would place intolerable limitations on Britain's use of the base".[14] Differences of opinion about the desirability of having the Singapore base under Malaysian control did not, however, diminish the eventual conclusion that "the Grand Design was the least harmful of the possible developments".[15] A merger between Singapore and the Federation, and the subsequent incorporation of the Borneo Territories, which were considered too "backward to survive on their own in the Cold War",[16] would do much, according to the calculations of British officials in the region, to secure a key area in Southeast Asia.

In the prevailing milieu of rising nationalism and growing assertions of local independence in the late 1950s, the British knew that their intentions had to be tempered by the concurrence and support of local leaders in the territories. As Anthony Stockwell explains, while the British occasionally "stimulated local interest in the concept... they knew it would be counter-productive to impose a scheme or issue a directive ... and steadfastly refrained from forcing the pace".[17] The ultimate amalgamation of the British territories in Southeast Asia would only happen when the political and economic conditions were deemed "right".[18]

As the British took soundings from the ground, they encountered a range of reactions to the idea of territorial consolidation. The most enthusiastic response came from Singapore where political opinions were strongly in favour of an eventual re-merger with Malaya, with most political parties agreeing that the colony's political and economic future depended on a return to Malaya. In 1957, Brunei's attitude notwithstanding, local opinion in Sarawak and the North Borneo Territories came out openly, if mildly, in favour of some form of closer association and of the need for more discussion in the territories to explore the idea further. As local political awareness in the territories was limited to small groups of urban élites, this enthusiasm was largely generated by British officials on the spot. Although they had not given firm direction on the policy to be pursued there,[19] the Commissioner-General in Southeast Asia, Robert Scott, and the Governors of Sarawak and North Borneo, Anthony Abell and Roland Turnbull respectively, called for the initiative to be considered seriously and tried to encourage local discussions on the issue of integration. They were convinced that eventually these territories would only be politically and economically viable states if they were part of some wider association.[20] There were also concerns that the territories were individually very vulnerable "both because of their geographical position and their racial make-up",[21] which made it easy for "powerful neighbours like China, Indonesia and the Philippines … to easily work up interests of one kind or another".[22] Sarawak's Chinese community was considered to be especially vulnerable to communist subversion and a clandestine Communist organization was known to be particularly active in the territory.[23] The nascent political organizations in North Borneo and Sarawak were receptive to British persuasions and agreed to explore the options. As the momentum on the ground gathered, the Secretary of State for the Colonies, Alan Lennox-Boyd, decided to authorize the governors of Sarawak and North Borneo to initiate public discussion on the closer association of their territories despite having personal reservations that the creation of a larger political unit "might stimulate the growth of nationalist parties and pressure for independence".[24] The potential dangers notwithstanding, a movement towards federation was seen as a necessary counter to the greater threat of separatism that was inherent in the existing situation. Officials were thus tasked to pursue the policy tentatively, and to ensure Brunei's participation, for without its oil wealth the association would not be feasible.[25] The Sultan of Brunei, unconvinced with the need for integration, shied away from talks.[26]

The least enthusiastic of the lot were the Malayans. The staunchly right wing leader of the UMNO, Tunku Abdul Rahman, was deeply distrustful of Singapore politics and was strongly opposed to merge with the island colony, fearing that this would lead to an influx of leftist Chinese into the Federation.[27] Not only was there opposition from his Malay heartland but his Chinese partners in the Malayan alliance government were similarly disinclined towards merger with Singapore.[28] The Malayan leadership was realistic enough to realize that the Singapore problem was not likely to go away, and that they would be subject to British and American pressures to play a part in securing the Singapore base. In private conversations, Malay leaders indicated readiness to keep the merger option open, but stated that future progress on this front would depend on the politics in Singapore returning to a state of "normalcy", and the possibility of incorporating Brunei, Borneo and Sarawak into a "Greater Federation".[29]

Within the British establishment, there was finally concurrence from the various departments in Whitehall on the desirability of the Grand Design. Duncan Sandys, Secretary for Commonwealth Relations, John Profumo, Secretary for Defence, and Louis Mountbatten, Chief of British Defence Staff and Admiral of the Fleet, had visited Singapore and Malaya in 1959 and following firsthand observations of the political conditions in the territories agreed that the idea was worth pursuing because local politicians were keen on the idea. By 1960, the Grand Design was very much on the cards.

In pursuing this policy, it was clear that politics and security were foremost considerations. Only through a greater Malaysia were the British confident of granting self-government status to the Borneo Territories and Singapore; the Grand Design would produce a satisfactory solution to the problem of the future constitutional status of the three Borneo Territories as well as Singapore. A stable federation would reduce the dangers that smaller units might be affected piecemeal by subversive elements from within or outside their borders. Most importantly, the British viewed the formation of an anti-communist super federation, and the securing of the Singapore base, as the surest way to provide stability in Southeast Asia and therefore minimizing their internal security obligations in the region.[30] Commonwealth links — involving the defence of Malaya, Australia, New Zealand and Hong Kong — as well as British relations with the United States, especially in the context of the Cold War in Asia, would be enhanced through this initiative. Political stability would provide the necessary conditions for economic development, which in turn would foster trade between the west and Asia. The Grand Design for a Greater Malaysia would maintain British influence in post-colonial Southeast Asia, allowing her to maintain her position in the world and yet keep the balance of payments healthy and defence costs down.

By the late 1950s, strategic interests, more than economic benefits, shaped British thinking about their position in Southeast Asia. Cold War and the containment of communism, defence and security obligations in the region, and Anglo-American relations dominated policy thinking about the future of Southeast Asia.[31] Although the Indonesian factor was not mentioned in official papers discussing the Grand Design, perhaps the allegation that this was part of an Anglo-American conspiracy to contain the revolutionary politics of Sukarno's Indonesia from spreading to other parts of Southeast Asia was not far off the mark.[32] Not unexpectedly, the Indonesian President was a vocal critic of the scheme, arguing that Greater Malaysia was a neo-colonial plot aimed at maintaining Britain's economic and political stranglehold in the region even after they have constitutionally relinquished their territories in the region. The economic value of the Grand Design was however less obvious. By 1960, rubber and tin were no longer essential to British balance of payments, and the balance sheet for the region indicated that more money was spent for political reasons "rather than for any prospect of financial gain".[33] As Stockwell and others have shown, while British businesses continued to dominate the trade in Southeast Asia, the region's economic significance for Britain had been declining.[34] Moreover, there was little evidence to indicate that the British Government and business interests took a unified approach to economic matters concerning the empire. The records and memoranda on the Grand Design were also largely silent on the economic benefits that the scheme would bring to Britain. In so far as the economic aspects were concerned, the British were more concerned about the implications for the component territories — common market, tariffs, etc., rather than possible benefits for Britain. Where the Grand Design was concerned, British ministers were clearly more concerned about "bases not markets, security not commerce, and international influence not investment opportunities".[35]

Although there was now a convergence of views that the Grand Design was the preferred policy, there were strong feelings among the officials in the territories that the scheme be undertaken in a cautious and consultative approach so as not to give the impression that the Grand Design was a neo-colonial scheme imposed on the people of the colonies. On 20 October 1960, at an inter-territorial conference held at Kuching, Sarawak, in which the Commissioner-General of Southeast Asia, Governors of North Borneo and Sarawak, the High Commissioner for Brunei, Minister of State for the Colonies, and the Commander-in-Chief of the Far East Land Forces were present, an agreed position was taken, the outline of which was communicated a few days later to the Colonial Secretary.[36] In essence, the Kuching meeting recommended that the British Government work towards bringing about a closer political association between Malaya, Singapore and the three Borneo territories, but the progress towards this goal "would be gradual and adjusted to the rate of political evolution in the Borneo Territories".[37] As a first step, ties between North Borneo and Sarawak should be strengthened with the intention of the two territories eventually forming a single unit, and if Brunei chose to join in, it should be encouraged. Such a broad association, the meeting at Kuching had concurred, would provide the only "satisfactory evolution that would safeguard in the longer term not only the security, economic development and welfare of the territories themselves, but also ... the United Kingdom's own essential defence interests consisting of the base in Singapore and the necessary deployment areas outside it".[38] It was further agreed that there are "growing interests of all territories concerned, despite the real and obvious differences between them, in some such eventual solution to their problems".[39] Selkirk, however, sounded a cautionary note in his missive to the Colonial Secretary:

> We hold it important to avoid any appearance that Her Majesty's Government are actively pursuing such a solution or seeking to impose it upon the peoples concerned....[40]

The above proposals were subsequently endorsed at an Eden Hall Conference in January 1961, in which the views of the Governors of Sarawak and North Borneo, as well as the High Commissioner of Brunei, Kuala Lumpur and Canberra, and the British ambassador to Indonesia were represented.[41] On 18 April 1961, the question of the Grand Design was considered at a meeting of the Colonial Policy Committee, during which it was decided that subject to the views of the governments of Australia and New Zealand, the British Government accepted the development of a political association between Malaya, Singapore and the three Borneo territories as "an ultimate aim of policy". Whenever opportunities arose, the British should discuss the matter in confidence with interested parties such as the Tunku, Lee Kuan Yew and the Sultan of Brunei, and with the support of these protagonists, the British should issue public statements to the effect that "a broad association between the Federation and Singapore and the Borneo territories [had] great possibilities for the future of the area".[42] While the Cabinet Colonial Policy Committee was prepared to endorse Selkirk's recommendations, it agreed to abide by the Colonial Secretary's advice against making a public statement of policy "in advance of evidence of some weight of local opinion in favour of such an association".[43]

It was from Malaya, the critical piece in the entire gambit, that the British had hoped the favourable "weight of local opinion" would come, but it was quite clear that the Tunku had no interest, at that point in time, to bring Singapore into the Malayan Federation. In his memoirs, the Tunku explained that the question of "Singapore *vis a vis* Malaya was not as simple as idealist[s] might think" for "the Malays [in Malaya] might without the protection of the Constitution, find themselves at a total loss in the only homeland they had". "This might eventually mean trouble as an outcome," he added, and asked, "and who wanted that?"[44] The Malayans were not convinced that a merger with Singapore would serve Malayan interests at that stage. Yet, the primary piece of the Grand Design puzzle was the merger between Singapore and Malaya, without which the whole scheme would not take place. Malaya was obviously the key to this entire scheme as she was already an independent country and a trusted British Commonwealth member. It would constitute the core of the Grand Design, and the Greater Malaysia Federation would have to be grafted on the Malayan state.

Without the merger with Malaya, independence for Singapore was almost a non-starter. The political danger and security implications of an independent and politically unstable Singapore were clearly of major concern to London. Although they were bound by an agreement to institute a constitutional review in 1963, four years after Singapore was granted self-government, the British were convinced that they would not concede further constitutional concessions to Singapore if the conditions were not right. The 1959 Constitution had stipulated that should the United Kingdom and Singapore governments not arrive at a mutual agreement in a constitutional review by 1963, the current constitution would "continue in force".[45] As far as the British were concerned, they were prepared to adopt an attitude of wait-and-see with regard to Singapore's political future, but this could not go on indefinitely.

While the British were committed in policy to bring Malaya and Singapore into a "single united nation",[46] they had to make sure that the terms and conditions of the merger would not jeopardize political conditions in Singapore (which should have a government that would be friendly to London) and thereby hurt British interests in the region. It was clear that even while policy directives and priorities were set in London, it was local politics that would define the progress and shape of the Grand Design. Each of the component states, driven by local circumstances and imperatives, as much by mutual distrust, wanted merger only on their own terms. From 1961, when the stage was set for the formation of a Greater Malaysia, it was local politics that was to determine the pace and content of its progress, although the British hoped to "be in a position to influence its shape and character..."[47] Having articulated a policy direction, the British now had to facilitate the negotiations and broker the necessary agreements between the principal players to bring about the Grand Design. The merger negotiations between Singapore and Malaya were to bear this out very dramatically.

NOTES

1 Matthew Jones, *Conflict and Confrontation in South East Asia, 1961–1965: Britain, the United States and the Creation of Malaysia* (Cambridge; New York: Cambridge University Press, 2001), p. 1.

2 Ibid.

3 Anthony J. Stockwell, "Colonial Planning during World War Two: The Case of Malaya", *Journal of Imperial and Commonwealth History* 2, no. 3 (1974).

4   Phillip Darby, *British Defence Policy East of Suez* 1947–1968 (London: Oxford University Press for the Royal Institute of International Affairs, 1973), p. 210.

5   Nicholas Tarling, "Some Rather Nebulous Capacity: Lord Killearn's Appointment in Southeast Asia", *Modern Asian Studies* 20, no. 3 (1986): 559.

6   Anthony J. Stockwell, ed., *Malaysia. British Documents on the End of Empire,* Series B, Vol. 8 (London: Stationery Office, 2004), p. xxxvii.

7   For this argument, see Greg Poulgrain, "The Genesis of Konfrontasi: Malaysia, Brunei and Indonesia 1945–1965" (Adelaide: Crawford House Publishing, 1998).

8   Cited in Stockwell, ed., *Malaysia*, p. xxxvii.

9   Minutes by H. T. Bourdillon (August 1945), CO 825/42, Public Records Office. In explaining its decision to separate Singapore from Malaya in 1946, the British had stated that it had been no part of their policy "to preclude or prejudice in any way the fusion of Singapore and the Malayan Union in a wider union at a later date". See *White Paper on Detachment of Singapore from the Straits Settlements* (January 1946), Cmd 6274.

10 Cheah Boon Kheng, *Malaysia: The Making of a Nation* (Singapore: Institute of Southeast Asian Studies, 2002), p. 2.

11 See Mohamed Noordin Sopiee, *From Malayan Union to Singapore Separation: Political Unification in the Malaysian Region, 1945–65* (Kuala Lumpur: Universiti Malaya, 1974), p. 128.

12 Stockwell, ed., *Malaysia*, p. xlix.

13 Ibid.

14 Ibid.

15 "Defence implications of an association of the British Borneo territories with the Federation of Malaya and the State of Singapore", Report by Joint Planning Staff, JP(61)57, 17 July 1961, DEFE 4/137, Public Records Office.

16 Anthony J. Stockwell, "Malaysia: The Making of a Grand Design", *Asian Affairs* XXXIV, no. III (November 2003), p. 228.

17 Stockwell, ed., *Malaysia*, p. xxxviii.

18 Stockwell, "Malaysia: The Making of a Grand Design", p. 228.

19 "Proposals for a wider association between the British Borneo Territories, Singapore and the Federation of Malaya", CO 1030/980.

20 Ibid.

21 Ibid.

22 Ibid.

23 Memorandum for Cabinet Colonial Policy by Mr Lennox Boyd, assessing the possibility of closer association of the Borneo Territories, "Borneo Territories", 29 November 1957, CAB 134/1556, CPC (57) 34. See also "The Origins and

Formation of Malaysia", FCO Research Department, Memorandum (10 July 1970, FCO 51/154 no. 15, para. 24, in Stockwell, ed., *Malaysia*, p. 591.

24 "Borneo Territories": Cabinet Colonial Policy Committee minutes approving initiation of public discussion of closer association, 4 December 1957, CAB 134/ 1955, CPC 14(57)2, Public Records Office.

25 Ibid.

26 Notes on the Future of Borneo Territories, n.d., CO 1030/977.

27 Memorandum of conversation between Dr Ismail, Minister for Commerce and Industry and Vice-President of UMNO, and Mr Thomas Wright, American Consul General, Kuala Lumpur, 1 June 1956.

28 Stockwell, "Malaysia: The Making of a Grand Design", p. 232.

29 Ibid.

30 Note to Prime Minister, "Singapore, the Malayan Federation and the Borneo Territories", 17 April 1961, PREM 11/3418, Public Records Office.

31 Stockwell, ed., *Malaysia*, p. xlviii.

32 See, for instance, Said Zahari, *Dark Clouds at Dawn: A Political Memoir* (Kuala Lumpur: Insan, 2001), p. 151.

33 "Future Developments in SE Asia": Committee on Future Developments in SE Asia minutes, 29 September 1960, CAB 134/1644, DSE (60) 15th meeting.

34 See Nicholas White, "The Business and Politics of Decolonization: The British Experience in the Twentieth Century", *Economic History Review* 53, no. 3 (2000): pp. 544–64; and Anthony J. Stockwell, "Malaysia: The Making of a Neo-Colony?", *Journal of Imperial and Commonwealth History* 26, no. 2 (1998): 138–56.

35 Stockwell, ed., *Malaysia*, p. xlvii.

36 "Prospects for closer association": despatch from Lord Selkirk to Mr Macleod reporting his personal views following high-level discussions in Kuching, 25 October 1960, CO 1030/977 no. 75.

37 Ibid.

38 Ibid.

39 Ibid.

40 Ibid.

41 Despatch from Lord Selkirk to Macleod following up his despatch on 25 October and urging a government statement of policy on the closer association, "The Grand Design", 30 January 1961, CO 1030/978 no. 119.

42 "The possibility of an association of the British Borneo territories with the Federation of Malaya and the State of Singapore", 18 April 1961, Cabinet Colonial Committee minutes, CAB 134/1560, CPC 4 (61) 1.

43 Memorandum by Mr Macleod for Cabinet Colonial Committee reporting on developments since July 1960, "The possibility of an association of the British

Borneo territories with the Federation of Malaya and the State of Singapore", 14 April 1961, CAB 134/1560 CPC (61) 9.

44 Tunku Abdul Rahman Putra, *Looking Back: Monday Musings and Memories* (Kuala Lumpur: Pustaka Antara, 1977), p. 79.

45 *Report of Singapore Constitutional Conference held in London in March and April 1957. Presented by the Secretary of State for the Colonies to Parliament by command of Her Majesty* (London: Her Majesty's Stationery Office, 1957), Cmd 147 para. 48(d).

46 C.M. Turnbull, *A History of Singapore, 1819–1988*, 2nd edn (Singapore: Oxford University Press, 1989, p. 266.

47 Selkirk to Macleod, 30 January 1961, CO 1030/978 no. 119.

CHAPTER TWO

Merger and Greater Malaysia: Political Attitudes towards Union between Singapore and the Federation

B y 1960 the Colonial Office, Commonwealth Relations Office and Ministry of Defence of the Government of the United Kingdom had reached a consensus that the merger between Singapore and Malaya, and the eventual incorporation of the Borneo Territories, individually or as a unit, into the newly extended Federation to form a Greater Malaysia should constitute the "ultimate goal of British policy in Southeast Asia". Preliminary soundings among British officials serving in the territories concerned had unanimously indicated that the Grand Design — the establishment of a Federation incorporating Malaya, Singapore, North Borneo, Sarawak and Brunei — was a logical policy that would serve well the interests of all concerned. Independence would be given to the remnants of the British colonies in Southeast Asia, and the post-independent political and economic viability of these erstwhile, smaller colonies (for whom the British regarded there was little future in individual independence or even independence in association together)[1] would be enhanced by their amalgamation into a bigger, more stable Federation. The inclusion of the North Borneo territories into a Malaysian Federation would effectively thwart whatever territorial designs Indonesia and the Philippines might harbour on those colonies. Most importantly, Britain's strategic and defence concerns and obligations in the region denoted "East of Suez" by policy-makers would in no way be diminished by the process of de-colonization. London would be able to create a friendly Commonwealth bloc in the region, containing an "independent" Singapore whose military bases would still be available for

British use,[2] with the added advantage that the thorny issue of internal security in Singapore would no longer be a British concern, but a burden for Kuala Lumpur to bear. All things considered, the formation of Greater Malaysia promised to be a propitious end to formal British Empire in Southeast Asia.

Reactions among the local politicians to the idea of a wider Malaysian Federation were, however, more varied. Since its separation from Malaya in 1946, all shades of political opinion in Singapore were agreed that the island-colony had no long-term political future on its own, and would eventually find its way back into the fold of its natural hinterland — the Malayan peninsula. The idea that Singapore could survive for long as an independent state outside the Federation was never regarded as realistic; the question that local politicians grappled with was not whether Singapore should eventually re-merge with Malaya, but when and how? Since coming to power in 1959, the People's Action Party (PAP) government had advocated unequivocally that "independence though merger" with the Federation was the ultimate constitutional aim of the self-governing island state. The cause of merger found an ardent and articulate champion in the person of Singapore's first Prime Minister, Lee Kuan Yew. Convinced then that there was no other political future for Singapore other than being a part of the Federation, Lee had, from the mid-1950s, worked consistently to achieve his goal of merger between Singapore and the mainland. To achieve that political objective, there were a number of "battles" that he had had to fight for not only did he face a Malaya that up to the middle of 1961 was totally uninterested to contemplate a singular merger with Singapore, but local political opposition that, while opposed to merger, was nonetheless prepared to utilize Lee's difficulties with Malaya as a political weapon against him.

Lee's counterpart in Kuala Lumpur, Prime Minister Tunku Abdul Rahman, had his own dilemmas to face. All along, he had been opposed to a direct merger with Singapore for fear of the adverse political impact that the incorporation of one million Chinese from the colony would have on the racial and political balance in Malaya. He knew that his domestic political opponents, especially the right-wing Malay opposition Pan Malayan Islamic Party (PMIP), were strongly averse to incorporating Singapore into the Federation, even if the Borneo Territories were included, for fear that this would not only upset the dominant position of the Malays in Malaya but that there was also the risk of the mainland being infected by the "communist contagion" from Singapore.[3] If the Tunku were perceived to be forthcoming to Singapore, he would be criticized by his opponents. Yet, he was acutely aware that keeping Singapore out by closing the causeway and leaving it to the mercy of the communists was a dangerous policy. Kuala Lumpur could better deal with the "red menace" in Singapore as an internal affair than to leave it as an external problem that would, if left uncontrolled, spread its insidious influence northward. The Tunku's solution was thus to bring Singapore in, but would limit the latter's influence within the Federation by bringing in the Borneo Territories as a counterweight. By so doing, he was able to fulfil his long-term ambition of creating a Greater Malaysia — a pan-Malayan entity anchored on the Federation of Malaya, and incorporating Singapore, Brunei, Sarawak and North Borneo.

This chapter seeks to explore and explain the development of the ideas of a direct merger between Singapore and the Federation on the one hand, and a Greater Malaysia that would incorporate the Borneo Territories on the other, and how the two eventually dove-tailed to form the basis of a policy that was to become Malaysia in 1963.

Singapore: Independence through Merger

Although Singapore was separated from the other Straits Settlements and Malaya and established as a Crown Colony in its own right in April 1946, British officials and policy-makers were convinced that the island's long-term existence as a state on its own was hardly viable given the economic and trade dependence of the tiny, resource-scarce island on the Malayan hinterland.[4] Indeed, when the British decided to excise Singapore from the mainland, largely as a measure to ease the acceptance of the Malayan Union plan by the Malay politicians and the Sultans,[5] the separation of the two territories was meant to be a temporary expedient; British officials actually foresaw their coming together again in the not too distant future.[6] Once out, however, it was to prove difficult for Singapore to get back in again. After

1946, Malcolm MacDonald, then Governor-General of Southeast Asia, claimed that although the British were prepared to return Singapore to Malaya, that decision was blocked by Malay leaders during the Anglo-Malay constitutional discussions in mid-1946.[7] When the Union experiment failed — its liberal citizenship provisions to non-Malays proved politically unacceptable to the Malay élites — and was replaced by a new arrangement in the form of the Federation of Malaya in 1948, the Malay political leadership continued to oppose the re-merger of Singapore, determined as they were to prevent "the submergence of the Malays by the economically superior and aggressive Chinese".[8]

While policy-makers in London doubted if Singapore could afford to stay out of Malaya for long, for the moment at least, the retention of Singapore as a separate Crown Colony had its own logic. For Britain, direct control over Singapore would mean that it was able to retain continued use of the military bases there for the purposes of maintaining its strategic policy east of Suez.[9] Further, there was the concern that if Singapore were to be incorporated back into Malaya, its economy, which was ultimately dependent on entrepôt and free trade arrangements, would be threatened as Kuala Lumpur would in all probability bring the island into some form of customs union with the rest of the Federation. For the time being, therefore, it was decided in the interests of all concerned that Singapore should remain separate from the mainland. By 1948, even political parties in Singapore, many of which still saw an eventual merger with Malaya as the only way by which Singapore would ultimately achieve its independence, had come round to the view that under the existing conditions, merger of the Federation was perhaps inappropriate as an immediate political goal for Singapore. The most prominent party of the time, the Singapore Progressive Party (SPP), an élite, moderate and pro-establishment party "without any mass support or an effective country-wide organization", had argued that "Singapore ... should press for self-government and then merge with the mainland [only] when the Federation Constitution had been liberalised to confer equal rights on the Malays and the pro-Malays".[10] SPP leader, C.C. Tan, a Singapore-born and London-trained lawyer, explained that any form of merger at this stage with a pro-Malay Federation would retard the political progress of Singapore.[11] The SPP's main political rival, the Singapore Labour Party, a party formed by trade unionists and dominated by English-educated Indians, similarly felt that merger was not a serious option at this stage. Its president, Lim Yew Hock, warned that an immediate merger was tantamount to "tying a millstone around [Singapore's] neck".[12] All that these parties, as well as the Chinese economic interests in Singapore, would support at this point in time was for the concept of a loose Confederation of Malaysia that would comprise Malaya, Singapore and the North Borneo territories.[13] Consequently, from the immediate post-war period, Singapore, as a separate colony, proceeded to develop on its own; its directions and destiny divorced, for the time being, from those of mainland Malaya.

By the early 1950s, as political parties in Singapore sought progress towards eventual self-government for the colony, the question of merger with Malaya began to generate interest again. All major political parties had accepted the view that Singapore was not likely ever to achieve sovereignty existing on its own and it was necessary, as the rhetoric of self rule and independence became more pronounced, that the question of merger now had to be addressed with a greater degree of urgency. Indeed, in the 1955 elections, following the adoption of the Rendel Constitution — which considerably increased the size of the legislative assembly, the franchise and the number of political parties in Singapore — merger with the Federation became a prominent electoral issue, eliciting encouraging comments from several prominent politicians. In January 1955, campaigning to form the first government under the Rendel Constitution, SPP leader, C.C. Tan, in a perceptible shift from his earlier position, called for an early tie-up between Singapore and the Federation, declaring that before Singapore could expect complete independence, "the question of her relationship with the Federation must first be settled".[14] Tan, however, did not expect any immediate moves in that direction, and urged that politicians from both sides of the causeway should "refrain from interfering in each other's affairs".[15] The following month, Lim Yew Hock of the Labour Front[16] spoke of the necessity of "bringing the two territories into a coherent whole", and argued that independence for Singapore would "automatically follow merger".[17] In a manner characteristic of his flamboyant style, the Jewish lawyer and leader of the Labour Front, David Marshall, confidently declared in March 1955 that "there will be a union of the two territories within three years", a view which he said, was based on information which he had gathered from London.[18] For all the keen rhetoric on merger in the Singapore political scene, the time was perhaps still not ripe for such a venture. The colony was still some way off in securing self-government — its next stage of political progress — and in any case, the Malayans had chosen to remain cool to any idea of union with Singapore. The Tunku made clear his government's stand when he announced that, "the question of merger was still a long way off and nothing much can be done about it until Singapore and the Federation achieved their [respective] independence".[19]

In the meantime, politics in Singapore took an interesting turn. Despite expectations that the pro-British and conservative SPP would emerge victorious in the 1955 elections and thus form the first government under the Rendel Constitution, it was the moderate democratic socialist Labour Front, led by David Marshall, which surprised everyone with their performances at the polls. With no single party winning enough seats to form the government, the Labour Front, which won 10 of the 22 seats contested, went on to form a coalition government with three additional seats from the Malay Union Alliance,[20] and David Marshall became the first Chief Minister of Singapore. Swept by the euphoria of his strong election showing, the new Chief Minister now took it upon himself to wrest early independence for Singapore from the British and staked his political reputation on the accomplishment of that task. He led an all-party delegation to London in April 1956 for negotiations, and when talks broke down, a discredited Marshall returned to Singapore and resigned. Marshall had demanded full internal self government by April 1957, and while he was prepared to leave foreign policy and defence in the hands of the British, wanted a veto on defence and rights of consultation on foreign affairs.[21] Marshall had clearly misread the British intent and underestimated their concerns on the security of Singapore. The Colonial Office had fears that Singapore might end up as an outpost of communist China, and would not entrust security in the hands of a government it had no confidence could deal effectively with the communist threat. The British Government was prepared to concede on most other areas — a fully elected Assembly, citizenship, local control of trade and commerce, but would not compromise on security, in which they demanded the casting vote in the defence council.[22] The talks thus broke down on the critical issue of security. Marshall was succeeded by Lim Yew Hock, his colleague from the Labour Front government. The Lim Yew Hock tenure, which lasted from 1956 to 1959, was dominated by the government's head-on collision with the increasingly militant activists among the politically-minded Chinese students, teachers and union leaders.[23] Violent strikes and riots that took place in 1956 and 1957 were met with a firm government reaction in the form of a number of arrests of labour and student leaders without trial. Notwithstanding the political turmoil that existed on the island during this period, the British proceeded with their plans for conceding self-rule for Singapore. Lim Yew Hock led a second all-party delegation to London for talks in March/April 1957, and succeeded where Marshall had failed; he was able to secure the promise of self-government for Singapore by 1959. Provisions for an extended franchise based on Singapore citizenship and a parliamentary system of government based on popular elections were eventually agreed upon. Defence and external affairs would, however, remain in British hands, and responsibilities for internal security would be shared jointly by the British, Singapore and Malayan governments.[24]

During the Labour Front governments of both Marshall and Lim, both Chief Ministers had made repeated overtures to the Tunku, urging him to consider merger with Singapore. To them, this was the only way in which Singapore could realistically convince the British to concede independence to the Colony. The Tunku chose, however, not to reciprocate. Although he liked Lim Yew Hock for the firm manner in which the latter had dealt with the militant Chinese students and workers in Singapore, once even describing his government as "courageous and good", he was still uncertain if the conditions for merger were right. Lim Yew Hock, who had good ties with the Alliance government in Kuala Lumpur, was nonetheless confident that merger would happen within the next five years.

If indeed merger were to happen, as Lim had so confidently predicted it would, it was not destined to happen under the auspices of a Labour Front Government, as things turned out. The 1959 elections,[25] which ushered in the period of self-government for Singapore, were swept by the left-wing People's Action Party (PAP), which won 43 of the 51 seats contested, garnering 54 per cent of the overall votes. The PAP had won over the ground with their effective campaigning strategies and the promise of an "honest and efficient government" that would give priority to tackling employment, housing and education — issues that appealed to the recently enfranchised working classes. Just prior to the elections, the PAP charged the Labour Front for receiving political funds from external sources through its Minister for Education Chew Swee Kee. This was proof, the PAP alleged, that the incumbent government was incurably corrupt and had "sold Singapore to foreigners for a few thousand dollars". Lee Kuan Yew then called for the resignation of the entire Lim Yew Hock government "in view of public disgust and loss of public confidence".[26] The old Labour Front, which had fallen apart and reorganized into a new Singapore People's Alliance party, on the other hand, had lost the support of the Chinese-educated masses, and was riven by internal dissent and tainted by the smear of corruption.[27] It won only four of the 39 seats contested.

Among the platforms upon which the PAP campaigned the 1959 elections was the pledge to work towards bringing Singapore into a united Malaya. Like its predecessors in government, the PAP had all along been committed to the goal of achieving political independence for Singapore within the framework of a united Malaya. From its very inception in November 1954, the PAP had declared as one of its main objectives the ending of colonialism in Singapore through the establishment of "an independent [and non-communist] national state of Malaya comprising the ... the Federation of Malaya and the Colony of Singapore".[28] Following the constitutional talks in London in 1957, Lee maintained his position that independence for Singapore was not possible until merger with the Federation was achieved, and just before the PAP fought the 1959 elections, he obtained an undertaking of full support, particularly from the pro-communists within his party whom he knew were ambivalent to the idea of re-integration with Malaya, for merger as the way to independence.[29] Having won the elections so convincingly, the PAP now believed that it had the mandate from the people to push vigorously for merger with Malaya, and promised that this would be achieved within their term of office.

From 1959, as self-governing Singapore's first Prime Minister, Lee Kuan Yew became the island's main advocate for merger. At the outset of his political career, Lee had held a deep personal conviction of the imperative of merger, firmly convinced that unification with the mainland was absolutely vital to the survival of a non-communist and prosperous Singapore. Indeed, he had argued that the frontier between Singapore and the Federation was a "freak man-made [one]...[created] by the fancy of planners and map-makers in London", and that "the relentless logic of geography and the force of historical, ethnic and economic forces all point to the inevitability of merger".[30]

Ever the pragmatic politician with a solid grasp of the realities of the day, Lee's belief in the necessity of merger was essentially borne out of his assessment of the problems that Singapore had to contend with as it moved towards political and economic independence. As far as he was concerned, separate independence for Singapore was a "dangerous illusion", and the island state would be "committing national suicide if [it] refused to merge in Malaysia".[31] Throughout the 1950s, the colony had been under mounting economic pressure brought about by the combined result of the explosive rate of population growth in the island and a declining entrepôt trade. Its exports to the region had been dramatically reduced, owing to import restrictions on the part of many of its neighbours to protect their own industries, and entrepôt trade, the mainstay of Singapore's economy, was threatened by countries which were increasingly engaging in direct trading. Amidst all this, there was the further problem of ensuring that opportunities for employment would increase at a corresponding pace to the rapid growth of the island's population. If Singapore were to create enough jobs for its young and fast growing population as well as cut its dependence on the entrepôt trade, its economy would have to embark on a course of rapid industrialization. But for this to work, integration with the economy and markets of the Federation was crucial.[32] Finance Minister Goh Keng Swee saw this very clearly and commented that "whatever we do, major changes in our economy are only possible if Singapore and the Federation are integrated as one economy".[33]

Without some form of economic integration or common market, the Singapore and Malayan economies would find themselves in direct competition with each other, particularly in attracting foreign investors. Singapore, with its smaller work-force and higher production costs, had found that it was in a particularly disadvantageous position as many local companies, such as local rubber footwear firms, were moving out of Singapore into the Federation, where costs of production were much lower. In the Federation, these companies could also secure tariff protection for their products, which they could not under Singapore's free port economy. Although Singapore could hope to overcome some of these problems by taking action to restrict imports of goods which competed directly with the island's industries, the island's free port status would be questioned if the government were to resort to those measures.[34] And while Singapore was having difficulties protecting its local industries from foreign competition, it found, at the same time, that the Federation's tariff barrier acted as a bar to the entry of Singapore manufactured goods across the causeway into the Federation markets.

The Singapore Government was therefore keen to establish an integrated industrial development programme with the Federation in the context of a common market. However, negotiations to that end had made little progress as the Federation government saw that it had little to gain from it. The Federation government quite rightly saw that as long as Singapore completely retained its free port status, while the rest of the Federation were imposed with a set of similar custom duties, common market arrangements would only give a preponderant advantage to the former. Presently, the Federation of Malaya had a normal range of tariffs on imported goods, including those bought from Singapore, while the latter was a free port which collects duties only on intoxicating liquors, tobacco and petroleum intended for domestic consumption. Goods manufactured in the Federation thus enjoyed free entry into Singapore, while goods made in Singapore had to pass through a tariff barrier before they could be marketed in the Federation.[35] If Singapore were to remain wholly a free port while a common market was instituted, the Federation would have to open their own markets to Singapore manufactures in return for no further advantages in the Singapore market which they did not already possess. The Malayans, therefore, saw little rationale in having a common market with Singapore.

While the Singapore Government had very strong and compelling economic reasons for merger, it was politics that propelled the PAP government to seek urgently an effective union with Malaya. From the very outset, the PAP was "divided between two ideologically diverse factions with incompatible ends and means".[36] While Lee and a number of his moderate, English-educated comrades were committed to achieving an independent, democratic and socialist Singapore through open constitutional struggle, there was a rival faction within the party, comprising powerful pro-communist union leaders like Lim Chin Siong, whose political aims were focused on the establishment of a socialist Malaya through radical political change, if necessary. In the first few years of the PAP's existence, for reasons of mutual political expediency, the two factions were able to forge a united front. Lee and the English-educated moderates needed the help of the Chinese-educated pro-communists members, with their control of the trade unions, cultural organizations and Chinese schools, to win the Chinese ground,[37] while communist elements saw in the PAP a legitimate left-wing party and a convenient legal political vehicle on which to carry out their activities, gradually subverting Singapore and ultimately using the island as a base to foment a revolution in Malaya. Lee knew that his attempt to ride the "communist tiger" was fraught with danger, and that once the British left, the two factions would have to scrape it out between themselves. By 1960, while the moderates still controlled the party through the central executive committee, there were growing signs that the influence of the pro-communists was growing stronger and more pervasive as Chinese chauvinism, fed by economic frustrations and the popular appeal of anti-imperialism (especially with the British enjoying full rights of occupation, control and use of the bases on the island), fuelled the popularity of the extreme left.

With the radical left stirring up an anti-colonial mood in Singapore, Lee knew that his political position would become increasingly tenuous as long as colonialism, or forms of colonial presence, was still evident in the island-state. As an anti-colonial party, the PAP was obliged to end Singapore's status as a colony, but Lee and his government knew that without merger, it was not likely that the British would concede independence; and unless the government was able to make some progress with the Federation on either political merger or common market and thus mark the road to independence with a degree of certainty, the pro-communists would continue to gain political mileage at the moderates' expense.[38]

While the gathering strength of Lee's political opponents made the securing of a merger agreement with the Malayans a matter of extreme importance for the PAP government, it was, ironically, over the very same question of merger that catalysed the seething tension between the pro-communists and the moderate wings of the PAP into an open conflict between the two groups.[39] All along, the extreme left-wing in the PAP had been fundamentally opposed to merger, which would see Singapore gaining independence as part of the Federation. For them and the communists, merger would mean internal security being placed in the hands of a rabidly anti-communist Kuala Lumpur government, which would certainly spare no effort in suppressing the communist movement in Singapore. Independence through merger would also remove in a single stroke the continued excuse to couch their political battle in the form of an anti-colonial struggle. However, for so long as the possibility of achieving merger seemed remote, the extremists had found it expedient to pay lip service to it. They were, after all, anti-colonialists who had regarded the split between Singapore and Malaya as a colonial act that had to be rectified. However, should Lee have a breakthrough, they would be prepared to sabotage the enterprise by staging a revolt against the PAP leadership. Encouraged by the British, which stipulated that they were prepared to allow the pro-communists, whom they were ready to accept as radical non-communists, to form the government should they acquire power constitutionally — an act of subterfuge, according to Lee — the militants began to openly challenge Lee and the moderates for control of the party and the government.[40] By 1960, Lee was clearly in a fix: without showing a stern hand in dealing with the militants, he was not likely to win the Tunku's confidence for merger; yet without the clear prospects of merger, Lee was in no position to politically defeat the militants that were out to get him. For the embattled Prime Minister of Singapore, the survival of his government and the future viability and stability of Singapore without merger was very bleak.[41] Indeed, the very political survival of the PAP would soon be staked on that very issue.

The longer the Malayans held out, the weaker would be his position. According to Philip Moore, the British Acting High Commissioner in Singapore, "the opposition to Lee was building up and he would find it increasingly difficult to carry Singapore with him in a merger with the Federation".[42]

But up to 1961, while faced with an increasingly desperate political situation at home, Lee, despite his best efforts, was not having any luck with the Tunku. Lee admitted that he had been trying for a long time to convince the Tunku of the need for merger between their two territories.[43] But each time the Singapore Government raised the issue, it would be met with an intransigent Malayan premier who would slap down any suggestions that the Federation was prepared to consider any form of merger with Singapore. The Tunku would be quick to deny that merger was possible in the foreseeable future, and to point out that Malaya had first to settle its own racial policies. For a long time the Tunku decided to shut his ears to all suggestions of merger,[44] and not wishing to lead Singapore into thinking that merger was indeed on the cards, the Federation government, also to avoid drawing flak from the right wing political ground in the Federation, would cautiously keep a safe distance from any proposals for common action which might be interpreted as the first steps towards a political merger of the two territories. With the position of the Tunku on a Singapore-Malaya merger made clear to him several times before, Lee knew that it would be naive of him to expect a positive gesture from the Federation at this stage; but he was concerned that the Federation should at least keep alive the hope of eventual merger and not encourage the idea that Singapore could be independent on its own.[45] Indeed, Lee Kuan Yew, mindful of the Tunku's firm rejection of any idea of merger with Singapore, had repeatedly said that he did not want the Malayan Government to welcome the idea of merger at this point in time, but merely to keep the door ajar, and to offer some immediate cooperation in the economic field.[46] In a meeting with the British High Commissioner of Malaya, Geofroy Tory, Lee explained that in speaking of merger, he was not trying to upset the Malayan or the Alliance government; he was simply expressing his belief that without Malaya, Singapore was nothing. He was, as it were, simply "putting his hand across the causeway and keeping hold of the Federation".

He genuinely regarded it as an essential part of the plan to contain and absorb communism in Singapore.[47] At present, he lamented that he was not even getting this minimal measure of assistance.

While the door across the causeway remained shut for the moment, Lee knew that he could not stop at rhetorical gestures, but had to continue creating tangible conditions in Singapore that would encourage the Tunku to be more favourably disposed to merger once the time was right.[48] Fundamentally, the PAP realized that it had to "resolve the …fears which make the Malay majority in the Federation not want the Chinese majority in Singapore".[49] From its inception in 1954, the party created a Malay Affairs Bureau, under the charge of an active Malay journalist, Othman Wok, who later became a cabinet minister. While in the Opposition benches between 1955 and 1959, the PAP had demonstrated its readiness to cooperate with the Federation government when Lee took the potentially problematic and unpopular position of supporting the institution of the Internal Security Council to control security in Singapore. Lee had then argued that as the PAP's ultimate aim was to effect merger between Singapore and Malaya, "it was logical to recognize that the Federation would have a decisive voice in the affairs of Singapore, including its security".[50] From 1959, Lee took steps to create a pan-Malayan outlook in Singapore, to create, in his words, "a Malayanised Singapore man who would talk, think and act like the exemplary Malayans of the Federation".[51] In attempting to facilitate the social integration of the predominantly Chinese population of Singapore with the Malayan hinterland, and hoping to impress the UMNO leadership in Kuala Lumpur at the same time, Malay was made the national language of Singapore, and a Malay Head of State (Yang di-Pertuan Negara) was installed. A Malay Education Advisory Committee was set up in 1959, and a Malayan school syllabus was introduced. By the end of 1959, the government agreed to provide all Singaporean Malay citizens with free primary education, with the privilege extended to secondary and university education for suitably qualified Malay citizens.[52]

By 1960, despite the PAP's policies of conciliation and goodwill, the Tunku still remained cool to the idea of merger. The PAP government was becoming increasingly worried if it could indefinitely hold on to the line of independence through merger without any promise of any concrete achievements. In the meantime, the government's position was further undermined by an open quarrel with one of its members in the Assembly, the former Mayor Ong Eng Guan. In June 1960, the increasingly ambitious Ong decided to mount a political challenge to Lee by charging the leaders of the PAP for being undemocratic and failing to make progress with independence. Ong's political manoeuvre failed to turn the party against the leadership, and instead was expelled from the Assembly by the party's central executive committee. In December 1960, Ong vacated his seat in the Hong Lim constituency but returned with a vengeance in the by-elections in April 1961 for the seat he had vacated. Using his charismatic personality and impressive skills in local dialects to great advantage, Ong decisively trounced the PAP candidate and won the by-election with 73.3 per cent of the votes. The defeat dealt a serious blow to the PAP government, and Lee and his ministers offered to resign, believing that the economic and social problems that had alienated the voters in Hong Lim against the PAP would never be resolved unless there was merger, or the establishment of common market with the Federation.[53] But the PAP's threatened resignation only drew a round of protests from the communists who were quick to promise their support for the government, a move, Lee believed, that was motivated less by their concern for Singapore than the fear that the PAP would be replaced by a more resolutely anti-communist government.[54] Lee knew that this would only be a temporary respite. With its position weakened by the Hong Lim by-election, the PAP government would soon be subjected to increasing pressure from the pro-communist hardliners to adopt the objective advocated by Marshall and never expressly abandoned by Lim Yew Hock: separate and outright independence for Singapore, or for independence before merger. Both these courses of action would well postpone merger indefinitely. Lee Kuan Yew, naturally, did not want this and indeed he was especially afraid of it, since he had the sense to see that an independent Singapore, standing by itself, would rapidly be engulfed.[55] The line had to be drawn, and the PAP announced that at the 1963 Constitutional Review Talks they would demand independence through merger with the Federation, or merger in a larger Federation. He then confided in the British that the party would stand or fall by this.[56]

The Hong Lim by-election, while it threatened to topple the government, proved to be fortuitous for Lee and the moderates in an unexpected way. Watching with great interest from Kuala Lumpur, the Tunku was beginning to realize that the moderates were rapidly losing ground, and unless he did something to bolster Lee's position, the government in Singapore would be taken over by the radical left. In April 1961, Lee and his deputy Goh Keng Swee were invited to Kuala Lumpur to meet the Tunku and Abdul Razak for a discussion on merger. According to Lee, the Tunku made it clear during the meeting that he was still strongly opposed to the idea of a direct merger between Singapore and the Federation but had spoken about the possibility of bringing in the Borneo territories first if Singapore had to be taken in at a later stage.[57] When Lee then spoke to Selkirk about the meeting, the latter assured that the British Government was in favour of the Grand Design — the overall amalgamation of the British colonies in Southeast Asia (including the independent Malaya) into a single entity — in principle, but omitted details on what the London had in mind.[58] Indeed, in an earlier meeting with the Governors of these territories in October 1959, the Commissioner-General had recommended that discreet "encouragement should be given to the interests that the Prime Ministers of both the Federation and Singapore had been taking in the wider association with these territories".[59] Lee was now offered a way out of his impasse: as the PAP's declared aim of independence through merger with the Federation was "vulnerable to destructive criticism from his political opponents because the Federation's attitude was so unforthcoming", he started to push for merger through a wider political association that would include the Borneo Territories.[60]

By the middle of 1960, with no headway on the venture of a single merger between Singapore and the Federation, Lee had become increasingly attracted to the idea of a larger grouping both as a solution to his own dilemma and as a desirable development in its own right. Through the Grand Design, which could proceed on the basis of a Malaya-Singapore merger with the three Borneo Territories coming in as a counterweight to the Chinese factor (which he knew the Tunku dreaded), Lee reasoned that he would probably have more success in talks with the Federation ministers.[61] The Grand Design, it seemed, was the only method by which the Tunku could be persuaded to accept Singapore. However, Lee was advised that it was politically inexpedient to switch his line too rapidly from merger to Grand Design, and any change on his part had to be gradual and must be presented as an expansion rather than an abandonment of previous ideas.[62] British officials were concerned that a sudden switch from the direct merger between Singapore and the Federation to the Grand Design, which would involve the Borneo Territories, could be seen as an acknowledgment of defeat of the PAP's merger policy, and this could have an adverse political effect on Lee's standing in Singapore.[63] Unsure of the Tunku's attitude, British officials were concerned that should Lee push his ideas of a Grand Design too enthusiastically, he might "cause revulsion in the Federation and also excite alarm in the Borneo Territories".[64] However, after the Kuala Lumpur meeting of April 1961, and following the Tunku's request for Lee to draft a paper on the "Grand Design", the British were more re-assured that the time was perhaps ripe for Lee to pursue the matter further. Lee was then advised by Philip Moore, deputy high commissioner in Singapore, that he should attempt to highlight the attractiveness of the Grand Design as an option of "general interest to the entire Malaysian region", while making references to the "possible dangers to the Federation of a movement in Singapore for complete independence".[65]

In early May 1961, Lee produced a paper on the Grand Design, which he sent to the British and Federation Ministers for consideration. In his paper, Lee listed two alternatives for the constitutional future of the British territories in Southeast Asia. The first was for the territories to be given independence on its own, to function as separate, independent political units. He then pointed out that if this alternative developed, merger between Singapore and the Federation of Malaya would be abandoned as a political objective, and "power in Singapore would pass to a China-minded group with strong cultural and economic links with Communist China".[66] A pro-communist government would emerge that would eventually achieve independence for Singapore with the help of communist China. With such a development, he warned that British interests and security in Southeast Asia would come under considerable threat, with a Chinese communist base right in the heart of Southeast Asia. The repercussions will be felt in Malaya, too. An independent Singapore would have to "pander to its 75% Chinese population and will end up with greater appeals to Chinese chauvinism and eventually all talk of Malayan culture, national language, national solidarity and nation-building will disappear with tremendous adverse repercussions on the Chinese in the Federation of Malaya".[67] The consequences would be frightening, according to him; "it would put to an end any hope of building a united multi-racial community in Malaya".[68]

The other alternative was for the establishment of a larger federation comprising the territories of Malaya, Singapore and the Borneo territories. This, to him, was the most satisfactory solution for the peoples of the territories concerned, and also one which the British could quite easily accede to. In broad terms, the scheme was to use the stable Malaya-based Federation government as the sheet anchor of the whole of this region. Each of these states could then be left to elect its own government based on its existing state arrangements, with the government of the Federation of Malaya, by virtue of its larger population, controlling the government of the larger federation. The seats in the Federation government would be apportioned in such a way as to give the Federation government an overwhelming majority,[69] and this would ensure that the "government of the Federation of Malaya [would] automatically control the government of the larger federation".[70] The powers of the larger Federation government should include defence, foreign affairs, police, security and such matters like currency and common economic development, which could be more efficiently handled by a central government, should be left to the Federation government. To protect the susceptibilities of the Borneo peoples and the present balance of power between Singapore and the Federation of Malaya, provisions would have to be built into the constitution to ensure that voting by citizens of the respective three states could only be done in their own states. This safeguard would prevent upsets in the balance of power.[71] In subsequent discussions with British officials, Lee, however, expressed reservations that the Borneo territories could be incorporated into the Malaysian Federation at once, since they were in a less advanced constitutional condition; the most that would be possible was for the British Government to give the Malayan Government an undertaking on the Borneo territories so that the process of merger between Singapore and Malaya would not be hampered.[72]

The thrust of Lee's argument was clear: separate independence for Singapore was too much of a political risk for British as well as Malayan interests. Merger with the Federation did not only promise economic viability for the small island state, but more fundamentally, its survival from the communist threat. There was no doubt in the mind of Prime Minister Lee Kuan Yew that "the Communists could only be beaten if it was clear that Singapore could not have independence except through merger".[73] But the position of his government, with whom the Tunku could still do business, was under the constant threat of the radical left and rebels like Ong Eng Guan. Unless the government's position was strengthened by its ability to achieve independence for Singapore through merger with the Federation, the moderates would fall, and if the communists were to come to power, the PAP would not be the only losers; Britain and Malaya would have to suffer consequences as well. He understood, however, that a straightforward merger between Singapore and the Federation would not be acceptable to the Malayan prime minister. Thus, a Greater Malaysia, incorporating the Borneo Territories, would be the solution that would satisfy all concerned.

By 1961, as the political situation in Singapore became increasingly threatening and desperate for the PAP, Lee decided that he had to appeal to Malaya's sense of self-interest in order to get the Tunku to respond more positively to his overtures. He thus decided to highlight the threat that Singapore would pose for Malayan security should the Tunku decide to keep Singapore out. He began arguing that the Singapore problem was an integral part of the wider Malayan problem, and that "it was easier if [the Tunku] were to include [Singapore] in his overall calculations ...than if he were to try to pass the problem child to the British".[74] Gradually, as Lee explained, "the unpleasant facts were placed before the Federation Government". "What had been publicly known was that Malaya was vital to Singapore. But what we did not emphasize ...was that Singapore was vital to their survival".[75]

By the middle of 1961 Lee's efforts seemed to have paid off, and the Tunku had begun indicating that he had had a change of mind, when he spoke for the first time, in May 1961, of the need for political and economic association with Singapore. Lee warmly welcomed the proposal for a Greater Malaysia in his National Day Rally speech on 3 June 1961:

> By the ties of sentiment as well as business, we in Singapore have always been closest to the Federation of Malaya. If merger and independence can come sooner and easier through the Borneo sister territories coming in together with us into political integration with the Federation, then we support it for it would also mean that we would have a larger and more powerful economic base for our new nation....We welcome and support the declaration of the Prime Minister of the Federation of Malaya that it is inevitable that we should look ahead to this objective of closer political and economic association between the Federation, Singapore, Brunei, Sarawak and North Borneo.[76]

Malaysia: In Pursuit of Greater Malaysia

Since the 1950s, although political developments in both Malaya and Singapore had, for a decade, progressed independently of each other, the political future of Singapore remained a source of direct and deep concern to the Tunku.[77] In August 1957, the Federation of Malaya had achieved independence and the question of Singapore's independence was set to follow in the not too distant future. The issue of merger between the two territories had already been raised several times before, but the UMNO-dominated Malayan Government had all along objected to that, fearing that the inclusion of over a million Chinese in Singapore would upset the delicate racial arithmetic in the Federation. In 1961 the population of Malaya stood at just over seven million. The biggest group comprised the Malays, who formed just below half of the overall population. The 2.7 million Chinese constituted about 38 per cent of the population. Together with the Indians who formed just under 10 per cent of the population, the non-

Malays actually outnumbered the Malay population in the Federation. However, as the largest ethnic group, the Malays had been able to maintain a position of political primacy in the country, a position which has been preserved by a coalition arrangement the dominant UMNO shared with the Malayan Chinese Association and the Malayan Indian Congress, the racial parties representing the Chinese and Indian communities respectively. Thus, although the Alliance government in Malaya was based on inter-racial cooperation, the political order had always been predicated on Malay political dominance.[78] But with a direct merger with Singapore, the Chinese population of the combined territories would then be greater than the Malay population; and this would lead to a further strengthening of the influence that the Chinese community already had on economic life of the country. The Malay leadership feared that economic predominance would eventually lead to political control, whatever constitutional safeguards may be put in place.[79]

But it was not just the one million Chinese that the Tunku was unwilling to incorporate into the Federation; it was also radical Chinese influence that he was most afraid of. As Lee Kuan Yew explains:

> The Tunku had all along opposed the idea of a merger, i.e. a merger with Singapore alone, fearful of its upsetting the racial balance which was Malaysia's main political problem, and also that Singapore was regarded as a communist power-house. He was basically fearful that the Chinese majority in Singapore might join with the Chinese minority in the Federation to the detriment of the interests of the Malays.

The Malayan Prime Minister had long held the view that Singapore was a "power-house" of communist subversion, and that the Federation, which had only recently defeated an armed insurrection, must at all cost insulate the peninsula from this pernicious influence from the south.[80] Since 1955, as he became increasingly aghast at the boisterousness of the trade unions and radical student organizations in Singapore, his policy had been one of systematic isolation and the cutting of all ties between Singapore and the Federation, believing that it was in Malaya's best interest that the British would continue looking after Singapore.[81] Given the state of politics in Singapore, the incorporation of the colony into the Federation, as he had been urged to do so many times, was simply out of the question. Malay politicians also believed that there was a higher proportion of Chinese sympathizers in the communist movement and if Singapore were to be annexed to the Federation, the left-wing votes in the combined territory would be increased significantly. For a long time, therefore, the Tunku and his Malay ministers had maintained their position that Singapore and its predominantly Chinese population had to be kept out of the Federation.[82]

The refusal of the Tunku to contemplate merger with Singapore was also based on his strong distrust of Singapore politics. The political differences between Singapore and the Federation were obvious. The Tunku had publicly described his Alliance government as right-wing, and he and his ministers harboured a strong suspicion of socialism, which they tended to regard as synonymous with communism.[83] Federation ministers were therefore unable and unwilling to place complete trust in a Singapore government that was openly committed to democratic socialism, an ideology that was believed to have widespread appeal amongst the Chinese population in Singapore.[84] Further, there was the fear that once the PAP or any left-wing Singapore party was able to organize itself on a pan-Malayan basis, they could eventually weld the opposition parties into an effective bloc, which could very effectively threaten UMNO political dominance.[85] In any case, the Tunku believed that the predominantly Chinese population in Singapore was never keen to assume a pan-Malayan identity as their natural tendency was to "make the Colony a little China".[86] He, therefore, doubted if the Chinese in Singapore would ever make Singapore or Malaya the focus of their loyalty. Having seen the state of affairs in Singapore, the Tunku was apparently unwilling to consider any form of federation with Singapore, fearing that in the future, a communist government in Singapore might destabilize the peninsula itself. In this regard, domestic politics played a part. The Alliance government was concerned that the PMIP, whose political fortunes were on the wane, would exploit anti-Singapore sentiments in Malaya to win back Malay electoral support.[87] As far as the Tunku was concerned, the interests of the Federation would best be served by keeping Singapore separate, and should the situation in the island colony get out of hand, the Federation could easily insulate itself from the effects by physical means, such as the closure of the causeway, and by relying on friendly western powers.[88]

While the Malayans had very strong political reasons against the proposed union between Singapore and Malaya, they saw, at the same time, little or no economic benefits from merger that would outweigh the political disadvantages. As mentioned above, even without merger, the Federation had been able to enjoy the commercial services which Singapore, with its financial and commercial expertise, could offer. Indeed, the Singapore economy depended to a large extent on its ability to provide these services to the Malayans economically and efficiently.[89] However, the Federation was already developing in a number of ways that would reduce her dependence on Singapore, for example, in the creation of a Central Bank, Stock Exchange, Rubber Market and international airport.[90] Certainly, the Federation did not require the small Singapore market of one and a half million people, when its own domestic market of over seven million people was more substantial. A common market, which the Singapore Government had vigorously pursued, was thus a non-issue from the Malayan's point of view as it was already enjoying duty-free entry for its goods into Singapore. Latching on Singapore with its volatile trade unions and politicized workforce might in fact prove a liability for the Federation's industrialization efforts; the Federation, on its own, with its stable labour conditions, right-wing government and larger domestic market, would be better able to attract industrialists.[91] Malayan ministers thus did not respond favourably to Singapore's proposals for an integrated industrialization programme and for a limited common market. Exploratory talks were held, but did not make much headway.

While rejecting the idea of any form of integration between Singapore and the Federation, the Tunku was, however, very much more receptive to the idea of a Grand Design of a closer association between the Federation and the Borneo Territories, in which it was doubtful if he saw any part for Singapore.[92] The Tunku's interests in forming a grand federation of Malaya and the British colonies in North Borneo had preceded the Federation's independence, and on many occasions he had publicly raised the possibility of the formation of such an association. Noordin Sopiee mentions a speech made by the Tunku at the UMNO General Assembly in December 1955 in which he suggested that Singapore, Sarawak, North Borneo and Brunei should consider joining the Federation as member states, if each felt that it was too small to achieve independence on its own.[93] Although he refused further comments on it when pressed by journalists to elaborate on his Greater Malaysia concept while on his way to the London constitutional talks in 1956,[94] he was to mention again, a few months later, and in clarification to his remarks that he "would not have Singapore at all", that he would welcome Singapore, Sarawak, Brunei and British North Borneo into a "greater Malaya" nation "if they themselves come in voluntarily".[95] He was, however, quick to add that he was merely "thinking of the distant future", and that at this stage, his priorities were not with territorial expansion but with developing the Federation itself.[96] In June 1956 Dr Ismail Abdul Rahman, Vice-President of the United Malays National Organisation (UMNO), revealed to the American Consul General in Kuala Lumpur, Thomas K. Wright, that the Tunku was already contemplating a Greater Federation of Malaya with Brunei, Borneo and Sarawak.[97] Immediately after independence in August 1957, the Malayan prime minister pursued the idea further when it was announced in a BBC broadcast that he was favourable to the idea of extending the Malayan Federation to the Borneo Territories, if these territories wanted this. He pointed out that the new Federation constitution had provisions for a "Greater Federation" to enable the inclusion of the Borneo territories, and eventually Singapore and the Malayans would be "happy if some of them will come in".[98] Clearly, even then, the Tunku was aware that at some stage, he would be asked to consider taking Singapore into the Federation. Should the British want the Malayans to take on board the problematic Singapore, the Tunku would ask that they concede his Greater Malaysia plan first.[99]

Prior to a visit to the Philippines in January 1959, the Malayan prime minister had informal talks with Malcolm MacDonald and Geofroy Tory, the British High Commissioner in Kuala Lumpur, in the course of which he referred to the long-term future of the Borneo territories. He then said that he had in mind some sort of political union between the Borneo territories, the Federation of Malaya, and that the long-term future of the territories obviously lay with Malaysia.[100] He also discussed this subject with the Governors of Sarawak and North Borneo when he passed through those territories on his way to the Philippines. He mentioned that his government would not consider a merger of Singapore and Malaya alone because the Malays could not regard with favour the idea of the Singapore Chinese re-enforcing the Chinese in Malaya with the effect of establishing in due course a Chinese political predominance. He had in mind that if the three Borneo territories came into a Five-Power Federation the non-Chinese populations of those territories would be a counterweight to the Singapore Chinese.[101] The British believed that the Tunku "looked upon the indigenous races of the Borneo Territories as almost Malays" and his appeal for the territories there to enter into some form of federation with Malaya was made on the grounds that "all Malays should stand together".[102] Talking to some American journalists in 1958, the Tunku once again reiterated that Malaya would be "only too happy to take into its fold the Malay territories of Brunei, Sarawak and North Borneo",[103] stating that "their people are within our group [and] have the same characteristics as we". He further added, "it would be good financially. They have oil."[104] In 1960, Senu Abdul Rahman, the Federation's ambassador to Indonesia, undertook a study tour of the North Borneo territories, probably to gauge response among the locals to the idea of Malaysia. He subsequently submitted a report to UMNO, in which he concluded that the indigenous peoples of Borneo were akin to the Malays, and that if Malaysia were to come about, the Malay races would predominate if the Borneo territories were incorporated.[105] This was of primary concern to the Tunku: on no occasion must Malay predominance, in absolute numbers and political power, be jeopardized.[106] Lord Selkirk, however, took a more cynical view of the affair; he knew that the Tunku was well aware that Borneo was not a Malay country but nonetheless regarded the indigenous people as natural allies against the Chinese.[107]

In June 1960, at the Commonwealth Prime Minister's meeting in London, the Tunku suggested to Lord Perth of the Colonial Office that "although merger was unacceptable to the Federation government, a package deal, including Singapore and the Borneo Territories was another matter".[108] In his overall plan, the Tunku indicated a particular keenness on Brunei, attracted as he was to the valuable addition of the resources of oil-rich Brunei to the Federation treasury, and where he had previously attempted to forge links with the Brunei administration by seconding Malayan officers to fill key posts in Brunei.[109] He was further lured by the prospects of a doubling of the Federation's territories if Brunei with Sarawak could be reunited — with the Sultan of Brunei taking over the latter — and then brought together into the Federation of Malaya.[110] And while he was interested in the integration with Brunei and Sarawak, also partly because he believed the two territories had racial affinity with Malaya, he was clearly less enthusiastic about North Borneo and Singapore, where the Malays formed a small minority within a non-Malay majority.[111] He was thus quite happy to let the British retain North Borneo for defence purposes, as a "British fortress" colony outside this association. However, this was rejected by the British on the grounds that retaining North Borneo as a Crown colony was an impractical proposition in the event that Sarawak assumed self-government status as part of the Malaysian Federation. British officials thus decided against giving any form of encouragement to the Tunku on this score.[112] As far as Singapore was concerned, the Tunku would prefer the British to remain in control, as at present, for a long time.[113] By 1960 it had become clear to the British that the Tunku and his Malayan ministers were demanding the Borneo Territories as "the necessary sugar to sweeten the pill of Singapore",[114] if the British were keen to push through its Grand Design. The Tunku was clearly out to impress the British Government that "it would be politically impossible for him to accept any kind of link with Singapore even in a limited kind of field such as internal security except on broad lines of a Greater Malaysia plan". His Malays would never forgive him if he were by connection with Singapore alone to create at any time a Chinese majority in the two territories.[115] While the Tunku was clearly concerned about Lee's position in Singapore and the pressing reasons for his desire to get some tangible link with Malaya in the near future, he was determined to hold his position that he will have none of Singapore by itself and it will be all of Greater Malaysia or nothing.[116]

While the Tunku remained adamant in his opposition to merger with Singapore, his cabinet colleagues were gradually becoming less sure if merger was such a terrible thing. Several of his ministers had privately expressed their willingness to seriously consider a merger with Singapore. Dr Ismail, Minister for the Interior, had on the sidelines of the Internal Security Council meeting at the Cameron Highlands on 25 June 1960 held a private conversation with H.T. Bourdillon, Deputy Commissioner in Singapore, in which he spoke of the possibility of bringing about a merger between the Federation and Singapore but which would embrace the Borneo Territories as well. [117] Ismail was not alone in having such a view. Tun Abdul Razak, the Federation Deputy Prime Minister and Minister for Defence as well as Rural Development, had a more sophisticated plan. He proposed a three-stage plan in which Sarawak and Brunei, united under the Sultan of Brunei, be brought into Malaya in the first stage. Following this, North Borneo would be brought into the Federation in an association similar to Penang or Malacca. Finally, Singapore would be brought in, but under special status and on different terms from the other states in the Federation. [118] These younger ministers, it had seemed, were alive to the dangers of allowing Singapore to drift towards a greater stage of independence, in which case Singapore would either fall into the hands of the communists, or be absorbed by Indonesia. [119] According to Lee, Tun Razak had seen the potential danger of Singapore outside Malaysia being turned into a potential Cuban base that could strike at the heartland of the Federation. [120] He believed that Razak was already converted and could in turn be expected to break down the Tunku's prejudices. That the Tunku was slowly coming round to the view that merger with Singapore was an option he could not dismiss lightly was indicated by his public remarks, in January 1961, that the Singapore government was "as good a Malayan Government as [his]" and that the Federation was ready to work in close cooperation with Singapore. However, he was quick to add that merger would have to wait for some time "as certain elements among Chinese [in Singapore] are China minded". [121] The Tunku was believed to have remarked to Geofroy Tory in early 1961 that he thought that Lee Kuan Yew was facing too many troubles in Singapore and needed "a little assistance" from him. [122] Towards the end of April 1961, the

Tunku seemed ready to discuss questions of merger with Lee, possibly because the arguments brought upon him by Razak and his other ministers that an independent Singapore would be a source of continuous danger and embarrassment to the Federation were beginning to sink in.[123]

There was little doubt that the British "in their own pragmatic ways" helped to bring the Tunku to this point of view. The British were getting increasingly anxious at the Tunku's stubborn refusal for any merger with Singapore. They knew that if the Tunku persisted in closing his doors to Singapore, the pressure towards separate independence for the Colony would strengthen, and the moderate PAP government would either have to give way or be overthrown. This was likely to lead to the emergence of a radically left-wing government which might resort to industrial unrest or even violence to force the issue of independence. The British Government would then have to face the difficult decision of either withdrawal or repression; the latter scenario was something which London wanted to avoid at all cost. British officials were thus encouraged to convince the Tunku and his ministers to take "a more sober view of their relations with Singapore".[124] During his visit to Malaya in January 1961, the idea of merger was very much on Duncan Sandys' agenda.[125] While attending a Commonwealth Prime Ministerial Meeting in London in February 1961, the Tunku had a number of meetings with Macmillan in which the latter expressed Whitehall's concerns of the political situation in Singapore, and spoke of the need for merger and the formation of Malaysia. Macmillan painted a distressing scenario of a deteriorating situation in Singapore for Malaya. A communist-controlled Singapore would be to Malaya what Cuba was to the United States. Once Singapore became an independent state, it would not be easy for the Tunku to exercise any control, as it would be regarded as external interference and would elicit world condemnation. To control Singapore's internal security situation, and thus protect the Federation, it was necessary for Tunku to bring Singapore under the control of Kuala Lumpur.[126]

But the Tunku was probably weighing the options himself. It was apparent to him that the situation in Singapore was changing, and that a constitutional review was due in 1963. The increasingly slender hold on government by the PAP highlighted the ever-ominous threat that Singapore would soon have a communist-led government. This and the realization that the British would not be able to look after Singapore indefinitely for him, led him to give serious consideration to a possible merger. With the deterioration of the PAP government in Singapore, with the risk in Singapore of a communist take-over, and with a growing conviction that the British could not be relied on to counter the risk, the Tunku decided to take the calculated risk of staying ahead of events.[127] That the Tunku was already preparing for a major decision was reflected in remarks which he was reported to have made to Reuters:

> On the question of merger between Malaya and Singapore, the Tunku said, there would be no problem if the politicians in Singapore had not been given too much rope. The British in Singapore have not been firm enough — they have wanted to please everyone and politicians and trade union leaders have been allowed to do what they want. Because of this and because the government in Singapore is now powerless to do anything in this matter, the people are looking to the Federation. I do not know what we can do but the time has come to do something.[128]

To the Tunku, the risk that popular support for Lee Kuan Yew in Singapore was rapidly dwindling was palpable and if a general election should be called in Singapore, there were fears that it would easily be won by the elements of the extreme left, which in Tunku's judgement and that of all his advisers, was a classical communist front manipulated by Lim Chin Siong, who was regarded by the Malayan leadership as a hard-core communist.[129]

Both the British and Lee had also brought the Tunku to the realization that the British, having given Singapore its constitution, would have to adhere to it themselves, which would preclude them from taking an active part in using undemocratic measures for the purpose of frustrating communism. In due course, too, when the constitutional review was due (in 1963), Singapore would demand independence which the British would be hard put not to grant. Thereafter, the Tunku foresaw that "Peking and Moscow would establish Missions in Singapore, and that as soon as the Communist powers had provided Singapore with the necessary guarantees, economic and military, British rights and interests in Singapore would be liquidated". If the British were eventually going to pull out of Singapore, the Tunku realized that he had little option but to step in for fear of Malaya's own security and integrity. In short, the Tunku reasoned "if Singapore is to be saved from communism, then [he] himself must do it".[130]

By 1961, the easy but short-term solution of keeping Singapore out was no longer a viable option for the Tunku. The long-term dangers of keeping Singapore outside the Federation were clearly unacceptable. The Tunku started to signal that he was gradually coming to the conclusion that Malaya would have to accept the responsibility for Singapore.

But to solve the problem of making the unpopular decision of merging with Singapore, he had to be sure he could bring in the Borneo territories as a counterweight, and then be able to devise a constitutional arrangement that would limit Singapore's political influence in the Federation. He would, however, be exposing himself to attacks from the Malay nationalists if the terms and conditions of merger with Singapore betrayed possibilities of increased Chinese influence and the loss of Malay predominance in the new and extended Federation.

The broad framework of a "Greater Malaysian" plan had by the middle of 1961 been formed in the Tunku's mind. Upon merger, Singapore would be given special status as a state within the Federation. Kuala Lumpur would take over the defence and internal security responsibilities of the island from the British, but Singapore would remain essentially responsible for other functions of local government as it stood. For that purpose, it would have to maintain its own civil service. But as a first step and a prerequisite — the "sugar that will sweeten the pill of Singapore" — the Federation would also take over responsibility for the administration of the three Borneo territories — North Borneo, Sarawak and Brunei, either united or separately, but on the same basis of the existing states of the Federation, and unlike Singapore, in a very subordinate position and with very little powers in their hands.[131] The Tunku expected Brunei to join the Federation almost immediately, with Sarawak and North Borneo joining a little later, once the British Government had given a firm lead in convincing the peoples of those territories of the desirability of joining the Federation.[132] And finally, in satisfying that most basic of British requirement, the existing defence treaty with the Federation would be extended to Singapore and the Borneo territories, thus ensuring that the British-led defence framework in the region would remain intact.

NOTES

1 Note for Secretary of State's discussions with Selkirk, 5 July 1961, DO 169/26, Public Records Office.

2 Ibid.

3 UK High Commissioner to Malaya to Secretary of State for Commonwealth Relations, 7 December 1960, DO 169/114.

4 Prior to 1867 Singapore, together with the Straits Settlements of Malacca and Penang, was administered by the Indian Government. In that year, the Straits Settlements became a British Crown Colony. From 1942 to 1945 the island was occupied by the Japanese. Upon the restoration of civilian government at the end of the War, Singapore was detached from the other Straits Settlements to become a separate colony. In a White Paper published at that time (Cmd. 6724, January 1946), it was stated that "in considering the need for a closer integration in Malay, His Majesty's Government consider that, at least for the time being, Singapore requires separate treatment... It is recognised, however, that there were, and will be, close ties between Singapore and the mainland".

5 For the story of the Malayan Union, see Anthony J. Stockwell, *British Policy and Malay Politics during the Malayan Union Experiment, 1945–48* (Singapore: Malaysian Branch of the Royal Asiatic Society, 1979); and Albert Lau, *The Malayan Union Controversy, 1942–48* (Singapore: Oxford University Press, 1990).

6 Nicholas Tarling, *Nations and States in Southeast Asia* (Cambridge: Cambridge University Press, 1998), p. 77.

7 Ibid.

8 Yeo Kim Wah, *Political Development in Singapore, 1950–55* (Singapore: Singapore University Press, 1973), p. 14.

9 For this, see Chin Kin Wah, *The Defence of Malaysia and Singapore: The Transformation of a Security System 1957–71* (Cambridge: Cambridge University Press, 1983).

10 Yeo Kim Wah and Albert Lau, "From Colonialism to Independence, 1945–65",

in Ernest Chew and Edwin Lee, eds., *A History of Singapore* (Singapore: Oxford University Press, 1991), pp. 124–25.

11 Ibid., p. 125.

12 *Straits Times*, 26 March 1953, quoted in ibid.

13 See Yeo, *Political Development in Singapore*, pp. 44–49; and Mohammed Noordin Sopiee, *From Malayan Union to Singapore Separation: Political Unification in the Malayan Region, 1945–65* (Kuala Lumpur: Universiti Malaya, 1974), chapter 5.

14 *Straits Times*, 24 January 1955.

15 Ibid.

16 In July 1954, following the publication of the Rendel Report, the Singapore Labour Party sought to extend its organizational base by drawing in former socialists together to form a Labour Front under the leadership of David Marshall.

17 *Straits Echo*, 7 February 1955.

18 *Straits Times*, 5 March 1955.

19 Sopiee, *From Malayan Union to Singapore Separation*, p. 110.

20 The Malay Union Alliance was a parliamentary coalition of UMNO and the Malayan Chinese Association.

21 C.M. Turnbull, *A History of Singapore, 1819–1988*, 2nd edn (Singapore: Oxford University Press, 1989), pp. 257–58.

22 Ibid.

23 Ibid.

24 *Report of the Singapore Constitutional Conference Held in London in March and April 1957. Presented by the Secretary of State for the Colonies to Parliament by command of Her Majesty* (London: Her Majesty's Stationery Office, 1957), Cmd 147.

25 Singapore attained internal self-government in June 1959. The new constitution provided for a legislative assembly with fifty-one elected members and a cabinet responsible for the assembly. While the local government assumed responsibilities for domestic development such as labour, education, culture, finance, health and national development, the key portfolios of defence, external affairs and some internal security responsibilities remained with the United Kingdom, overseen by its Commissioner in Singapore. An internal security council was set up, comprising the UK Commissioner and five other members, two appointed by the UK, two by the Prime Minister of Singapore and one by the Government of the Federation of Malaya.

26 Ong Chit Chung, "The 1959 Singapore General Election", *Journal of Southeast Asian Studies* 6, no. 1 (March 1975): 66.

27 Ibid.

28 "An assessment of the present situation and the future outlook in Singapore", Department of External Affairs, Canberra, 20 August 1957, 'Singapore — Internal

Affairs', A1838/318, no. 3024/1/7, Part 1, Australian National Archives, Canberra.

29 Han Fook Kwang, Warren Fernandez, Sumiko Tan, *Lee Kuan Yew: The Man and His Ideas* (Singapore: Singapore Press Holdings and Times Editions, 1998), p. 70.
30 Han, Fernandez and Tan, *Lee Kuan Yew*, p. 67.
31 Speech by Lee Kuan Yew at the luncheon of the Singapore National Union of Journalists, 24 May 1963.
32 Ibid.
33 Cited in Turnbull, *A History of Singapore*, p. 267.
34 Economic Relations between Singapore and Malaya, CO 1030/972.
35 Ibid.
36 Yeo and Lau, "From Colonialism to Independence, 1945–65", p. 133.
37 Lee Kuan Yew, *The Battle for Merger* (Singapore: Government Printing Office, 1962), p. 16
38 Selkirk to Secretary of State (Colonial Office), 2 May 1961, CO 1030/979.
39 Lee Kuan Yew, Radio Broadcast, 25 September 1961.
40 *Singapore Legislative Assembly Debates*, 20 July 1961, Col. 1668.
41 Note on "Lee Kuan Yew, Merger and Malaysia" by British Secretary of State, DO 169/249.
42 Note of Meeting on 26 June 1960 in Singapore, DO 169/26.
43 Han, Fernandez and Tan, *Lee Kuan Yew*, p. 280.
44 M. J. Moynihan, to Commonwealth Relations Office, 12 October 1961, DO 169/30; and Tunku's speech in Parliament on 16 October 1961, as given to the press.
45 Note of meeting between UK delegation and Singapore delegation on Internal Security Council, which took place on Saturday, as enclosed in Acting UK Commissioner (Singapore) to Secretary of State (Colonial Office), 28 June 1960, CO 1030/977 no. 256.
46 Enclosure no. 1 to Selkirk's despatch no. 2 of 30 January 1961, to the Colonial Office, CO 1030/978.
47 Report of meeting between Lee Kuan Yew and Sir Geofroy Tory, UK High Commissioner (Kuala Lumpur), on 21 and 22 December 1959, CO 1030/972.
48 *Petir*, 4th Anniversary issue (Singapore, 1958).
49 People's Action Party, *Sixth Anniversary Celebrations Souvenir* (Singapore, 1960).
50 *Singapore Legislative Assembly Debates*, 8 October 1958, Col. 804.
51 Sopiee, *Malayan Union to Singapore Separation*, p. 116.
52 Lily Zubaidah Rahim, *The Singapore Dilemma: The Political and Educational Marginality of the Malay Community* (Kuala Lumpur: Oxford University Press, 1998), p. 189.
53 Yeo and Lau, "From Colonialism to Independence, 1945–65", p. 140.

54 Lee Kuan Yew, Radio Broadcast, 27 September 1961.

55 Selkirk to Macleod, 15 March 1960, CO 1030/925.

56 Selkirk to Macleod, 27 June 1961, CO 1030/980.

57 Record of conversation between Lee Kuan Yew and Selkirk, 24 April 1961, DO 169/25.

58 Ibid.

59 Draft brief for Prime Minister's Conference, 13 February 1961, CO 1030/978.

60 Selkirk to Macleod, 30 January 1961, CO 1030/973.

61 Proposals for a Wider Association between the British Borneo Territories, Singapore and the Federation of Malaya, n.d., CO 1030/980.

62 Ibid.

63 H.T. Bourdillon to Melville, 17 December 1960, CO 1030/973.

64 Ibid.

65 Record of conversation between Lee Kuan Yew and Philip Moore, 28 April 1961, DO 169/25.

66 Paper on the future on the Federation of Malaya, Singapore and the Borneo Territories by Lee Kuan Yew, n.d., CO 1030/979.

67 Ibid.

68 Ibid.

69 According to the paper, Malaya would be entitled to the 68 seats with Singapore and the Borneo Territories taking 16 and 12 seats respectively. See ibid.

70 Ibid.

71 Ibid.

72 Moore to H. T. Bourdillon and Selkirk, 6 June 1961.

73 Note of a meeting between UK delegation and Singapore delegation on Internal Security Council, which took place on Saturday, as enclosed in Acting UK Commissioner (Singapore) to Secretary of State (Colonial Office), 28 June 1960, CO 1030/977 no. 256.

74 Ibid.

75 Singapore *Legislative Assembly Debates*, 30 July 1963, Col. 301.

76 Lee Kuan Yew, National Day Rally Address at the Padang, on 3 June 1961.

77 "Greater Malaysia", a paper by the Commonwealth Relations Office, n.d., DO 169/247.

78 Although the Tunku had effectively developed a form of inter-racial cooperation with which he was able to win independence from the British and the maintain the government of the Federation, he and his Malay ministers had always maintained that the interests of the Malays were paramount, and would never agree to anything that would result in the political subordination of the Malay race. See A. J. Brown (Kuala Lumpur), to W. F. G. Le Bailly (Commonwealth

Relations Office), "Malayan Attitudes to 'Grand Design' and Singapore", 13 July 1961, DO 169/10.

79 Brown to Le Bailly, 13 July 1961, DO 169/10.

80 Tunku Abdul Rahman to Commonwealth Relations Office, 16 August 1961, PREM 11/3418.

81 Han, Fernandez and Tan, *Lee Kuan Yew,* p. 280.

82 "Greater Malaysia", a paper by the Commonwealth Relations Office, n.d., DO 169/247.

83 Brown to Le Bailly (Commonwealth Relations Office), "Malayan Attitudes to 'Grand Design' and Singapore", 13 July 1961, DO 169/10.

84 Ibid.

85 Ibid.

86 Tunku's speech to Foreign Correspondent's Association, 27 May 1961.

87 Brief by Commonwealth Relations Office to the Cabinet Committee on Greater Malaysia, 6 November 1961, CAB 134/1949.

88 Selkirk to MacLeod, 27 June 1961, PREM 11/3418.

89 Ibid.

90 Memorandum on Greater Malaysia, September 1961, CO 1030/992.

91 Brown to Le Bailly, 13 July 1961, DO 169/10.

92 British High Commissioner in the Federation of Malaya to the Secretary of State for Commonwealth Relations, "Federation of Malaya: Background to the Greater Malaysia Plan", 20 October 1961, DO 169/30. See also note of meeting in Colonial Office on "Relations between the Federation of Malaya and Singapore", 26 July 1960, CO 1030/972.

93 Mohamed Noordin Sopiee, "The Advocacy of Malaysia — before 1961", *Modern Asian Studies* 7, no. 4 (1973): 724.

94 Ibid.

95 *Singapore Standard*, 23 June 1956, as cited in Sopiee, "The Advocacy of Malaysia — before 1961", pp. 725–26.

96 Ibid.

97 Memorandum of conversation between Dr Ismail (Vice President of UMNO) and Thomas K. Wright, (American Counsul General, Kuala Lumpur), 1 June 1956, File 350, US State Department Files.

98 *Singapore Standard*, 25 September 1957, as cited in Sopiee, "The Advocacy of Malaysia — before 1961", p. 728.

99 Ibid.

100 Note by Moynihan on Malaysia, 12 October 1961, DO 169/30.

101 The Future of the Borneo Territories, n.d., CO 1030/977.

102 Brown to Le Bailly, 13 July 1961, DO 169/10.

103 *Sunday Standard*, 16 February 1958, cited by Sopiee, "The Advocacy of Malaysia — before 1961", p. 729.

104 *Sunday Times*, 16 February 1958, cited by Sopiee, "The Advocacy of Malaysia — before 1961", p. 729.

105 Sopiee, *Malayan Union to Singapore Separation*, pp. 136–37.

106 Despatch from UK High Commissioner in KL to the Secretary of State for Commonwealth Relations, 12 October 1961, PREM 11/3422.

107 Note on Meeting in Singapore, 26 June 1961, DO 169/26.

108 Brown to Le Bailly, 13 July 1961, DO 169/10.

109 Ibid.

110 Selkirk to Macleod, 16 May 1961, DO 169/25.

111 Note by Colonial Office for Cabinet Committee on Greater Malaysia, Draft Brief for Minister on Race in the Borneo Territories, 7 November 1961, CO 1030/1003.

112 Memorandum from Secretary of State for Colonies to Cabinet Colonial Policy Committee, April 1961.

113 Tory to Sandys, 1 December 1960, CO 1030/978.

114 Brown to Le Bailly, 13 July 1961, DO 169/10.

115 Kuala Lumpur to Commonwealth Relations Office, 5 August 1961, CO 1030/981 no. 576.

116 Ibid.

117 Memorandum no. 1020, Critchley to Secretary, Department of External Affairs, 14 July 1960, A1838/333 no. 3006/10/4 Part 1.

118 Critchley to Secretary, Department of External Affairs, on his private conversation with Razak, A/1838/280 no. 3027/2/1 Part 1.

119 Moore to Selkirk, 7 April 1961, CO 1030/979.

120 Lee Kuan Yew's speech to Singapore National Union of Journalists, 24 May 1963.

121 FCO Research Department Memorandum, "The Origins and Formation of Malaysia", 10 July 1970, FCO 51/154, in Anthony. J. Stockwell, ed., *Malaysia. British Documents on the End of Empire*, Series B, Vol. 8 (London: Stationery Office, 2004), p. 597.

122 Ibid., p. 598.

123 Record of Conversation between Lee Kuan Yew and P. B. C. Moore, United Kingdom Commission (Singapore), 28 April 1961, DO 169/25.

124 "Background Note on Singapore-Malaya Relations", n.d, CO 1030/973.

125 Milton Osborne, *Singapore and Malaysia* (New York: Cornell University, 1964), p. 13.

126 Sopiee, *Malayan Union to Singapore Separation*, p. 138.

127 British High Commissioner in the Federation of Malaya to the Secretary of State

for Commonwealth Relations, "Federation of Malaya: Background to the Greater Malaysia Plan", 20 October 1961, DO 169/30.

128 Reported in telegram from British Commission (Kuala Lumpur) to Commonwealth Relations Office, 6 November 1961, DO 169/30.

129 Ibid.

130 Ibid.

131 Commonwealth Relations Office note for Secretary of State's discussions with Selkirk on Wednesday, 5 July 1961, DO 169/26.

132 Ibid; and Commonwealth Relations Office memorandum on Committee on Greater Malaysia, "Summary of Malayan Proposals and Issues to be considered by the British government", 25 September 1961, CAB 134/1949.

CHAPTER THREE

Setting the Stage:
Tunku's Ulster-type Merger and
Singapore's White Paper Proposals

By May 1961, although the Tunku was evidently prepared to contemplate the possibility of a merger between the Federation and Singapore, he was nonetheless adamant that two essential conditions first be satisfied. First, before being committed to an agreement to bring Singapore into the Federation, he wanted to be absolutely certain that he would be able to incorporate the three Borneo territories, with their predominantly non-Chinese population, to form a wider Malaysian Federation. Second, the Singapore Government would have to agree to have a smaller representation in the federal parliament than they would otherwise be entitled to on a population basis.[1] In return, the Tunku was prepared to concede to Singapore the retention of much wider local powers than the other member states of the Federation. The intention behind the conditions was obvious: it was vital to the Malayan Government that the terms of the merger with Singapore should contain provisions that would safeguard the Federation as a whole against what the UMNO and Malay politicians feared most — the possibility of Chinese political domination. The Tunku was clearly caught in the horns of a dilemma. He knew, on the one hand, that pro-communist forces were gaining ground in Singapore, and that a communist-controlled independent Singapore would give him no end of trouble. The only way he could control the situation was to bring Singapore into the Federation and then deal with the communist threat there as an internal security issue directly from Kuala Lumpur. Yet, he knew of the political cost of bringing Singapore into the Federation — the addition of 1.3 million Chinese on the island would upset the racial balance in the Federation, and "ruin the calm atmosphere there". Lee Kuan Yew was aware of the Tunku's deep-seated mistrust of the Chinese — "many Chinese educated and new immigrants to the country", the Tunku was reported to have said, "will always be loyal to China and they are less Malayan-minded".[2] Earlier overtures on the part of the Singapore Government to merger with Malaya had repeatedly been rejected by the Tunku primarily because of the Chinese factor. But Lee knew that by 1961 the Tunku was beginning to take notice of the increasingly tenuous political situation in Singapore. The Tunku would have to act, but, clearly, he would only do so on his own terms.

Accordingly, the Tunku laid down his specific conditions for the effecting of his Greater Malaysia scheme. As a first step, he wanted Brunei, North Borneo and Sarawak to be brought into the Malayan Federation as constituent units on the same basis as the existing states (although he had also indicated to certain Borneo leaders his preparedness to give the Borneo territories a large measure of self-government). This move was regarded as a necessary step to strengthen his political position if Singapore was later to be part of the Federation. The incorporation of Borneo, with its non-Chinese population, would correct the imbalance in the racial arithmetic of the Federation. As the Tunku admitted, "without the Borneo territories, I would find it impossible to contemplate the integration of Singapore and the Federation or to persuade my political colleagues and the country to accept it".[3] Ghazali Shafie, permanent secretary of the Malayan external affairs ministry, and one of the Tunku's key lieutenants in the merger negotiations, was later to note, "it [was] imperative that Malaysia had to have the Borneo territories; a single merger with Singapore was a non-starter".[4]

Once the above had been secured, the Malayan Government would then allow Singapore to join the Federation "as an autonomous state with absolute rights to determine its own internal affairs, except in matters of Defence, External Affairs and Internal Security".[5] In return for that special status, Singapore would have to accept a proportionately smaller representation in central parliament than it could claim on a population basis.[6] The administrative structure in Singapore would be retained, and the state would maintain its own civil service. On the issue of the use of military bases in Singapore, the Tunku's proposals were that the British bases in Singapore should cease to be used for SEATO purposes, but could be maintained as bases for Commonwealth defence.

The type of merger that the Tunku was contemplating with Singapore was borne out of certain political realities that the Malayan Prime Minister was facing at home. He had no doubt that merger would provide Singapore with what its people wanted — economic security and freedom from outside interference and intervention in its affairs. But the form of association should be such that it should at the same time provide protection for the people of the Federation. In a speech to the Federal Parliament on the subject of merger, Tunku explained that

> We cannot admit Singapore to complete merger without great [sic] deal of unhappiness and trouble, and we must find a middle course. Federation and Singapore Governments have set up working party to study question. Its terms of reference are to look into all aspects of merger with Singapore including defence, administration, finance and economics with wide powers for Singapore without prejudice to the principle of strong central government. Terms also include examination of separate citizenship for Federation and Singapore with single nationality, without one citizenship being inferior to the others.[7]

He indicated, at the same time, that he was prepared to consider Singapore as a special case, and that it should join the Federation of Malaysia on a partnership basis "like that which exists between the United Kingdom and Northern Ireland".[8] As in the case of Northern Ireland's relations with the United Kingdom of Great Britain, Singapore would enjoy a measure of local self-government with powers to deal with local affairs. In other words, Singapore would, therefore, become part of the Federation and yet remain outside, a case of "partners in one identity".[9]

British officials had noted that as early as June 1961, the Tunku, who evidently had been giving much thought to the issue of merger, seemed to have already made up his mind that the only possible association with

Singapore, from his standpoint, would be an Ulster pattern with Singapore maintaining extensive local autonomy, but with some representation in Federal parliament in Kuala Lumpur.[10] In August 1961, Tunku confirmed that he would propose to Lee the "broad outlines" of his proposed association between the Federation and Singapore before they both met in London. He instructed Ghazali Shafie, now specially appointed by the Tunku as a project officer for the formation of Malaysia,[11] to do some research into the Ulster Constitution with a view to adapting it to the Federation/Singapore conditions.[12] Shafie was instructed that the concept of merger that he was to draw up had to be acceptable to all parties concerned, namely the Malayan Government, the British Government, and the people of Singapore.[13] He had already had a series of dialogues with Lee Kuan Yew on the question of Singapore's merger with the Federation, and was confident that the Singapore leader wanted merger badly enough to support the concept of a wider Federation of Malaysia,[14] and on the terms that had been suggested by the Tunku.

Having sounded the possibility of a wider Federation of Malaysia in his 27 May speech, and encouraged by the positive sentiments from Singapore and the Borneo territories,[15] the Malayan Government decided that it now had to influence the British Government to think seriously of the subject. The Tunku then wrote to the British Prime Minister on 26 June 1961, enclosing a memorandum outlining his preliminary thoughts on the proposed merger, in which he had envisaged that while Singapore would be taken into the Federation in a special position and retaining a certain amount of local autonomy, the Borneo territories would enter the wider Federation as units on the same basis as the existing states of the Federation. In response to the Tunku's letter, Harold Macmillan, following discussions with Selkirk in London in July, replied to the Tunku on 3 August 1961, inviting him and Lee Kuan Yew to come to London in late October or early November to discuss the proposals. Both Lee and Tunku accepted the invitation, but the Tunku, in a letter to Macmillan dated 11 August 1961, made it clear that he could not agree to the integration of Singapore into the Federation without the Borneo territories. Subsequently, the Tunku indicated that he would like to visit London starting on 5 November, but without Lee present in the first place.

The Tunku felt that he could not present a Federation/Singapore merger design to Macmillan until he had arrived at some agreement on some general principles. In particular, the Tunku needed to be clearer about British intentions concerning the Borneo territories before he could go any further with Lee Kuan Yew.[16] Lee, for his part, was informed by his Malayan counterparts, in particular, Ghazali Shafie, that "he should not push too hard his idea of merger or whatever he had in mind regarding the Malaysia concept but should wait for the Tunku to work out the concept".[17]

Meanwhile, the region came abuzz with talk of the impending Greater Malaysia plan. On 24 July a Commonwealth Parliamentary Association Conference, convened in Singapore and comprising representatives from Sarawak, Brunei, North Borneo and Malaya, issued a communique declaring "the necessity and inevitability of the united states of Malaysia".[18] To ensure that the momentum for Malaysia would not be lost, the Conference agreed to create a Malaysia Solidarity Consultative Committee to carry on discussions as to the final shape and form the Malaysian state would take.[19] Ten days later, following a meeting in Kuala Lumpur, the Singapore and Federation governments agreed on approaching the United Nations to look into the setting up of a common market between the two territories.[20]

On 23 August the first meeting between the Prime Ministers of the Federation and Singapore on merger was held, essentially to discuss the terms on which a merger between their two countries might be arranged. Lee Kuan Yew and Goh Keng Swee, having spent a few days in the Cameron Highlands discussing the Internal Security Council, immediately proceeded to the Residency in Kuala Lumpur for discussions with the Tunku, Tun Abdul Razak and Ghazali Shafie.[21] During the meeting, Lee had apparently explained to the Tunku that the situation in Singapore had become "extremely serious and urgent", and that he (Lee) needed to secure some form of progress on the question of merger, from both the British and the Malayan governments. Lee emphasized that he would want to go to London by the end of the year to see the British premier and to get negotiations going. The Tunku agreed with Lee that it was perhaps necessary that both of them should call on Harold Macmillan by the end of the year, but pointed out "that they should go there with one mind, [and] not even a comma should be the subject of argument".[22] This suited Lee, who was anxious to secure some form of merger, apparently to counter the claim of his political opponents "that the Alliance government in Kuala Lumpur would accept the merger of Singapore only if the government was made up of the new Singapore Alliance".[23] During the meeting, the possibility of a referendum in Singapore on the question of merger was raised. Lee suggested that the Tunku should offer Singapore the status of a state similar to Penang but with local autonomy in education and labour. He would then proceed with a referendum which would ask the people to choose between a 100 per cent merger or merger less education and labour.[24] According to Ghazali Shafie, who was present at the meeting, "the Tunku quite simply said that the best procedure was to go straight to the point by simply asking the people on what Lee Kuan Yew could offer".[25]

According to available accounts, there were no major disagreements raised during the meeting. This suggested that earlier proposals of the broad terms of merger had been largely agreed upon. In principle, once merger was effected Kuala Lumpur would gain control of defence, foreign affairs and internal security, but Singapore, being admitted on a status of a state with greater autonomy, would have local control over education and labour. Without major disagreements of the above terms of merger, both parties then agreed at the meeting that a working party would be formed to study the implications of merger and to go into financial and related arrangements. Ghazali Shafie later scribbled on a piece of paper the draft of a press communiqué which was then approved by the Tunku and Lee. On the evening of 24 August 1961, an official communiqué was issued jointly by the Singapore and Federal governments announcing that "an agreement was reached in principle between the Prime Ministers of the Federation of Malaya and Singapore for a merger of the two territories". It further stated that

Among many matters examined was the question of Federation responsibility for defence, external affairs and security. The Singapore Prime Minister laid particular stress on the necessity of Singapore's retaining local autonomy, especially on matters of education and labour. Both Prime Ministers have agreed in principle on these proposals. They have also agreed that a working party should be set up to go into the overall financial and other implications arising out of arrangements whereby local autonomy is retained by Singapore on agreed matters, and to consider the financial contribution Singapore would be required to make to the National Government.[26]

Even before these terms were formally announced, Lee felt confident enough to intimate to Lord Selkirk and Philip Moore, acting UK High Commissioner in Singapore, that he had obtained agreement in principle on proposals for merger between Singapore and Malaya. Merger, it had seemed by then, was already in the bag, and all that needed to be done in the meantime was for a working party of officials to be set up to consider the financial implications, and other matters, including civil aviation, telecommunications, the port authority and other services.[27] Lee felt fairly confident that the working committee would be able to hammer out the details to the satisfaction of both sides, although he was wary that Razak and Tan Siew Sin might raise difficulties on the financial issues.

On 14 September, after three days of talks in Kuala Lumpur involving the Prime Minister and the Deputy Prime Minister of the Federation of Malaya and the Prime Minister and the Minister for Culture of Singapore, a joint statement announced that agreement had been reached and that a Working Party would be established to work out the details of merger with a view to bringing about the integration of the two territories and its peoples on or before June 1963. It was also announced that the two Prime Ministers were satisfied that all legitimate local and special interests of the people on the two territories could and would be safeguarded with merger of Singapore as a state within the Federation. A time-table had thus been set for the details of the merger to be worked out, and the joint statement announced that "it was decided that the two Prime Ministers would meet from time to time to review the work and decide on the recommendations of the Working Party". After the meeting, Lee felt sufficiently upbeat to announce to the press that "merger is off the launching pad and the latest developments have put it in orbit, with June 1963 as the target landing date".[28] On 22 September 1961, the Acting British High Commissioner in Singapore received a paper from Lee Kuan Yew setting out the proposed basis for agreement. Among other things, the paper elaborated that elections to the Singapore legislative assembly and for Singapore representation to the Federal parliament would be based on Singapore citizenship and election laws, and in view of greater autonomy to be enjoyed by Singapore, it would be accorded about two-thirds of the number of seats in the Federal Parliament that it would otherwise be entitled as a proportion of its population. The paper further stated that both Singapore and Federation citizens would become Federal nationals with a common passport. Other provisions included modifications to the Federal list that would give Singapore exclusive powers over civil and criminal law, banking, trade, commerce, industry and exclusive control of taxes of a national character.[29]

A month later, on 23 October, the Working Party met in Kuala Lumpur to discuss the many administrative problems on the judicial, legal and financial implications of merger. In judicial and legal matters, because of the separate evolution of two systems for the past sixteen years since 1945, the general attitude taken was that there should be no outright absorption of the Singapore judiciary into the judiciary of the new Federation, while at the same time all measures adopted should be based on the basic principle of maintaining a strong and efficient government, while ensuring the largest measure of domestic latitude possible. The Prime Minister of the Federation also stated that the terms of reference of the Working Party should include the examination of the question of separate citizenship for the Federation of Malaya and Singapore but with a single nationality with a view to "ensuring that such an arrangement does not render one citizenship inferior to the other".[30]

However, Federation authorities were still reluctant to comment on press reports that, according to the Tunku, merger was inevitable. Some Malayan ministers had insisted that the first sentence of the final paragraph of the joint statement should in their view be read to mean that merger between Singapore and the Federation was at best only a possibility. All that had been settled was an in-principle agreement between the Federation and Singapore Prime Ministers that should a merger be effected, responsibility for defence, external affairs and security should rest with Federation while Singapore would retain local autonomy in matters such as education and labour.[31]

The Tunku was also reported to have "disliked" Lee's idea of publishing the proposed terms of agreement in advance of London's discussions. Without an official undertaking from the British that the Borneo Territories would be included in Malaysia, the Tunku was still hedging his bets on Singapore. The British, too, felt that any published proposals would make for undesirable rigidity and felt that general interests would best be served if any statement on the subject which Lee would make in the Assembly or in public were kept to as broad lines as possible. There were concerns that detailed published commitments could seriously limit the freedom of the London discussions. The Acting British Commissioner in Singapore, Philip Moore, was therefore asked to discourage the idea of publishing the White Paper if it was felt that it would contain contents that would embarrass the British.[32] Nonetheless, on 19 September 1961, the press announced a recent meeting between Lee and Tunku, and spoke of bringing about the integration of the two territories on or before June 1963. It also stated that the two prime ministers were satisfied that "all legitimate local and special interests of people in the two territories can and will be safeguarded with merger of Singapore as a state within the Federation". Commenting subsequently, Lee said Singapore would merge with the Federation "as a very special state", on the basis that Singapore would retain education and labour, would receive a share of Federal taxes for those departments and would have representation proportionately reduced in Federal Parliament.[33]

By securing an "in-principle" agreement to the broad terms under which merger would be effected between Singapore and the Federation, Lee had achieved a considerable milestone in the progress towards Singapore's eventual entry into Malaysia. But Lee was constantly aware that further progress was only possible if the Tunku was satisfied that the Grand Design would include the North Borneo Territories, a key provision to which the British had yet to make a firm commitment. If the British were unable to accommodate the Tunku on the issue of the Borneo territories,

Lee was aware that the entire merger enterprise would fall through. But he was determined to strike while the iron was hot. Anxious to get the momentum going, Lee announced his intention of publishing a White Paper that would explain the detailed form which a merger of Singapore with the Federation would assume. Once he could get the Tunku to agree to accept the White Paper as a document supported by both the Federation and Singapore governments, he would have it debated in the Assembly, and opened to the public at a later stage through a referendum.

Soon after the announcement of the joint communiqué the Singapore Government decided to invite all parties in the Legislative Assembly to state their respective positions on the two basic points in the in-principle agreement on merger, i.e., Kuala Lumpur to control defence, external affairs and internal security while Singapore retained autonomy in education and labour. The Barisan Sosialis reacted swiftly, and, as expected, negatively. It stated that the party would support either

> Immediate complete merger with Singapore as the twelfth state in Federation like Penang or Malacca, with proper proportionate representation in Federal Parliament, full Malayan citizenship for Singapore citizens, Malay as national language and merger to be followed immediately by Federal General Election; or

> An interim stage during which Singapore would be autonomous unit within a Confederation (including Borneo Territories if possible), solely responsible for its own affairs, except Defence and External Affairs, which would be conceded to the Confederation Government by treaty.[34]

The Barisan's statement acknowledged that their aim was to unite with the Socialist Front in the Federation and fight the policies of the present Federation government, which they had bitterly denounced. Merger as proposed by the PAP was dismissed as "phoney", a "sell-out", in which the Federation government would be acting to police British interests in Singapore and the citizens of Singapore would become second-class citizens.

The Barisan tactic in calling for a complete merger, or for a confederal relationship that would retain internal security in the hands of the Singapore Government, was that they were confident that these would be totally unacceptable to the Tunku. Having posed the impossible, they now urged the third course, which was for an anti-colonial struggle for genuine internal self-government including the abolition of the Internal Security Council.[35] The main Barisan attack on the Tunku/Lee merger proposals concentrated on the handing of the internal security to Kuala Lumpur without full proportionate representation in the Federal Parliament. This argument would undoubtedly carry weight with a large number of Singapore Chinese who did not want their civil liberties to be curbed by the Malays in Kuala Lumpur. The only other reaction came from David Marshall who dismissed the PAP move as party propaganda and called for the immediate sitting of Assembly to discuss merger. He described the joint statement by the Prime Ministers as evasive and the proposed merger as likely to give the Federation more control over Singapore than the British have at present.[36] The Barisan Sosialis aim was to force Lee to resign and then hold a General Election, since it was commonly felt in Singapore that the PAP would be defeated in the General Election and the Barisan would emerge as the majority party. The PAP had only 26 seats out of the 51 seat Legislative Assembly and, on the face of it, their position in the Assembly was regarded as weak.

Lee was not unduly concerned about the tact that the Barisan Socialis was adopting in regard to the merger proposals. He told the UK High Commissioner that his answer to the Barisan call for complete merger would be to ask the people of Singapore whether they would prefer to retain local autonomy on matters of vital importance to the Chinese and the trade unions such as the education, labour and voting rights or to hand over control of Chinese education and trade unions to the Federation and to accept Federal citizenship laws which would reduce the electorate of Singapore from about 600,000 to 300,000.[37] Indeed in a radio forum on 22 September in which the question of merger was put to party leaders, Goh Keng Swee said that in the event of a full merger as the twelfth state of the Federation, federal citizenship laws would apply with the result that nearly half of the present Singapore electorate would be disenfranchised. This was because of the differences between citizenship provisions of Singapore and the Federation, and from the fact that only 320,000 out of 630,000 electors in Singapore were born in the state. Goh challenged the Barisan to convince the majority of the people that there should be full merger, with the consequence that half the voters would lose their political rights.[38] Lee also mentioned he would finally repulse the Barisan attack by taking them up on their promise to accept complete merger. He would do this by asking the people of Singapore in a referendum whether they wanted complete merger or a limited merger as at present agreed by Tunku and Lee.[39]

In the meantime, Lee and Federation officials were trying to fix a date to meet and discuss the details of the merger in London. It was suggested that a meeting be fixed in London towards the end of October 1961. In the lead-up to the London negotiations, Goh Keng Swee and Lee had several meetings with their Malayan counterparts in Kuala Lumpur. Goh Keng Swee had discussions about finance with Tan Siew Sin, who was mainly concerned with the technical questions connected with approval by the Federal Parliament of the state budget and taxation proposals. Goh was apprehensive that Tan should press for all revenues to be paid into the Federal treasury with Singapore getting a state allocation, whereas the Singapore position was keen on the other way around (for Singapore to manage its own revenue, but subject to tax from Federal Government). In this respect it seemed, Goh was reassured.[40]

Razak meanwhile had intimated to Lee that he was not yet prepared for details to be discussed by the Working Party of Officials and he asked the Singapore Government to produce a comprehensive merger plan covering all major points which would then be considered in the first instance by Tunku and Razak. Lee was getting down to this and hoped to complete a paper by early 1961 to be discussed in Kuala Lumpur as soon as possible.[41] Lee had agreed that it would be undesirable to be committed to a White Paper before he went to London. He said it would be necessary to reveal a certain amount of detail for public consumption but finally took the point that it would be wrong to tie his hands too tightly in advance of the London discussions.

The Singapore White Paper on Merger

In September, Lee submitted a paper on his proposals for merger. The following month, he held a long discussion with the Tunku in Penang about the merger paper and although the Tunku had not read the paper in detail, they were able to reach full agreement on all the main points. He was expecting Razak, Ismail and Ghazali to come up to the Camerons for a detailed discussion of the paper and then hoped for further discussion with the Tunku a few weeks later. Lee would then return to Singapore and go ahead with publishing the merger paper in time for the meeting of the Legislative Assembly on 31 October 1961.[42]

On 26 October, Lee showed his latest draft of the merger White Paper to Philip Moore, Acting Commissioner in Singapore, following his talks with the Federation ministers and a meeting of the official Working Party. It had been heavily amended and counter-amended, and according to Lee was the only draft in existence in Singapore.[43] In essence, the proposals as embodied in the draft White Paper reflected the broad terms of the earlier agreement that the two governments had arrived at. It was proposed that Singapore would be constituted as a state within the Federation, but on special conditions and with a larger measure of local autonomy than the other states forming the Federation.[44] Defence, external affairs and internal security would be federal subjects, while education, labour and a number of relatively minor subjects would be reserved as state subjects. However, according to Moore, all reference to details had been cut out at the wish of the Federation. There was no reference to how the internal security would be directed from Kuala Lumpur. Lee said that the Federation was insisting on direct control of the police and also that the internal security responsibilities of the Singapore Ministry of Home Affairs should be removed. However, as a compromise, the Malayan Government agreed that the Federation was prepared to have a Ministerial Consultative Committee on security in Kuala Lumpur as long as Lee and his colleagues remained in power.[45] The paper made references to the need to safeguard Singapore's special position in regard to entrepôt trade. The Singapore Port and Harbour would come under a State Port Authority but the implication seemed to be that ultimate control might rest with Kuala Lumpur.

The Singapore Government laid particular emphasis on the necessity of her retaining local autonomy, especially on labour and education.[46] In demanding his government's continued control of these areas, Lee wanted to assure the local population that their interests and future would not be jeopardized. In this respect, education was particularly important as Lee wanted to maintain English as the main medium of instruction in Singapore. He knew that once education came under the purview of the Kuala Lumpur government, he would be hard put to replace English with Malay, and his support for the Chinese schools, which was so politically important for the PAP, would have to cease. With regard to labour, Lee was anxious that workers in Singapore would continue to be protected by its labour laws, and would not be subjected to the tougher Federation laws, which were less liberal and thus less favourable to Singapore workers.[47] As Lee explained in one of his radio broadcasts in 1961, "Chinese parents who want their children to be educated in Chinese want to be assured that their present policy of equal treatment of all streams will go on.... and workers want to be assured that their pro-labour policy will continue".[48]

With regard to the representation of Singapore in the Federation, the draft White Paper proposed that Singapore should have 15 seats in the Federal legislature. If Singapore were to join the Federation on the same terms as the existing member states, it would be entitled to 25 seats by virtue of the size of its electorate. This later arrangement was clearly unacceptable to the Federal Government. Lee was prepared to agree to some smaller number, which can be justified on account of the greater autonomy that Singapore would enjoy in comparison with the existing states. The present Singapore legislature would continue as a state legislature after merger, but with reduced powers. The judiciary and the legal services would become a separate branch of the Federal judicial and legal service. After merger, the Singapore Civil Service would continue to exist as a state civil service. The subject of the police force was not fully covered in the draft, but it was indicated that while Lee wanted some measure of local control of police establishment matters, the control of the police would be wholly vested in Kuala Lumpur. Lee felt that it was important to have local control of the police in order to handle social unrest that may arise, for example from the hawkers and the taxi-drivers. Lee was particularly upset by the provision that was made for the control of personnel in the Singapore Police Force to come under the Federation Police Commission. He felt that this would be damaging to the career prospects of the Singapore police and would invite unfavourable comparison with the rest of the Singapore Civil Service, which would retain their own career structure. Lee was hoping to persuade the Federation to modify their views on this. Where financial arrangements were concerned, the White Paper proposed that whatever arrangements made should reflect the measure of local autonomy enjoyed by Singapore. Therefore, while the Federal Government would control all monetary policies and assume legislative authority over all taxation in Singapore of a national character, the proceeds of the national taxes raised in Singapore would be used to pay the cost of government and public services in Singapore and the contribution to the Federal Government for federal services.

As the economic benefits to be gained by Singapore through a merger with the Federation was one of the main reasons put forward by the PAP for its policy of wanting merger with the Federation, it was ironic that the terms of the White Paper were particularly vague when it came to economic issues. While a Common Market was the major plank of the PAP's merger strategy, the White Paper contained no mention of Common Market whatsoever. Another glaring omission concerned the proportion of Singapore's revenue that would have to be paid to the Federation after merger. The agreement merely stated that details of the appointment would be worked out by a Joint Working Committee.[49] All this perhaps suggested that in the negotiations leading to the White Paper, political issues took precedence over economic issues and in search for a quick political agreement, both sides were prepared to leave the more complicated economic issues to a later date.

Where citizenship was concerned, the arrangement envisaged in the draft White Paper was that after merger, the separate Singapore citizenship, presently recognized in the British Nationality Acts, should be retained and Singapore citizens should enjoy the same national rights and have the same passport as Federal citizens. The term "Federal Nationals" had been suggested to cover both categories of citizenship. The draft White Paper further proposed that the merger should be implemented by June 1963.

Singapore's White Paper on merger was considered by the Federal Government on November 1961, but failed to achieve an outright endorsement. The response was as follows:

> The Federation Cabinet considered on 1 November the Singapore White Paper. The Cabinet wish to emphasize that the White Paper represents entirely the views of the Singapore Government and in no way commits the Federation Government. However, at a later stage the Cabinet may propose an interim measure to cover the transitional period, during which the implications of the Singapore White Paper can be thoroughly considered.[50]

Up to November 1961, Lee was still experiencing considerable difficulty in persuading the Tunku to allow him to publish the Singapore White Paper on merger as a document agreed by both the Federation and Singapore governments. It seemed that the major opposition was coming mainly from Razak and Ismail.[51] According to Lee, who had been talking to the Tunku, the latter was quite content to take only defence, external affairs and internal security and leave the rest to Singapore. The Tunku's ministers, on the other hand, were anxious to obtain greater control over certain aspects of Singapore's life. Razak had tried to lower the number of Singapore representatives in the Kuala Lumpur Parliament from 15 to 12, a point on which Lee flatly refused to give in. Federal finance minister, Tan Siew Sin, clearly had a difference of opinion with his Singapore counterpart, Goh Keng Swee, on the financial arrangements of merger, particularly on the question on whether Singapore revenues would be paid directly into the Singapore Treasury. Lee had also been forced to concede to the Federation complete control of the Singapore Police Force, and as a corollary, the Federation had also insisted on taking over the Singapore judiciary. The issue of control of broadcasting was also tentative as Lee was determined to keep control of this.[52]

Following further discussions with the Federal Government, the Singapore Government submitted a revised draft of the White Paper. The merger plan as set out in the revised paper left very little within the control of Singapore, except in the fields of education, labour and health services; and even in those fields, the effectiveness of Singapore's local autonomy would depend upon the financial relations between Singapore and the Federation, which had yet to be worked out. In broad economic terms, the Federation would be dominant, subject only to the understanding that nothing will be done to affect the free port status of Singapore without the consent of the Singapore Government.[53] Although the revised draft represented a tighter document, and essentially left little room for further negotiation once the merger was effected, there were still a number of issues which were left unclear or unsaid, and which were to be the issues of some contention later.

The first concerned citizenship, a subject that had already generated extensive and heated debate between the Singapore Government and the opposition parties. It was also clearly one of the most vital issues as it affected closely the question of Singapore representation in the Federal Parliament. Lee was convinced that it was unrealistic to expect the Federal Government to admit all Singapore citizens automatically as Federal citizens on merger. His argument had been that only those born in Singapore would qualify "automatically by operation of law" and that the rest would have to seek citizenship by registration. His view was that only perhaps 100,000 out of a total of 327,000 Singapore citizens not born in Singapore would qualify for registration as Federal citizens, the tests for which were essentially residence and knowledge of the Malay language. The issue of citizenship was to feature prominently in the later stages of negotiations (see Chapter 4).

The other issue, which remained knotty, concerned the financial arrangements that would be effected upon merger. The revised paper made clear that the Federal Government would control all taxation except for the relatively trivial revenues assigned to the states in the Tenth Schedule to the Federal Constitution. The paper was, however, totally silent on how the proceeds of federal taxation attributable to Singapore were to be collected and apportioned. It was merely noted that the Joint Working Committee would work out these details at a subsequent stage. But there clearly was a substantial difference in approach to this question by the Singapore and

Malayan governments and the matter was to be the subject of tough negotiations. It appeared that the Singapore Government would have liked the whole proceeds to be paid first into their Consolidated Fund and for a contribution then to be paid to the Centre for Federal Services. The Federal Government, however, would have liked it the other way round. The revised paper made no indication as to how the amount of revenue to be retained by Singapore and the amount to the paid to the Federal Government was to be determined. This was clearly an issue of vital importance to Singapore, as the government would need sufficient revenue to run local services connected to education, health and welfare. With the Federal Government controlling the purse-strings, local autonomy in these matters would be but an illusion.

In early November 1961, Lee travelled to Kuala Lumpur for further talks with the Tunku and his ministers to finalize his proposed White Paper. Again, he had little difficulty securing from the Tunku the broad political agreements, particularly on the number of seats that would be given to Singapore in the Federal Legislature.[54] However, when he got to the nitty-gritty matters of the State and Federal lists, he was subjected to a round of extensive bargaining with Tan Siew Sin, Ismail and Razak.[55]

However, there arose some consternation when the Tunku mentioned that the White Paper was designed to cover a transitional period. Although the term transitional did not appear in the White Paper itself, it was nonetheless used by the Malayan Government to describe the means by which a merger of Singapore with the Federation could be achieved at short notice without running into constitutional difficulties. Lee wanted the White Paper to be an agreed document that would bind both parties to merger on the terms spelt out in the paper. The Tunku and his ministers, on the other hand, did not wish to be too strictly bound by the terms, and while agreeing to the principles as set out in the proposed White Paper wanted to have the flexibility of amending it.[56] Both Lee and the British representatives could see how the use of the word "transition" to describe the merger agreement that had been reached between Singapore and the Federation could lead to misunderstandings and trouble in Singapore as it could be taken to argue that the published arrangements whereby Singapore would join the

Federation on special terms were not as permanent as they seemed. In subsequent discussions, it emerged that the use of the word "transitional" in describing the proposed arrangements for merger between Malaya and Singapore was not intended to mean temporary, but could be described as provisional until they have been approved by the authorities concerned. Eventually, it was agreed that the White Paper would serve as a provisional arrangement which could be amended by agreement between the governments of Singapore and the Federation. Once the Singapore Legislative Assembly had approved them, they would be submitted for approval by the British Government as part of arrangements for Greater Malaysia as a whole. This agreement, the Tunku stressed, would not become effective until it had been ratified by the Federation Parliament, and there was to be no question of the transfer of sovereignty pending such ratification. Thereafter, they would be subject to alteration only by agreement between the Malaysian and Singapore governments.

The Singapore White Paper was published on 16 November, substantially in the form of the revised draft. This was published as Command 33 of 1961, as "Memorandum Setting out Heads of Agreement for a Merger between the Federation of Malaya and Singapore", and the agreement was signed by the Tunku and Lee. The Heads of Agreement were then discussed in London and on 22 November 1961 were endorsed by the British Government.

The Heads of Agreement and the general principle of merger were debated in the Singapore Legislative Assembly in November and December 1961. Although the PAP had only 26 seats in the 51-seat Legislative Assembly, Lee was fairly confident that he could push through with his proposals for merger. Since the defection of the 13 PAP members three months earlier, and although there have been rumours of waverers, no further defections took place and the 26 remaining PAP members had publicly re-affirmed their loyalty to the party. In addition, Lee was reasonably assured that the seven Alliance members and the independents would either abstain or vote with him on merger. The opposing vote, Lee reckoned, was likely to come from 17 members, comprising 13 Barisan Sosialis, Ong Eng Guan and his two supporters and David Marshall. The debate on merger was convened on 20 November, and Lee's White Paper was debated for over ten days in the Assembly. Lee successfully moved the motion in the House, and a motion accepting the Heads of Agreement as an immediate practical step towards merger was carried by 33 votes to none, with Lim Yew Hock's seven votes securing a majority of 33 for the PAP. Lee was fortunate in that there had been no breakdown in the negotiations with the Tunku and the British Government to prejudice the vote in the Assembly.[57]

Having secured a majority of 33 votes in a house of 51 seats, and having a two-thirds majority in the Assembly from the 1959 General Election in which merger had constituted the main platform of the PAP, Lee could have left it at that. But a successful vote in the Assembly was not sufficient. The PAP had earlier committed itself to a referendum in which the issue of the merger would be referred to the people of Singapore. However, there were considerable risks involved as the PAP's perceived unpopularity, as was shown by their defeats in Hong Lim and Anson, could turn the referendum on the merits of merger into a vote simply for or against the PAP. Lee was therefore anxious not to have to put the referendum question in the form of "are you in favour of merger with the Federation on the terms agreed by me with the Tunku — yes or no?" Lee had been disturbed by the recent referendum vote in Jamaica, and considered that there was too much at stake in a question as important as this to put it to a vote of the people in a straight "yes" or "no" form.[58]

Lee, therefore, decided to hold a referendum in which there would be no final defeat for him, whichever way the vote went. As all political parties have openly stated that they wanted merger, there was no need for the government to put the question again to the people of Singapore, whether or not they were in favour of merger. As far as the government was concerned, it was clear that everyone wanted merger; the question was how should merger be achieved. Lee's problems was that having secured overall approval for merger, he had to take the issue to the people of Singapore, and convince them that the PAP government would secure for them the best possible terms for a merger with the Federation. He, therefore, contemplated that the referendum should ask the people of Singapore whether they wanted merger on the terms agreed by the PAP with the

Tunku, or a complete merger, on the model advocated by the Barisan Sosialis. The PAP had already pointed out the drawbacks of a complete merger for Singapore. Not all the 630,000 present Singapore electors would automatically qualify for Federal citizenship and voting rights; labour relations would be in the hands of the Federation, and therefore the trade unions in Singapore could expect much stricter governmental control that existed presently in Singapore; and Singapore may have to accept the full implications of the Federal Government's Chinese education policy. In this way, Lee naturally hoped that the people of Singapore could be persuaded to vote in favour of the first option, i.e., merger on the terms as spelt out in the PAP White Paper. However, if the vote should fall in favour of the second option for a complete merger, it would still be a vote for merger, and in that event, Lee would undertake to go to the Tunku to try to negotiate merger in the form more acceptable to the people of Singapore. There would be no question of his having suffered an adverse vote, demanding the resignation of the PAP government.

The obvious obstacle to Lee's plan was that the Tunku would stipulate from the outset that the Federation could not agree to a full merger. Lee had earlier negotiated with the Malayan ministers on the questions that would be asked in a referendum that he was proposing to hold in Singapore. Not wanting to flounder on the referendum, Lee had indicated to the Malayan ministers that he had preferred for two questions to be asked, whether the people preferred an Ulster type merger, or a full merger. But Razak was opposed to that. He wanted the referendum to present a simple "yes" or "no" to an Ulster-type merger with the Federation, and to avoid the question and possibility of a full merger with the Federation. Both he and Ghazali Shafie were concerned with the awkwardness of the situation if the referendum should indicate popular preference for a full merger. It was quite impossible for Malaya to agree to a full merger with Singapore and it was fundamental to their agreement on merger that it should only be in the Ulster form. As far as the Malayans were concerned, Lee's second alternative was clearly a non-starter. They agreed that Lee would enjoy some tactical advantage if the game was played this way, but only at the Federation government's expense.[59] Although Lee had faced objections from Razak and Tunku on his referendum proposals, Lee was nonetheless trying his utmost to persuade the Tunku to agree to the referendum being put in this manner. For their part, the British were keen to support Lee's tactics, as they realized that they could not afford to allow Lee and his government to be toppled if a merger was to be achieved.[60]

Opposition from the Malayans notwithstanding, Lee's greatest challenge in the proposed referendum was to convince the people of Singapore that the PAP government was aiming to bring Singapore into the Federation on the best possible terms. But his government had been be-devilled by the constant opposition refrain that the Ulster-model merger would make Singapore a second-class partner to the Federation. Particularly potent was the issue of citizenship as that had direct relevance to every man in the street. Lee's next great battle was to secure from the Federation a form of citizenship agreement that would put to rest, once and for all, the fear that Singaporeans would be second-class citizens upon entering Malaysia.

NOTES

1 Note on "Greater Malaysia" by P. A. Clutterbuck, Chairman of Official Committee, n.d., DO 169/30.

2 Lee Kuan Yew, *The Singapore Story: Memoirs of Lee Kuan Yew* (Singapore: Federal Publications, 2000) p. 362.

3 Tunku to Commonwealth Relations Office, 16 August 1961, PREM 11/3418.

4 Ghazali Shafie, *Ghazali Shafie's Memoir on the Formation of Malaysia* (Selangor: Penerbit Universiti Kebangsaan Malaysia, 1998), p. 28.

5 Tunku to Sandys, 15 June 1961, DO 169/25.

6 Ibid.

7 Tunku's Speech in Parliament, 16 October 1961.

8 Ibid.

9 Ibid.

10 UK Commissioner (Kuala Lumpur) to Commonwealth Relations Office, 3 June 1961, PREM 11/3418.

11 Tan Sri Ghazalie Shafie later rose to become a senior Cabinet Minister in Malaysia (1970-84). See Shafie, *Ghazali Shafie's Memoir*, p. 26.

12 Kuala Lumpur to Commonwealth Relations Office, 12 August 1961, CO 1030/981 no. 597.

13 Shafie, *Ghazali Shafie's Memoir*, p. 26.

14 Ibid., p. 27.

15 Immediately after the Tunku's 27 May announcement, the British gave a coordinated series of favourable statements. On 13 June, Selkirk described the Greater Malaysia concept as a "sound, long term plan". A week later, Harold Macmillan, answering a question from parliament, said that "it was a good thing that this matter had been raised and provoked discussion". In June, the Governor of North Borneo, William Goode, spoke of "the need to seize the right moment to push through the Tunku's Mighty Malaysia plan". See Lee, *The Singapore Story*, p. 367.

16 Kuala Lumpur to Commonwealth Relations Office, 18 September 1961, CO 1030/983 no. 675.

17 Shafie, *Ghazali Shafie's Memoir*, p. 32.

18 Lee, *The Singapore Story*, p. 400.

19 Ibid.

20 Ibid.

21 Shafie, *Ghazali Shafie's Memoir*, p. 66.

22 Ibid., p. 67.

23 Ibid., p. 41.

24 Ibid., p. 67.

25 Ibid.

26 *Straits Times*, 24 August 1961.

27 Acting UK High Commissioner to Secretary of State for the Colonies, 25 August 1961, DO 169/28.

28 Lee, *The Singapore Story*, p. 400.

29 UK Commissioner (Singapore) to Secretary of State for the Colonies, 23 September 1961, no. 357, containing merger proposals prepared by the PAP, DO 169/29.

30 The Yang di-Pertuan Negara's address at the opening of the 3rd Session of the legislative assembly, CO 1030/985.

31 Telegram no. 632, Kuala Lumpur to Commonwealth Relations Office, 25 August 1961, CO 1030/982.

32 Telegram no. 357, Secretary of State (Colonial Office) to Acting UK Commissioner (Singapore), 30 August 1961, CO 1030/982.

33 Telegram no. 676, Kuala Lumpur to Commonwealth Relations Office, 18 September 1961, CO 1030/983.

34 Telegram no. 359, Moore to Secretary of State (Colonial Office), 30 August 1961, CO 1030/982.

35 Telegram no. 363, Moore to Secretary of State (Colonial Office), 1 September 1961, CO 1030/982.

36 Telegram no. 359, Moore to Secretary of State (Colonial Office), 30 August 1961, CO 1030/982.

37 Telegram no. 363, Moore to Secretary of State (Colonial Office), 1 September 1961, CO 1030/982.

38 Ibid.

39 Ibid.

40 Telegram no. 364, Moore to Secretary of State (Colonial Office), 1 September 1961, CO 1030/982.

41 Ibid.

42 Telegram no. 443, Moore to Secretary of State (Colonial Office), 20 October 1961, CO 1030/984.

43 Moore to Selkirk, 27 October 1961, CO 1030/996.

44 Draft of White Paper, DO 169/247.

45 Moore to Selkirk, 27 October 1961, CO 1030/996.

46 *Memorandum Setting out the Heads of Agreement for a Merger between the Federation of Malaya and Singapore* (Singapore: L. K. Heng, Government Printer, 1961), Singapore Legislative Assembly Command 33 of 1961, Article 2 — "The Agreement in Principle".

47 Lee Kuan Yew, *The Battle of Merger* (Singapore: Government Printing Office, 1962), pp. 78–79.

48 Ibid.

49 *Memorandum Setting out the Heads of Agreement for a Merger between the Federation of Malaya and Singapore*, p. 5.

50 Moore to Selkirk, 27 October 1961, CO 1030/996.

51 UK Commissioner (Kuala Lumpur) to Secretary of State (Colonial Office), 6 November 1961, DO 169/30.

52 Moore to Ian Wallace (Far Eastern Department, Colonial Office), 2 November 1961, DO 169/247.

53 See commentary of revised draft of the Singapore government's White Paper on merger, DO 169/247.

54 Shafie, *Ghazali Shafie's Memoir*, p. 138.

55 Ibid.

56 Ibid., p. 139.

57 Philip Moore to Ian Wallace, 18 October 1961, CO 1030/986.

58 Ibid.

59 UK High Commissioner (Kuala Lumpur), to Commonwealth Relations Office, 24 October 1961, DO 169/30.

60 Ibid.

CHAPTER FOUR

The Citizenship Issue

At the start of 1962, the PAP's White Paper proposals for merger with the Federation were officially endorsed by the Singapore Legislative Assembly. After 13 days of debate that began on 20 November 1961, during which the government's main political opponents, the Barisan Sosialis (BS), had tried their best to defeat the White Paper through what Lee Kuan Yew remembers as "tedious and repetitious" arguments, the Assembly carried the motion by 33 votes to nil for the Heads of Agreement as set out in the White Paper, with the opposition BS members opting to abstain by absenting themselves during the voting.[1] On 30 January 1962 the Legislative Assembly voted 35 'ayes' (PAP, UMNO, SPA), 13 'noes' (BS), three abstentions to support "in principal the plan proposed by the Tunku for the establishment of the Federation of Malaysia comprising the 11 states of Malaya, the states of Singapore and Brunei, and the territories of Sarawak and North Borneo".[2] By 1962, it had become clear that merger with the Federation would certainly happen, and on the PAP's terms as spelt out in the 1961 White Paper.

The PAP was on strong, defensible grounds in making its arguments for merger. Few could argue with the fact that a Malayan hinterland was critical for Singapore's political and economic survival. With a growing population, limited physical and natural resources and an economy that was stagnating, Singapore simply could not survive as an independent country on its own. Unable to contest the PAP's argument that merger was an absolute economic and political necessity for Singapore, all that the BS could resort to was to question the Tunku's motive for agreeing to merger with Singapore, and to arguing that the terms of the merger as proposed by the PAP were essentially detrimental to the interests of the people of Singapore. The BS argued that the Tunku's scheme was nothing but a neo-colonialist plot, hatched by the British to help the Federation suppress the radical anti-colonialists in Singapore and thus save the increasingly right-wing PAP government.[3] To support its claims, the BS pointed to the various provisions for merger as stipulated by the Heads of Agreement between the Tunku and Lee. The arrangements, particularly on citizenship and Federal legislative representation for Singapore, the BS alleged, were clearly designed to isolate Singapore politically.[4]

In response, the PAP pointed out that it could not afford to jeopardize the merger initiative by imposing impossible conditions which the Federation were likely to reject.[5] The White Paper proposals were, therefore, designed to facilitate Singapore's entry into the Federation on the best possible terms for the people of Singapore. For the time being, therefore, the proposed Ulster-type merger plan, in which the people would enjoy a greater degree of autonomy as compared with the other states of the Federation, particularly with local control over labour and education, would work to the advantage of Singapore. The PAP admitted, however, that it had to seize present opportunities when the Tunku was favourably disposed to the idea of a merger and that its White Paper arrangements were meant for a transitional period, during which adjustments and changes for a complete merger would be made.[6] The internal fight that was shaping up between the PAP and the BS over merger revolved not so much around the issue of whether or not there should be merger between Singapore and the Federation. On that, Lee knew he was on solid ground and had declared that "no political party, no one, has dared raise his voice against merger".[7] Rather, the issues of contention between the PAP and its opponents were to be focused on the terms of merger, and among the many points of the White Paper proposals that the BS took issue with, the most severe and politically damaging criticisms centred on the citizenship provisions. Indeed, Lee admitted during the Assembly debates on merger, his "main difficulty was not with [representation in the Federal parliament], or with complete merger, which the people of Singapore did not want. It was with the question of citizenship".[8]

Yet, while Lee faced criticisms from his political opponents on the citizenship provisions, he was, at the same time, up against a Tunku determined not to grant Malaysian citizenship for Singapore, fearful as he was of the political repercussions in the mainland of giving the vote to an additional one million Chinese. Indeed, the question of citizenship, although seemingly lacking in controversy during the White Paper discussions, was to be one of the thorniest issues that was to plague Lee Kuan Yew and his government for the better part of 1962. This chapter explains the nature of the citizenship controversy, and will narrate how Lee was able to fend off critics to the citizenship proposal, persuade the Tunku to re-define the terms of the White Paper concerning citizenship, and finally secure a successful referendum in Singapore, with citizenship as the key issue.

The Citizenship Controversy

The terms of agreement where citizenship was concerned were embodied in the White Paper as follows

> All Singapore citizens will keep their citizenship and automatically become nationals of the larger Federation. Citizens of the present Federation will similarly become nationals of the larger Federation. Nationals of the larger Federation, whether Singapore citizens or Federation citizens, will as nationals have equal rights, carry the same passport, enjoy the same protection and be subject to equal duties and responsibilities under the Constitution of the larger Federation. Singapore citizens will continue to enjoy their State rights and privileges within Singapore. Singapore citizens will vote in Singapore for their representatives to the new Federation Parliament and the citizens of the present Federation of Malaya will vote in the present Federation for their representatives to the same new Federation Parliament.[9]

The Heads of Agreement therefore clearly spelt out that the citizens of Singapore would automatically retain their Singapore citizenship, and like citizens of the Federation of Malaya, would automatically become new nationals of the new Federation with equal rights and responsibilities. In other words, while the Agreement provided for a common nationality, it maintained a differentiated citizenship for the people of Singapore and the Federation. And while the Agreement clearly stated that Singapore citizens and Malayan citizens would enjoy the right to vote only in their respective territories, i.e., Singapore citizens were allowed to exercise their electoral rights only in Singapore and *vice versa* for Malayan citizens, it was totally silent on areas in which citizens of Singapore could or could not do in the Federation. For instance, would Singapore citizens continue to be excluded from activities and occupations in the Federation that were reserved for Malayan citizens?[10]

This provision of common nationality but differentiated citizenship was instantly seized upon by the BS and other critics of the Singapore Government as an inherently one-sided arrangement that would work against the interests of Singapore citizens. Lee Siew Choh castigated the idea of a Federal nationality, arguing that the concept was redundant as it did not exist in the then Federal Constitution.[11] To Lee Siew Choh, nationality referred simply to a person's international status regarding his state, whereas citizenship defined his rights within the state. Thus, under Federal nationality, the leader of the BS mocked that "the Prime Minister has not been able to give anything more than the right to a national passport".[12] In the debates, Lee Siew Choh had launched a direct attack on the PAP's assurances that Federal nationality would guarantee that Singapore citizens would enjoy equal rights with their Federation counterparts. In taking this tact, the BS had seized on an issue that would resonate with the man in the street; by belonging to a separate category of citizenship within the Malaysian state, Singapore citizens would be easily discriminated against. Not surprisingly, other opposition members joined the chorus of criticisms against the citizenship provision. David Marshall, leader of the Workers' Party, was opposed to the citizenship provision, and argued that he would continue his opposition to merger unless "the Tunku [was] prepared to agree either to a common citizenship for Malaysia with the right to vote limited to the state in which the citizen was living, or that any alteration in the rights and privileges of Singapore citizens after merger would have to be confirmed by a vote in the Singapore Assembly".[13] He further pointed out that it was not good enough that assurances of equal and fair treatment to Singapore citizens were given orally; any such undertaking had to be enshrined constitutionally.[14]

The citizenship issue had opened up a weak flank in the PAP government, and the BS was determined to make maximum political capital out of this. It pointed out that the PAP was trying to effect a phoney merger with the Federation, and the terms that Lee had secured from the Tunku were indeed detrimental to Singapore, especially when Singapore citizens would have restricted rights of citizenship within the Federation.[15] Lee Siew Choh repeatedly questioned the differences that existed between the terms "Malaysian nationals" and "Malaysian citizens", pointing out that the two were indeed very dissimilar. He pointed out that while a "national" would only be entitled to a Malaysian passport, a citizen could, among other things, enjoy the "right to influence people...throughout Malaysia; for example, the citizen could stand for elections in any constituency in the Federation".[16] Other than voting rights, the BS questioned if under the present provisions, Singapore citizens would be allowed to enter directly into the Federation civil service as well as other jobs without discrimination.[17] Playing on the instinctive fears among Singapore citizens that they would be treated differently in Malaysia because the White Paper was especially vague on citizenship rights, the BS raised the potent cry that "if merger were effected [along the terms provided by the Heads of Agreement], Singapore citizens would be 'second class' citizens in Malaysia".[18] This was tantamount, the BS argued, to a continuation of colonial rule over Singapore, with control and power now transferred to Kuala Lumpur. Singapore would indeed be worse off with the PAP merger. The only way out of this, the BS argued, was for Singapore to enter Malaysia as the 12th state of the Federation, or complete merger, as this was the only way Singapore citizens would automatically become Federal citizens, and would have the same rights as citizens in the various states of the Federation.[19] However, if this was not possible at the time, Singapore should be made an autonomous unit in a Confederation, with full internal autonomy in all internal matters including security, and with external affairs and defence in the hands of the Federation.

At the level of practical politics, the PAP did not find the BS argument difficult to demolish for their demands were simply unworkable. To begin with it was quite clear that the Tunku would never agree to accepting Singapore as a full state of the Federation, with similar status as Penang or Malacca as the BS had insisted. Since 1946, when the Malayan Union scheme was scuttled because of its liberal citizenship provisions, the Federation had consistently enforced stringent citizenship restrictions for non-Malays, with the intention of preserving Malay dominance. The conservative and stringent policies of awarding citizenship to non-Malays were further reinforced during the Emergency in Malaya, which saw dominant Chinese participation and heightened communal tensions between the Chinese and the Malays. The Tunku was, therefore, extremely wary of the Chinese of Singapore, who, if given equal citizenship rights, would upset the political equation in the Federation and threaten not only the political dominance of the Malays but also of his own political party, UMNO, as well.[20] The political cultures of Singapore and Malaya had become so different having undergone nearly seventeen years of separate political development that the Tunku wondered if the Chinese in Singapore would be able to accept what the majority of Malayan citizens had accepted — "of Kingship and Sultanate, of Malay as the national language, and of Islam as the official religion of the nation".[21] If he were to admit all Singapore citizens as Federal citizens, it would intensify pressure from the Chinese community in Malaya, where acquisition of citizenship had been extremely restrictive,[22] to be admitted to Federal citizenship on terms no more onerous than those on which Singapore Chinese could then obtain Singapore citizenship.[23] The Tunku would, therefore, find it politically impossible to accept Singapore on terms that would be detrimental to his political position in Malaya. The Malayan Government, therefore, made it a necessary condition of merger that Singapore citizens would not be given automatic Federal citizenship by insisting that the Heads of Agreement would provide for the people of the two territories to keep their respective citizenship after merger.

The Tunku's opposition aside, the BS argument that full and complete merger would mean automatic Federal citizenship for Singapore citizens was shown to be completely erroneous. At a press conference on 15 October 1961, Lee explained that "while Singapore-born citizens would automatically become federal citizens under complete merger, others — some 327,000 of them, those born in China, India and even Malaya — would first have to meet federal [sic] residence qualifications and would also have to pass a language test in Malay before they could become federal citizens".[24] Unlike the citizenship proposals of the Federation Constitution, the Singapore Citizen Ordinance (1957) was more liberal in awarding citizenship. Under its provisions, a person could obtain citizenship quite simply by having parents who were citizens, by registration, if he was born in the Federation, a Commonwealth country, or if he had resided in Singapore for a total of 12 years. He could be a naturalized citizen if he had resided in Singapore for an aggregate 10 years during the preceding 12 years, if he had spent three to four years service in the armed forces in Singapore.[25] The BS had earlier invoked Article 22 of the Federal Constitution that provided the Federal Government the constitutional rights to incorporate Singapore citizens as Federal citizens upon merger, arguing that "there was no such thing as automatic disenfranchisement except when agreed upon by the two parties".[26] The PAP did not disagree that many of the citizens who were not born in Singapore but who had obtained their citizenship by other means would have to apply for Federal citizenship anew if there were a full merger between Singapore and the Federation. However, it was quick to point out that under the circumstances, with a working knowledge of Malay a fundamental requirement for Federal citizenship, large numbers from Singapore would have difficulties qualifying for citizenship if they reapplied under Federal laws.[27] K.M. Byrne, Minister for Health and Law, argued that Article 22 was but a red herring thrown in by the opposition and asked if it was reasonable at all to expect "… that the Federation Parliament … would agree to grant the Singapore-born more favourable terms that it has been prepared to concede to those who were born in the … Federation".[28] The PAP had thus exposed the flaw in the BS case: with full and complete merger, half of the voting population of Singapore would lose their citizenship and effectively be disenfranchised in Malaysia. In any case, Lee pointed out that even if full rights were given to Singapore citizens, "the Tunku could very easily deny these rights to Singapore citizens by other, admittedly more laborious, methods than by denying Federal citizenship".[29] The BS stand on merger, it is believed, had been framed in such an unrealistic manner that it either reflected the political naiveté of the party and its leaders or a deliberate attempt to demand terms which it knew the Federation would reject, thereby sabotaging the merger enterprise. The BS had a publicly stated commitment to reunify Singapore with the Malayan Peninsula, to correct an anomaly that had been created by colonialism. However, there were many in the ranks of the BS who were privately concerned that merger would place them at the mercy of anti-communist internal security machinery controlled by Kuala Lumpur. Lee Siew Choh had admitted, however, that the BS policy on merger was designed with the primary aim of attacking the PAP.[30]

While it was relatively easy for the PAP to challenge the logic of the BS arguments for automatic Federal citizenship under full and complete merger, the anxieties that without common citizenship, Singapore citizens could end up being "second-class" citizens within Malaysia was harder to dispel. The PAP tried their best to downplay the disadvantages of not being accorded Federal citizenship. Minister for Culture, S. Rajaratnam, questioned the value of Federal citizenship for Singapore citizens when he argued that they would still be subjected to the Federation's educational policy, labour policy, and complete domination over Singapore's finances and trade. Goh Keng Swee, Singapore's Minister for Finance denounced the opposition's accusations by pointing out that they had not produced the "slightest bit of relevant evidence" in support of the claim that without Federal citizenship, Singapore citizens would end up being second class.[31] The PAP's counter-arguments notwithstanding, the suspicion that "Malaysian nationals" would not be the same as "Malaysian citizens" continued to cause great unease, and Lee admitted that the fear of becoming second-class citizens did strike a chord and arouse alarm in Singapore.[32] Lee had tried his best to argue that the citizenship agreement in the White Paper had indeed given Singapore the best possible deal under the circumstances, and all that he could go on about was that with the exception of voting rights, Singapore citizens would have equal rights and privileges within Malaysia. In a publication released in 1961, the PAP government highlighted that

> The most important interest that will be protected in a merger based on the principle of partnership is that Singapore citizens...will keep their present citizenship rights and in addition acquire national rights as nationals of the new Federation. Nobody will lose any rights. On the other hand, every new citizen will gain new national status as a member of an independent and larger political unit.[33]

Lee was not wrong in pointing out that Singapore citizens would not lose any of their rights in Singapore. However, the burning issue remained: with the existence of two separate citizenships within the Federation of Malaysia, and without full political and voting rights in the Federation, would Singapore citizens be easily subjected to discrimination? The possibility was not lost on the British:

> Many of the existing laws in the Federation of Malaya refer to the citizens of the Federation and reserve rights to them which are not available to non-citizens. Unless these laws are amended singly or unless an Act is passed by the Parliament of the Federation of Malaya, which has the effect of interpreting a citizen of the Federation wherever it appears in Federation legislation to include citizens of Singapore, certain rights will be denied to citizens of Singapore. Singapore citizens could thus be excluded from holding office in trade unions outside Singapore if the Trade Union Ordinances are not amended; employment in the Government could be denied to Singapore citizens; Singapore citizens could be banished under the law from Malaya to Singapore; and administratively, in countless ways Singapore citizens could be discriminated against.[34]

The British assessment was not far off the mark. While the White Paper had specifically indicated that the maintenance of a differentiated citizenship between Singapore and the Federation was meant to restrict voting in their respective territories, it left too many issues to the discretion of the Federal Government. While the Singapore Government would like to observe the spirit of the agreement and argue that other than voting rights Singapore citizens would enjoy all other rights and privileges as their Federal counterparts,[35] the Federal Government could choose to interpret the letter of the agreement and, therefore, restrict rights and benefits of citizenship strictly within the boundaries of their respective territories. As long as the Malayan Government maintained the distinction between Malaysian nationals and citizens, this would remain a distinct possibility.

Given that Singapore had agreed to join the Federation on the Ulster model, there was little that Lee could do to persuade the Tunku to concede common citizenship. This was the trade-off that the Tunku had insisted upon: a limited merger and therefore greater local autonomy for Singapore for limited citizenship rights. The Tunku had repeatedly pointed out that if Singapore wished to retain considerable self-autonomy, as provided for by the Heads of Agreement, its citizens could not expect to have voting rights in the Federation. As far as the Tunku was concerned, this was a simple *quid pro quo*; either Singapore enjoyed local autonomy or full Federal citizenship, but she should not have her pudding and eat it.[36] Full federal citizenship was, however, never an option for Singapore but the Tunku was careful to point out that there was nothing inferior in Singapore's citizenship under Malaysia.[37]

Despite the nagging concerns of a separate citizenship for Singapore, particularly in the minds of the Chinese, the PAP's position was still defensible had there been no difference in the citizenship arrangements for the Borneo Territories on the one hand, and Singapore on the other. But in this particular matter, Lee's position was getting less and less tenable. In January 1962, at the third meeting of the Malaysia Solidarity Consultative Committee, the Borneo Territories were being coaxed into joining Malaysia by the promise that the Borneo people would share the special position of the Malays in the Federation, and would thus become founder-citizens of Malaysia by operation of law.[38] This, according to Lee, already emphasized the superior status of "citizens" over "nationals".[39] But this was still acceptable to the Singapore population if the Borneo Territories would not get "Ulster" status but would join Malaysia on essentially the same terms as the existing states of Malaya. In April 1962 Lee, perhaps sensing that a deal was being worked out between Kuala Lumpur and the Borneo Territories, indicated to the British that "if the Borneo Territories were offered a 'considerable degree of autonomy' separate citizenship would be unacceptable …and could no longer be justified as a corollary of the Ulster Status".[40] Indeed, Lee indicated to Selkirk that as he had come under much criticism in Singapore for his White Paper citizenship provisions, it would not be possible for him to go ahead with merger in these circumstances.[41] He had already been taunted by Lee Siew Choh, who claimed that while the Borneo Territories would join the Federation as equal wives, Singapore was but a mistress, and "children of mistresses were going to be treated as illegitimate".[42] The BS continued to fire salvos at the PAP, claiming that while the Borneo Territories had been offered both federal citizenship and state autonomy in some matters, the PAP had sacrificed Singapore's rights for "illusory autonomy in labour and education".[43]

In June 1962, after seeing the recommendations about citizenship for the Borneo Territories in the Cobbold Report, Lee felt that he would be hard put to explain to his detractors in Singapore why the people of the Borneo Territories were to have Federation citizenship with the right to vote in the Federation while this was denied to Singapore.[44] The Cobbold Report had recommended that "a citizen of the United Kingdom and the Colonies, before the date on which Malaysia comes into effect should, on operation of law, become a citizen of the Federation of Malaysia".[45] The Report further stated that the Borneo Territories had agreed to come into Malaysia on the consideration that they be given a considerable degree of autonomy in the new state. This added an unpleasant twist for Lee's position on the citizenship issue. Like Singapore, the Borneo Territories would enjoy autonomy within Malaysia, but unlike Singapore, the inhabitants of the Borneo Territories could become Malaysian citizens without a separate Borneo citizenship.[46] Lee was fully alive to the implications: with the Malayan Government agreeing to concede Malaysian citizenship to Borneo citizens, Singapore would be left with a "separate and diminished status" in the Federation.[47]

The proposals on citizenship, Lee pointed out, and "the way they were presented would not go down well with the Chinese in Singapore".[48] While he accepted that there need not be the same citizenship rules for both citizens of Singapore and citizens of Borneo, they should at least be seen in some "parallel relationship with the central authority".[49] What was important, Lee argued, was that the citizens of Malaya, the Borneo Territories and Singapore should all become citizens of Malaysia, but with the distinction that each would only have the right to vote in their respective territories. In this way, the Chinese citizens of Singapore would not feel that they were being discriminated against, but could be brought to accept a situation in which "they would not vote in Federal elections on the same weightage as Federal citizens, nor would they be able to cross the Causeway and vote in Johore and other Malayan states without first qualifying under the Malayan rules".[50] By effecting a change in name, but not necessarily the substance of common citizenship, the Chinese citizens in Singapore would be appeased and yet Malay fears of possible Chinese domination in the Federation would be allayed. It seemed to him that this was the best way out of the citizenship conundrum.

Lee at first hoped that the British help by either "making the terms of the Borneo Territories citizenship less generous than recommended by the Cobbold Report" so that there would be no obvious disparity with the citizenship provisions for Singapore, or by "persuading the Malayans to be more forthcoming to Singapore".[51] The British ruled out the first option as "unacceptable" as they were keen to get the Borneo Territories on board with the Malaysia Plan and did not wish to complicate matters there. They were also unsure if the time was right for them to approach the Tunku on the matter of citizenship arrangements with Singapore.[52] The British were, however, concerned that the citizenship issue threatened to be an explosive one between Singapore and the Federation, and if "ventilated in public could lead to a breakdown in the arrangements for merger and so for Malaysia itself". They were therefore prepared to play the role of "honest broker" only when the time was ripe.[53] For the time being, however, all they were prepared to do was to advise Lee to secure an agreement with the Tunku for a revision of the terms agreed in the White Paper of 1961.

The political situation was, however, hotting up with the BS gaining ground on its suggestion that Singapore citizens would be "second-class" types in Malaysia. The BS had clearly chosen to focus their attacks on the government on the question of citizenship. Lee had to respond, and decided to "tackle the question head-on".[54] On 3 June 1962, at the third anniversary of Singapore State Day celebrations, Lee announced that before Malaysia was implemented, he would make it clear in the constitution "that Singapore citizens would be equal to all others in the Federation".[55] He reasoned that if the unhappiness in Singapore was caused by the issue of differentiated citizenship, then the problem would be solved if the Tunku could be persuaded to drop the term "Malaysia nationals" and adopt the common term "Malaysian citizens" for all citizens of Malaysia, including Singapore, with assurances of similar rights and privileges, other than voting.[56] The pressure was building up. On 30 June, the Workers' Party, Parti Rakyat, United Democratic Party, the Liberal Socialist and the BS banded together to form the Council of Joint Action (CJA) to oppose the PAP's merger plans.

In early July, when Lee received news that the British had assured the Tunku that the Borneo Territories would join Malaysia, he thought it opportune to visit Kuala Lumpur to raise the matter of citizenship with the Malayan Prime Minister, hoping to catch him in the right frame of mind to tackle this tricky issue. However, after having "tentatively sounded Tun Razak...over a proposal for granting 'the name but not the substance' of common citizenship for Singapore" and evidently receiving no encouragement on that front,[57] he decided against raising the issue with the Tunku then. He was, however, certain that the change in nomenclature would be perhaps the best tactic for him to pursue, to overcome the opposition from the BS and to win popular support for merger on the basis of the White Paper. He would visit London "to thrash the matter out with the Tunku and the British government".[58] But before heading to London, Lee showed up at the United Nations to defend his stand on merger, following a memorandum protesting the PAP merger submitted by nineteen opposition assemblymen of the CJA to the United Nations' 17 Nation Committee on Colonialism.

Citizenship Re-Negotiated

During the second half of July 1962 representatives of the Malayan Government were invited to London for talks with their British counterparts to work out the details of the proposed Malaysia Agreement. Lee Kuan Yew joined them on 29 July, and it was during this round of negotiations that the question of citizenship was discussed. On 17 July 1962, the Tunku had met with the British Prime Minister, Harold Macmillan, at the Admiralty House in Whitehall. On the issue of citizenship, the Tunku reiterated his stand on citizenship to the British Prime Minister, stating that "because the majority of Singapore citizens might not be loyal to the Federation they could not be given Malayan citizenship but a Singapore citizenship". He was, on the other hand, quite prepared to allow citizenship rights to the people of the Borneo Territories. Although not explicitly stated, the Chinese factor was clearly at play here. The Tunku would like to maintain this position for the time being, but he admitted that "the situation might change in the future, when the people have settled down".[59] He further emphasized that the distinction between "internal" and "external" citizenship was an important one. When citizens of Malaysia went abroad, they would automatically be entitled to the protection of the country's ambassadors. But because of differences in internal citizenship, they would not be allowed to vote anywhere in the Federation except in their place of residence. Singapore citizens would not get suffrages as an automatic right, but they could acquire voting rights in the Federation if they had at least five years residence there.[60] This was where the matter of citizenship between Singapore and the Federation stood at the moment. As far as the Tunku was concerned, he had already reached a satisfactory agreement with Lee on the basis of the Heads of Agreement as set out in the White Paper of 1961. Why should he make any changes now, especially if the entire thing could back-fire on him politically?

The Malayan ministers were equally determined to maintain their interpretation and position on the citizenship provisions of the White Paper. At a separate meeting with the Acting British Commissioner in Singapore, Malayan Deputy Prime Minister Abdul Razak confirmed that all along "the Federation interpretation of Paragraph 14 (on citizenship) of the White Paper was that although Singapore citizens will, as federal Nationals, have common rights and privileges externally, their rights as citizens will be exercisable internally only within the state of Singapore".[61] It is interesting to note that Razak was not referring specifically or merely to voting rights. Both Razak and Ghazalie Shafie knew that once common citizenship was given, "nothing could be done if Kuala Lumpur, for some reason later, would want to discriminate against Singaporeans".[62] Although the Federation ministers were persuaded that they would give nothing away by calling Singapore citizens Federation citizens, since Kuala Lumpur could still control matters such as immigration, trade unions and the quota of Malays in the public service by other means, Razak and his colleagues remained strongly opposed to the change of nomenclature, fearing that this may lead to more substantive changes in citizenship provisions for Singapore.[63]

Malay intransigence notwithstanding, the Singapore Prime Minister decided that he had to persuade the Tunku to change his mind. Lee submitted an *aide-memoire* underlying his argument for a change in the terms of the White Paper agreement where citizenship was concerned.[64] It was understood that Lee had visited Kuala Lumpur prior to the London talks and had shown his proposals to the Malayan Finance Minister, Tan Siew Sin, hoping that the latter might be more sympathetic to his case as a Chinese and would help pursue the matter with the Tunku at a later date. Lee emphasized that "the terms under which the Borneo Territories [were] to come into the new Federation must be offered to Singapore as an alternative to the arrangements already agreed to between the Singapore Government and the Federation of Malaya Government as set out in Singapore Command 33 of 1961".[65] He pointed out that the recommendations and the recent Federal Constitutional Amendment (1962) which made it difficult for Chinese to get citizenship in the Federation was regarded as anti-Chinese. To disprove the lie and allegations being spread, the Federal Government should offer Singapore the terms of citizenship that they were offering to the Borneo Territories. He proposed that the term "Singapore Citizen (National of the new Federation)" be changed to "Citizen of the new Federation (Singapore)", as this would provide a "major psychological victory" against the communists by dispelling their allegations and allow his government to win the Chinese over.[66] As Lee saw it, this change involved no more than a change of nomenclature since voting rights would still be restricted. Goh Keng Swee, whom Lee consulted and confided in on the citizenship negotiations, had reassured his Federation counterparts that "the Federation would be giving nothing away by calling Singapore citizens as Federation citizens since they could still control by other methods such as immigration, trade union activities and quota of Malays in the civil service".[67] Although Razak had his doubts seeing that this was a "purely verbal device which people would in any case see through",[68] it was a desperate gesture by Lee, who knew that unless he managed to secure an agreement from the Tunku to amend the White Paper proposals and provide for a common "Malaysian citizenship" to the people of Singapore, the entire enterprise of Malaysia might have to be called off. Fortunately, the crisis was averted when the Malayan delegation, after negotiations with Lee and the Commonwealth Relations Office, agreed to a new agreement on citizenship. On 30 July the Malayan delegation in London issued a statement stating that the governments of Singapore and the Federation have agreed that with merger, Singapore citizens will be citizens of Malaysia. The change in nomenclature was along the lines that Lee had suggested, in that Singapore citizens will be known after the establishment of merger as Federation Citizen (Singapore). In addition to the change in nomenclature, the Malayan representatives further agreed that Singapore citizens, as full citizens of Malaysia, would enjoy all rights of Federation Citizenship throughout Malaysia, except for voting and in fields where the State of Singapore had been granted autonomous powers (e.g., Labour and Education).[69] The Tunku agreed to make a statement from Kuala Lumpur to confirm the London Agreement on Citizenship, and Lee had decided to make a statement on citizenship on Radio Singapore while simultaneously releasing the London Agreement on citizenship. The agreement, which Lee had extracted from the Tunku, was a compromised solution. It was clear that there was little that Lee could do to persuade the Tunku to grant common citizenship to all constituent states of Malaysia. The implications, from the Federation's point of view, were simply unacceptable.[70] The Tunku was, however, to concede to a change of nomenclature, perhaps convinced by Lee that the political destiny of the PAP and of the final merger hinged on the outcome of the proposed referendum, which would be won or lost on the citizenship issue. In any case, the Tunku believed that he was not conceding anything of substance with the change in nomenclature. Even if he were to call Singapore citizens Malaysian citizens, their voting and franchise rights would still be restricted to Singapore. The politics of both territories would still remain separate.[71]

The change was, however, significant enough for the PAP for it now gave Lee Kuan Yew the psychological effect he was looking for. Having secured the concession of federal citizenship from the Tunku in London, Lee returned triumphant to Singapore and made his radio broadcast, announcing on 14 August 1962 that "instead of a common nationality there will be a common citizenship — citizenship of the new Federation of Malaysia.... All citizens of Singapore will automatically become citizens of Malaysia".[72] The following day, Lee was able to generate more political mileage by announcing "my job is to get what my people want. And if they want citizenship, I get them citizenship".[73] Taking advantage of his "trump card", Lee announced at the same time that the referendum he had promised would be held two weeks later, on 1 September.[74] Initial reactions in Singapore were upbeat, and newspaper articles generally agreed that the new arrangement had contributed to squelching fears and rumours about second class citizenship.[75] Lee's announcement had taken away the opposition's main argument against the PAP merger proposals, and had left them wondering how Lee Kuan Yew had been able to secure what he had once admitted as unrealistic and impractical. Not content to accept defeat, the BS issued a press statement on the following day pointing out that all that had happened was a change in nomenclature, where the word "national" was replaced with "citizen". Common citizenship was given in name, not in fact, and that the political status of Singapore citizens remained precisely as that provided in the White Paper of 1961.[76] The party continued to denounce Lee's "trump card" as a fraud. But the winds had been taken from the opposition sails and "the only effective criticisms they could levy against Lee was that Singapore citizens were still limited in the exercise of their political rights".[77]

While the PAP was able to fend off the local opposition, Lee's comments, however, immediately drew flak from the Malayan government for having "made such a statement without the fuller consultation in advance which on such an important matter of common concern it would have been normal to expect".[78] The Australian High Commissioner in Singapore, T.K. Critchley, reported that Lee's statement "caused irritations among the Federation Ministers, not so much because of what it says as what it left unsaid".[79] Lee's statement which implied that there would be complete equality other than in voting rights was seen to be "far too sweeping".[80] The Tunku stated that the Federation would not accept the statement that Lee had made as it stood, but would nonetheless avoid accentuating differences between them and Lee when he addressed the Malayan parliament on 15 November. Razak complained that Lee's account of the citizenship issue was one-sided, and that the only change that has been agreed to in paragraph 14 of the 1961 White Paper related only to nomenclature and franchise.[81] The Tunku later provided his version of the agreement that had been reached in London between his delegation and Lee. He stated that the agreement had been reached between Lee and his government, and had not been brought about by the intervention of the British Government. The Tunku then reiterated that the citizenship agreement of the White Paper provided for equal rights and protection as Nationals of the Federation. He pointed out that after further consultation with the Singapore Government in London, it has been agreed that constitutionally, Singapore citizens will not only be nationals of the Federation but "will be Citizens of Malaysia and will, as Citizens, enjoy in Singapore rights corresponding in all respects to those enjoyed by other Citizens of Malaysia as a whole". The catch here was the emphasis on the territorial restriction — that the rights would only be enjoyed exclusively "in Singapore". Rights of citizenship would not apply across all parts of Malaysia. He was quick to qualify that even with the change of nomenclature, Singapore citizens would not be entitled to all rights enjoyed by Federation citizens. As he explained:

It must be appreciated that there are rights which are reserved for Federal Citizens only as well as there are rights reserved for Singapore Citizens only, and the people of the Borneo Territories. These are the corresponding rights and those rights will remain with the Citizens of those Territories, e.g. rights to vote, jobs in the state services, etc... Where it is provided that Singapore citizens are to enjoy rights exclusively in Singapore, it will be provided that other citizens of Malaysia will enjoy corresponding rights exclusively in the remainder of the Federation. The converse will also apply so that there will be no question of discrimination against class of citizens.[82]

A careful reading of the Tunku's statement reveals that the Federation Government was attempting, in fact, to retract from the agreement reached in London and to revive the claim that paragraph 14 of the White Paper merely conferred upon Singapore citizens common external rights.[83] In the first place, the Tunku deliberately kept alive the concept of "Malaysian Nationality", "despite the agreement in the exchange of letters with Lee that references to 'national' in paragraph 14 of the White Paper should be abandoned and replaced by citizen".[84] Additionally, in his statement, the Tunku continued to refer to "rights" which would be reserved for "Federal citizens" — a term which it was stated in the London Agreement should lapse — and for the people of Borneo Territories alone, thus emphasizing the separateness of Singapore. What was perhaps most damaging was that having agreed that Singapore citizens should be able to enjoy all the rights in the Federation, the Tunku now qualified the statement by indicating that Singapore citizens would only enjoy those corresponding rights within the area of Singapore, thus denying them the substance of equal rights and privileges with all other citizens of the Federation.

Thus although Singapore citizens will be called Malaysian citizens, they will, outside their own state, not enjoy the fundamental citizenship rights provided in the Constitution; e.g. freedom of movement and residence under Article 9(2), freedom of speech and expression, of assembly and of association under Article 10, and so on.[85]

It had seemed that soon after the agreement in London, the Federation was seeking to revert to their previous position on citizenship. In this apparent volte-face by the Tunku, the British were sympathetic to Lee. The legal advisor in the colonial office had made it clear that "the common sense interpretation of paragraph 14 was that given by Lee Kuan Yew".[86] However, it was clear that the Federation government had clearly not changed their minds on the substance of citizenship, whatever transpired in London. Except for nomenclature and franchise, they still held that their interpretation of paragraph 14 counted, that it was meant to confer external rights, and not internal rights. By equal rights, the Federation were referring to corresponding rights, not identical ones. They had conceded what Lee sought was a change of name to create a psychological effect which they were prepared to assist with, but became concerned when Lee sought to turn a psychological concession into a constitutional one.[87] The Tunku felt it necessary, therefore, to press home the point, after Lee's announcement on 14 May, that the essence of the citizenship issue had not been changed. As Geofroy Tory, UK High Commissioner to Malaya, explained to Lee

> The Tunku wanted these provisions intact so as to prevent Singapore citizens from holding office in (and thus the communists from taking control of) Malayan trade unions; to prevent them from being employed in the Federal Government Service; and to be able to banish them from the Federation. Many Federation laws reserved rights to Federation citizens and the Tunku did not want these rights to be extended to Singapore citizens by giving them Federal citizenship.[88]

The Federation ministers have insisted that on several occasions, the Tunku had made it clear that there would be areas of special rights that would be reserved for the existing Malayan citizens, other than voting rights. To the Tunku, although it was not stated, it was important that he held the constitutional right to prevent undesirable Singaporeans and extremist political activities from spreading across the causeway.[89]

Lee, clearly exasperated by the Tunku's remarks, nonetheless insisted upon the true position being set out when it came to drafting the constitutional provisions. He knew that his personal political reputation would be at stake especially when his referendum campaign had made the claim that Singapore citizens would have common Malaysian citizenship.[90] He sought the intervention of the British, but the latter, while sympathetic, were unwilling to intervene, considering that they might do more harm than good, and pointing out that citizenship was a domestic issue that had to be resolved between the Federation and Singapore governments.

At home, Lee continued to fend off criticisms of the citizenship provisions for merger, especially when he had not actually succeeded in removing separate citizenship for Singapore. In a 45-minute broadcast debate with David Marshall, leader of the Worker's Party, Lee defended the need for maintaining a distinct Singapore citizenship as opposed to the suggestion by Marshall that Singapore adopt the formulae for the Borneo territories and drop the need to preserve a separate Singapore citizenship. Lee argued that Singapore citizens would continue to have special rights and privileges not accorded to any of the other Malay states in Malaya. Singapore state citizenship still carried with it tangible privileges such as priority in housing, education, jobs in the civil service, social welfare, sickness benefits, etc.[91] Marshall attempted to draw out from Lee if indeed there would be inherent disadvantages for the people of Singapore in the agreement made between the governments of the Federation and the PAP. Lee denied that there would be any disadvantage, potential or real, that would accrue to a separate citizenship for Singapore, and that he had made no secret deals with the Tunku on the question of citizenship.[92] Lee further made the assurance that except for "gangsters and subversives", who would be denied legal rights to move freely in the territories constituting Malaysia, regular citizens should be free to move about in the Federation, work and own property there.[93] Lee explained, however, that there was reciprocity of disability between the two territories — "[Federation citizens] can't stand for elections in [Singapore] so long as they are on the Malayan electoral roll, and

[Singapore citizens] can't stand for elections there as long as we are on the Singapore electoral roll".[94] Finally, Lee assured Marshall that there was no secret deal with the Tunku, and that the draft constitution of Malaysia would be submitted to the Singapore Legislative Assembly. Marshall was evidently convinced following the radio debate, and agreed to support the PAP's merger proposals.[95] In the upshot, despite the differences in interpretation between the Singapore and Malayan governments on the extent of rights that a Malaysian citizen in Singapore could enjoy upon merger, Lee Kuan Yew seemed to have averted a major crisis and was determined to press ahead with the referendum now that he had acquired the psychological advantage over his opponents.

Referendum

Having secured from the Tunku the agreement that citizens from Singapore would be called Malaysian citizens after merger, Lee believed that the final obstacle to merger on the PAP's White Paper proposals had at last been removed. He, therefore, felt that the time was ripe to execute the *coup de grace*, and announced that the promised national referendum would be scheduled for 1 September 1962. The PAP would use the referendum not merely to ascertain the collective opinion of the people on the type of merger that they would want with the Federation, but to compel the opposition parties to make their stand on merger. As expected, the Referendum elicited another bout of contest between the PAP and its rivals, the BS, Workers' Party and the United People's Party, mainly in the questions that should be asked in the referendum. The opposition had asked the government to allow a straight "Yes" or "No" question to the merger White Paper proposals in the referendum.[96] The government refused to concede on this, and favoured, instead, for a referendum with alternatives, rather than straight "Yes" or "No". Indeed, in late 1961, when Lee first indicated to the Tunku his plans to hold a referendum on merger, his original idea was "to present to the people the option of agreeing to the Northern Ireland type of merger or a complete merger".[97] He felt that there was no need to ask the people if they actually wanted merger or not as "they all wanted merger".[98] On hearing Lee's proposals, the Tunku suggested that the referendum should first ascertain if the people wanted merger or not, and if they did want a merger, they would then choose between a limited or a full merger.[99] He made it clear, however, that if the people should choose a full merger, the final say of whether that would come about would still rest with the Malayan Government. By doing so, the Tunku explained, "Lee Kuan Yew would be free from any blame if complete merger was found to be unacceptable, as it was likely to be".[100] But, as Ghazali Shafie explained, this "opened the way for the merger not to take place which obviously would not be agreed to by Lee Kuan Yew".[101] According to Ghazali Shafie, the Tunku was concerned that Lee would use the referendum to force the Malayan Government to accept Singapore even without the Borneo Territories. As the British had not yet given their full commitment that the Borneo Territories would come on board, the Tunku did not want to be left holding the Singapore baby should the Malaysia Plan fall through, and was "preparing for a way out".[102] Later on, however, the Malayan Government seemed to have a change of mind and Razak wanted Ghazali Shafie to convey to Lee that a referendum should be a "straightforward question of either a merger of the Uslter kind ...or no merger". Razak was insistent that the question of complete merger should not be posed as he did not want the "refusal of the Federation Government in the face of the people's wish for complete merger".[103] Subsequently, in a discussion with the Malayan ministers, where Lee, Goh Keng Swee and S. Rajaratnam were present, Lee said that after a great deal of thought and consideration, his colleagues and advisors agreed that "the best and most effective approach was to pose the referendum in the form of either reserved merger or complete merger, instead of a straight 'yes' or 'no' to the reserved merger". He was confident that when confronted with these options, the people of Singapore would choose reserved merger, as they were aware that half of them would be disqualified from voting with Singapore entering the Federation on full merger.[104] He was nonetheless told that complete merger was a non-starter with the Malayan Government, whether or not the people of Singapore chose it.

In March 1962 the PAP, with the support of the SPA-UMNO alliance in the Legislative Assembly, managed to push through its National Referendum Bill which provided a referendum in which the electorate would be asked to choose between three types of merger which the PAP said were proposed by the PAP government, the BS and the SPA-UMNO alliance respectively. The three alternatives presented were (A) — the White Paper Proposals, (B) complete and unconditional merger for Singapore as a state on an equal basis with the other eleven states in accordance with the constitutional documents of the Federation of Malaya, and (C), merger on terms no less favourable than those given to the Borneo Territories.[105] The questions were cleverly crafted as to make the PAP's alternative as the most attractive, since the second alternative was an arrangement that would lead to the disenfranchising of half of Singapore's adult population, and one that the Tunku would never concede to,[106] while the terms for option C were as yet unconfirmed. Fearing that the BS might well advise their supporters to put in blank votes since the alternatives the government were offering might not be acceptable to them, the PAP forced through the Select Committee a clause in the Referendum Bill that provided for all blank ballot papers to be regarded as accepting the vote of the Assembly, i.e. White Paper merger.[107]

Because the referendum did not carry an option for a total rejection of merger with the Federation, Lee's opponents, in particular the BS, had called the entire exercise a "sham and a farce".[108] Lee, however, defended his position claiming that the issue of merger had been decided in the Legislative Assembly, which had given it a resounding endorsement. Furthermore, the PAP had been elected to office in the 1959 General Elections with merger as one of the key election issues. The electoral victory of the PAP, by that logic, suggested that the people of Singapore had accepted merger as the desired political objective to be achieved as soon as possible, and with the best possible terms for Singapore. The PAP leadership had done just that, and now the people were asked to decide not whether they wanted merger, which was an issue already settled, but on whether they were satisfied with the terms which the PAP had secured for them, under the White Paper Proposals. The British, concerned that Lee might discredit himself and his government by holding a referendum that was loudly touted as "dishonest and phony", tried to talk Lee out of holding his referendum. Their exhortations, however, fell on deaf ears. Lee was quite determined to go ahead with the referendum to avoid, as he had often said to the British, being "labelled as the man who sold the Singapore Chinese to the Malays".[109]

The lead-up to the Referendum was marked by a flurry of activities from the ruling party and the opposition. The BS started its island-wide campaign, mobilizing cultural organizations, trade unions, rural residents and other associations to campaign against the PAP. In two weeks, they held nearly 300 rallies, big and small, and went on house to house visits. The PAP made use of the radio and the print media and visited market places and rural areas day and night to call on the people to vote Alternative (A).

It is impossible to verify if indeed, as the BS had claimed, it was the PAP tactics of "threats and tricks" that had a significant bearing on the outcome of the referendum.[110] It is also difficult to ascertain if the government's intention of allocating blank votes to Alternative (A), as a way of scaring the Chinese into voting for the PAP's proposal, had worked to the PAP's advantage. Two things were, however, clear from the referendum. First, there was little doubt that it represented a firm victory for the PAP, whatever the BS might allege. Of an electorate of 624,000 voters, 397,626 voted for Alternative (A). The BS suffered a stunning blow as the alternative that was described as their choice only obtained 9,422 votes, while Alternative (C) had 7,911 votes.[111] However, what probably had not escaped Lee's attention was that there were still a quarter of the voters (144,077) who chose to cast a blank vote, thus indicating that a significant portion of the population were still against the idea of a political merger with the Federation.[112] Lee was convinced that of the 25 per cent who indicated their opposition to the merger by casting blank votes, 10 per cent were communists, who had to be dealt with firmly, and the other 15 per cent were Chinese chauvinist, who needed to be handled with a gentler hand.[113]

By the end of 1962, Lee had clearly obtained the upper hand internally, where the question of merger was concerned. He had weathered the political uncertainties of the past few months, and the referendum results had all but put him and his government in an unassailable position. Although the BS had refused to accept the results of the referendum, there was little doubt that the 1962 national referendum had marked the triumphant end of the PAP's domestic battle for merger.

Malaysian historian Cheah Boon Kheng has argued that the most significant reason why Malaysia was formed, from the perspective of the Tunku's administration, was the ethnic factor. In an enlarged Malaysia, the racial scales would be tipped in favour of the Malays and "natives" of Malaya over the Chinese, Indians, and other "non-natives" and "non-Malays".[114] Going by Cheah's assertion that racial demography was a primary factor in the formation of Greater Malaysia, the debates on citizenship are thus critical in highlighting the nature and substance of the Malaysia Federation that was being constructed in 1962. The citizenship arguments demonstrate very clearly that there was a tussle between policies of inclusion and exclusion based on race. The Tunku was prepared to integrate the territories of Malaya and Singapore, but he was certainly less keen to unite the peoples of these two territories based mainly on his concern that the incorporation of the Singapore Chinese population would threaten the political primacy of the Malays. He wanted to adopt the politically safe policy of exclusion through restrictive citizenship arrangements for Singapore. He thus introduced the distinction between Malaysian "citizens who are Singapore citizens" and "citizens who are not Singapore citizens".[115] The PAP understood this, and was prepared to accept these restrictions in return for greater autonomy following merger. The opposition in Singapore, however, argued for an inclusive citizenship fearing that anything less would make the citizens of Singapore "second class" in the new state of Malaysia. The Tunku was not averse to creating a Malaysian identity, as is evident in his use of the term "common Malaysian nationality", defined in terms of individuals and groups identifying with the Malaysian state. But the nationality was based on two types of citizenship in one state.[116] This was made clear in the open arguments over the formal elements of citizenship; however, the substantive aspects, how the rights of Malaysian citizens (Singapore) would be accommodated in the new state were largely left vague. For the moment, the provisions that were agreed had served their purposes. The referendum was done, and the path cleared for the PAP to press on with their merger plans. However, there were still battles ahead, not least a general election. But, as the date for merger drew nearer, a major one that was looming concerned Singapore's negotiations with the Malayan ministers on the financial details and common market arrangements of merger, a battle that would once again unsettle the already shaky progress towards merger.

NOTES

1 The PAP received support from one independent, two UMNO, and three SPA members. Lee Kuan Yew, *The Singapore Story: Memoirs of Lee Kuan Yew* (Singapore: Federal Publications, 2000), p. 408.

2 Ibid.

3 See *Far Eastern Economic Review* 37, no. 3 (1962), Hong Kong.

4 *Singapore Legislative Assembly Debates*, 20 November 1961.

5 Ibid.

6 *Straits Times*, 18 September 1961.

7 Lee Kuan Yew, Radio Broadcasts, 13 September 1961.

8 Lee, *The Singapore Story*, p. 407.

9 *Memorandum Setting out the Heads of Agreement for a Merger between the Federation of Malaya and Singapore* (Singapore: L. K. Heng, Government Printer, 1961), Cmnd 33.

10 Colonial Office note, "Citizenship Arrangements for Singapore within the Proposed Federation of Malaysia", n.d., CO 1030/998.

11 *Singapore Legislative Assembly Debates*, vol. 15, 20 November 1961, Col. 334.

12 Ibid.

13 Telegram no. 262, Moore to Sandys, 17 May 1962, DO 169/250.

14 Ibid.

15 Note of a meeting between Lee Kuan Yew and members of the Colonial Office, including John Martin, C. G. Eastwood, P. R. Noakes and C. S. Roberts, 16 May 1962, DO 169/250.

16 *Singapore Legislative Assembly Debates*, 20 November 1961.

17 Ibid.

18 *Straits Times*, 23 September 1961.

19 See Barisan's stand on merger between Singapore and the Federation. Barisan Sosialis, *Letter to the Secretary-General, United Nations, from Lee Siew Choh* (Singapore: Barisan Sosialis, 1963).

20 Sandys to Selkirk, 5 October 1962.

21 Malaysia, *Parliamentary Debates. Dewan Ra'ayat (House of Representatives) Official Report*, vol. 3, 16 October 1961, Col. 1592.

22 In the Federation, a person who was born in Malaya did not automatically get rights of citizenship. A person who was born in the Federation before Merdeka

Day, and who had not already been a citizen of the Federation, had to apply for registration as a citizen. The applicant would have to reside for five years out of the preceding seven years before his application, have intended to reside permanently in the Federation, and had to possess an elementary knowledge of the Malay language. See Citizenship Provisions in Federation of Malaya Agreement, 1948; the Federation Constitution of 1957; and the Constitution (Amendment) Act of 1962.

23 Note of UK delegation meeting on 25 July 1962 under Chairmanship of Lord Lansdowne, 26 July 1962, CO 1030/1158.

24 Lee, *The Singapore Story*, p. 408.

25 See Singapore Citizen Ordinance, 1957.

26 *Singapore Legislative Assembly Debates*, 20 November 1961, Col. 320.

27 Moore to Wallace, 21 June 1962, DO 169/250.

28 *Singapore Legislative Assembly Debates*, 22 November 1961, Cols. 473–80.

29 Brief record of meeting between Lee Kuan Yew and Geofroy Tory, UK High Commissioner to Malaya, 6 July 1962, CO 1030/1029.

30 See Sunny Tan, "Barisan Sosialis: Years at the Front Line, 1961–1966" (Unpublished Honours Thesis, Department of History, National University of Singapore, 1997/98), p. 15.

31 *Singapore Legislative Assembly Debates*, 21 November, 1961, Cols. 407–09.

32 Lee, *The Singapore Story*, p. 429.

33 *A Year of Decision* (Singapore: Ministry of Culture, 1961), p. 8.

34 Colonial Office note, "Citizenship Arrangements for Singapore Within the Proposed Federation of Malaysia", n.d., CO 1030/998.

35 Note, for example, Lee's talk to the leaders of the Chinese-speaking community on 13 January 1962 at the Victoria Memorial Hall. Cited in Lee, *The Singapore Story*, pp. 414–15.

36 Tunku's address to the Singapore Chinese of Commerce, 27 March 1962, CO 1030/988.

37 Telegram no. 84, Tunku's speech at the foundation laying ceremony of the new UMNO house in Singapore, March 1962, CO 1030/988.

38 Lee, *The Singapore Story*, p. 415.

39 Ibid.

40 "Citizenship Arrangements for Singapore Under Malaysia", n.d., DO 169/250.

41 Ibid.

42 Lee, *The Singapore Story*, p. 407.

43 Selkirk to Sandys, 29 March 1962, CO 1030/988.

44 Moore to Wallace, 15 May 1962, DO 169/250.

45 *Report of the Commission of Enquiry, North Borneo and Sarawak, 1962* (London: Her Majesty's Stationery Office, 1962), Cmnd 1794, CO 947 paragraph 148 (K).

46 "Malaysia: Singapore Situation". Note of United Kingdom Delegation Meeting, 26 July 1962, CO 1030/1158.

47 F. Mills, "Note for Record: Lee Kuan Yew's Meeting with Duncan Sandys, Secretary of State, Colonies", 15 May 1962, DO 169/250.

48 Ibid.

49 Ibid.

50 Ibid.

51 "Citizenship Arrangements for Singapore Under Malaysia", n.d., DO 169/250.

52 Ibid.

53 Ibid.

54 Lee, *The Singapore Story*, p. 429.

55 Ibid.

56 Moore to Wallace, 21 June 1962, DO 169/250.

57 "Citizenship Arrangements for Singapore Under Malaysia", n.d., DO 169/250. See also extract of letter from Philip Moore, ibid.

58 Telegram no. 332, Moore to Sandys, 9 July 1962, DO 169/250.

59 Record of a Meeting at Admiralty House between the Tunku and Harold Macmillan, 17 July 1962, CO 1030/1024.

60 Ibid.

61 Telegram no. 348, Moore, to Sandys, 14 July 1962, DO 169/250.

62 Shafie, *Ghazali Shafie's Memoirs*, p. 262.

63 Ibid.

64 Telegram no. 332, Moore to Sandys, DO 169/250.

65 Aide-Memoire on "Citizenship" by Lee Kuan Yew, n.d., DO 169/250.

66 Ibid.

67 Telegram no. 348, Moore to Selkirk, 14 July 1962, DO 169/250.

68 Telegram no. 427, Moynihan to Selkirk, 10 July 1962, CO 1030/1024.

69 Minutes of Fifth Meeting of Steering Committee on Malaysia, 30 July 1962, Commonwealth Relations Office, DO 169/250.

70 Telegram from Acting High Commissioner (Kuala Lumpur) to Commonwealth Relations Office, 10 July 1962, CO 1030/1024.

71 Telegram no. 526, Moynihan to Selkirk, 6 August 1962, DO 169/250. See also Cablegram no. 3759, Australian High Commissioner to Kuala Lumpur, 3 August 1962, A 1838/280.

72 Lee Kuan Yew's talk over the Radio, 14 August 1962, PREM 11/3868.

73 Cited from transcript of a news conference at Radio Singapore on 15 August 1962.

74 John Drysdale, *Singapore: The Struggle for Success* (Singapore: Times Books International, 1984), p. 308.

75 Telegram no. 404, Moore to Secretary of State for the Colonies, 16 August 1962, DO 169/250.

76 *Straits Times*, 15 August 1962.

77 Ibid.

78 Telegram no. 555, Moore to Commonwealth Relations Office, 15 August 1962, DO 169/250.

79 T.K. Critchley, to Secretary, Department of External Affairs, 17 August 1962, A 1838/280.

80 Ibid.

81 Telegram no. 555, Moore to Commonwealth Relations Office, 15 August 1962, DO 169/250.

82 Telegram no. 556, from Kuala Lumpur, 15 August 1962, DO 169/250.

83 Telegram no. 404, Moore to Sandys, 16 August 1962, DO 169/250.

84 Ibid.

85 Ibid.

86 Ibid.

87 Telegram no. 596, Moynihan to Commonwealth Relations Office, 28 August 1962, DO 169/250.

88 Brief record of talk between Geofroy Tory and Lee Kuan Yew at Paya Lebar Airport, 6 July 1962, CO 1030/1029.

89 Ibid.

90 Telegram no. 404, Moore to Secretary of State for the Colonies, 16 August 1962, DO 169/250.

91 Transcript of a recording of a radio dialogue between Lee and Marshall on the citizenship issue, 19 August 1962, DO 169/250.

92 Ibid.

93 *Straits Times*, 20 August 1962.

94 "Transcript of a recording of a radio dialogue between Lee and Marshall on the citizenship issue", 19 August 1962, DO 169/250.

95 "Transcript of a Radio Forum on the Citizenship Issue broadcast over Radio Singapore on 25 August 1962", in *Prime Minister's Speeches, Press Conferences, Interviews, Statements, and etc.* (Singapore: Prime Minister's Office, 1962–63).

96 *Singapore Legislative Assembly Debates*, Singapore, 14, 15 and 16 March 1962.

97 Shafie, *Ghazali Shafie's Memoir*, p. 130.

98 Ibid.

99 Ibid.

100 Ibid.

101 Ibid.

102 Ibid.

103 Ibid.

104 Ibid.

105 Moore to Wallace, 21 June 1962, CO 1030/998.

106 Ibid.

107 See *Select Committee on the Singapore National Referendum Bill: Official Report* (Singapore: Government Printing Office, 1962); and *Singapore Legislative Assembly Debates*, 5 July 1962.

108 Dr Lee Siew Choh (Chairman, Barisan Sosialis Party), Memorandum of the Barisan Sosialis Party of Singapore on "Malaysia", 11 March 1963, DO 169/248.

109 Moore to Wallace, 21 June 1962, CO 1030/998.

110 Ibid.

111 *Report of the Superintendent of the Singapore Referendum on the Results of the Referendum held on 1st September 1962* (Singapore: Government Printer, 1962), Cmnd. 18.

112 Ibid.

113 G.W. Tory, "Notes of a talk with Lee Kuan Yew in Kuala Lumpur", 9 November 1962, CO 1030/1159.

114 Cheah Boon Kheng, *Malaysia. The Making of a Nation* (Singapore: Institute of Southeast Asian Studies, 2002), p. 93.

115 Jayakumar S. and Trindade, F.A., "Citizenship in Malaysia, Singapore", *Malayan Law Journal* (reprint, 1964), pp. 2–3.

116 See Michael Hill and Lian Kwen Fee, *The Politics of Nation Building and Citizenship in Singapore* (London & New York: Routledge, 1995), p. 58.

CHAPTER FIVE

Financial Arrangements and the Common Market

For the better part of 1961 and throughout 1962 the governments of Singapore and the Federation had preoccupied themselves with the settlement of the major political issues concerning merger, involving political representation in the Federal Government, citizenship and local autonomy in labour and education. The acceptance of the Singapore White Paper of 1961 and the successful referendum in Singapore endorsing the White Paper proposals for merger had removed the major obstacles to merger, and by the beginning of 1963, with the thorny issue of dual citizenship seemingly settled, it looked as if the target date for establishing merger by 31 August 1963 would be achieved easily. The remaining tasks were straightforward enough: both the Singapore and Federation governments simply had to work out the details of financial and tax arrangements that would be effected when Malaysia came into being. The negotiations in earnest on the financial arrangements started only in 1963, as previously, the two governments were trying to iron out the politically more sensitive issues of parliamentary representation and citizenship. However, as the planned date for the Malaysia agreement drew near, the nitty-gritty matters of tax collection and the sharing of revenues between state and centre came to the fore, leading to hard bargaining between the two governments. On a number of occasions, the disagreements over financial arrangements threatened the progress towards Malaysia. The nature of the disputes reflected the divergent aims and underlying assumptions which both the Singapore and the Federation governments adopted with regard to merger. As far as Malaya was concerned, merger was meant to solve a political-security problem: to allow Kuala Lumpur to exert direct control in Singapore and thereby nip the growing threat of communism there. The Tunku was thus satisfied that as long as he could do that without Singapore politics jeopardizing his Malayan political base he was quite happy to include Singapore within the Federation. Thus, according to Lee, "the bargain between [the Tunku] and [him] was: You be the New York, do exactly what you like; don't give me trouble in internal security and foreign affairs and defence, you be New York, don't worry".[1] With the big issues of citizenship and parliamentary representation in the bag, the Tunku was thus prepared to leave the bargaining of the non-political details to his advisors and ministers.

But from the Singapore perspective, while the political issues were indeed weighty, the economic arrangements of merger were just as crucial, if not more. The referendum had been won, and for the time being, the PAP's position was secure. However, if Singapore went into the Federation without assurances that its economic future would be protected if not enhanced, then the earlier political gains would have been a pyrrhic victory. Since the mid-1950s, the PAP's rationale for pressing for merger with the Federation was essentially borne out of an economic imperative. A Singapore economically divorced from the Malayan hinterland was simply inconceivable. From very early on, the PAP had regarded the formation of a customs union as absolutely "vital to the future economic existence of Singapore".[2] Lee Kuan Yew and Goh Keng Swee therefore placed the greatest importance on common market terms that they considered to be the key to the whole question of Singapore's future prosperity within the Federation.[3] Even before the negotiations began, Lee knew that he was in for a round of hard bargaining. The British acting High Commissioner noted that Lee was "apprehensive about the negotiations which he expect[ed] to be difficult". It was an observation that was to prove prophetic.[4]

The negotiations for economic details relating to merger took place within the framework of an Inter-Governmental Committee (ICG) on Federation/Singapore Merger, a joint committee headed by senior ministers from both governments. The key issues which drew agitated and protracted arguments from both sides centred on the control of the finances of Singapore, and, subsequently, the establishment of the common market. The 1961 White Paper had spelt out in general terms the financial arrangements that should take effect upon merger, but it was only when the IGC started working out the detailed terms of the merger in December 1962 that the problems of the financial arrangements emerged, with both sets of ministers and officials getting involved in endless rounds of argument and bargaining. The subsequent disputes over the financial terms of merger, as well as the related issue of common market, threatened to de-rail the progress towards an agreement between the two governments. This chapter analyses the nature of the disagreements in the negotiations over financial arrangements and the common market, and the eventual agreement that was arrived at, literally, on the eve of Malaysia Day.

The Tussle over Financial Control

The 1961 Singapore White Paper announcing the Heads of Agreement between Singapore and Malaya stipulated that

> In view of the larger measure of local autonomy and the consequent larger expenditure on Singapore services and development, the financial relations between the Federal Government and the states set out in the Federal Constitution will not be applicable in their entirety to Singapore.

> The Federation will retain legislative authority over all taxes of a national character…subject to the maintenance of a free port status of Singapore which will not be changed without the concurrence of both the Federal and Singapore governments. The present machinery for the collection of taxes in Singapore will be retained.

> …The proceeds of national taxes will be used to pay the cost of government and public services in Singapore and the contribution to the Federal Government for federal services. The details of the apportionment will be worked out by the joint working party.[5]

Although the general principles concerning the financial arrangements between Singapore and the Federation were laid out in the White Paper, no detailed arrangements had been agreed upon, and no decisions had been made on the manner or the amount which Singapore should contribute for Federal expenditure. A committee of officials of the Singapore and Federation Governments met in early 1963 to discuss "whether Singapore should, after Malaysia, continue to collect taxes, and pay an agreed proportion to the Federation Government for federal services (Defence, External Affairs etc), or whether the Federation should take over the collection of taxes and allocate funds to Singapore to meet local commitments".[6] It was precisely on these two matters, "the apportionment of expenditure and the quantum of Singapore's contribution for Federal Expenditure, as well as responsibility for collection of national taxes in Singapore after merger", that the negotiations got mired in disagreement and dispute.[7] Consequently, the unresolved issues were referred to the plenary session of the Inter-Governmental Committee.

On 28 February 1963, during the first IGC meeting convened at the instance of the Federation government to discuss financial arrangements, Lee offered on behalf of his government that Singapore should keep all its revenues, including tax collections, after merger and pay a lump sum each year to the Federal Government to meet its share of Federal services, such as the maintenance of police and prison services.[8] The Singapore Government also agreed to contribute to pan-Malayan services which was estimated at between S$50 – S$60 million a year. The Federation Finance Minister, Tan Siew Sin, rejected outright the proposal from Singapore, demanding that fiscal policies were a central responsibility and that the Federal Government should control all major taxation, collect virtually all taxes and allocate money according to Singapore's needs and requirements.[9] Singapore, however, contended that the 1961 White Paper had agreed to the contrary, that because there would not be a full merger, Singapore would keep all her revenues while making a contribution to the Federal Government, and that the arrangements in the present Malayan Federal constitution would not apply to Singapore. It was a *quid pro quo* agreement — in return for a smaller representation in the central government, Singapore would enjoy greater autonomy, and this included control of its finances. The White Paper, Lee argued, implied that sources of revenue to be assigned to Singapore would include all present taxes collected by the Singapore Government which would become federal taxes upon merger. The White Paper also stated that "financial relations between the Federal Government and the States in the present Federation Constitution would not be applicable in their entirety to Singapore".[10] Although the Federal Government would retain legislative authority over all taxes of a national character, the present machinery for the collection of taxes would be retained.[11] Reference was also made to an undertaking by Tunku that Singapore would keep "more than three-quarters of her revenue for the discharge of responsibilities".[12] Tan Siew Sin, however, would have none of it, maintaining his ground that revenue and finance matters were Federal responsibilities, which under no circumstances should be devolved to the state government. A deadlock subsequently ensued as no agreement was reached at the meeting, and Lee suggested a joint board to decide the Singapore contribution for Federal services.

While the Singapore Government accepted that fiscal policies were a matter that resided within the jurisdiction of the Federal Government, it was nonetheless determined to maintain control of its surplus revenue after contributions for Federal expenditure, arguing that these revenues were absolutely vital for the future economic development of Singapore. Since World War II, economic development in Singapore had progressed on a tangent that was very different from the Federation. The state in Singapore had put more emphasis on development, and had committed larger sums of its revenues on social services and municipal development than the Federal Government.[13] Unlike the Borneo territories that would have to depend on the Federation for help in its internal development plans, Singapore needed to develop on its own resources.[14] The PAP government was, therefore, anxious that it retained sufficient control over its internal revenues to allow it to carry on developing along the lines it had adopted, having already engaged in a one hundred million sterling pound plan to promote industrialization and develop social services to match the rapid growth of its population. To maintain the plan, revenue as well as loan finances were required, and the Singapore Government feared that Federal control would give Kuala Lumpur a potential stranglehold on the state's progress.[15]

Malaya, on the other hand, was concerned that Singapore's potential capacity as an entrepôt, commercial, and developing industrial centre would lead to a state where it would be able to enrich itself and attract an unfair share of industrial development at the expense of Malaya, possibly to the point where it could economically eclipse the mainland.[16] Such unhealthy competition between the state of Singapore and the Federation, after merger, was deemed by the Malayan ministers as highly unsatisfactory. Although this had not been raised at the negotiating table, there was also a political dimension to the Federation's stand on the issue of revenue control. T.K. Critchley, Australian High Commissioner to Kuala Lumpur, noted Malayan fears that "if a wealthy Singapore [were] able to control its Federal revenues, it [would] be able to use them to exert political influence in the rest of Malaysia. This would give opportunities for the ruling party in Singapore (possibly in the future the Barisan Sosialis Party) to expand into politics on a Malaysian-wide basis".[17] Lord Selkirk and Geofroy Tory shared similar views, pointing out that the "Federation [feared] Singapore gaining economic hegemony which would be followed by political control".[18] Added to this was the MCA's "fear of encroachment by Singapore and Borneo on Malaya's wealth", especially when the institutional interests of its core supporters — the industrialists — stood to be threatened. The Malayan Chinese leaders were thus staunch opponents of granting "unnecessary financial concessions to the new territories", especially Singapore.[19] Little wonder then that the Federation Cabinet decided to send Tan Siew Sin and Lim Swee Aun (the Malayan Minister for Commerce and Industry) to London for the financial negotiations with Singapore in July 1963 to ensure that the more amenable Razak did not make too many compromises that would imperil Malay dominance in Malaysia.[20] Tan had indeed taken the position that he would not allow any deal that could potentially hurt the financial interests of Kuala Lumpur.[21]

After a period of acrimonious haggling, it was decided that Singapore would be allowed to go on collecting the taxes within its territory, but this was to be done under Federal supervision. The question of control of taxes to be collected was put aside, but remained unsettled. The attention of the financial arrangements was subsequently turned to the actual amounts of Federal revenue in Singapore that should be apportioned respectively to the state and towards the cost of Federal services. In a memorandum put forward by Malaya to Singapore on 18 March 1963, the Federation outlined the factors that would be taken into account in determining Singapore's share of payment for Federal services. In the memorandum, the Federation government proposed that it would calculate the amount of Federal expenditure on the basis of the "provisional expenditure incurred in Singapore in 1962 which would be classified into Federal or state expenditure according to the interpretation of the Federal Government of the Singapore White Paper of 1961".[22] Revenues would similarly be classified according to the White Paper agreement. The Federation then proposed that the Singapore Government should bear a 21.2 per cent share of common pan-Malaysian expenditure incurred by services such as defence, internal security, parliament and external affairs, etc.[23] The percentage was based on the average of the 1961 actual revenue collected by Singapore and the 1962 provisional actual revenue collected in each of the territories to comprise Malaysia.[24] The Federation government claimed that their proposals were based on the projected overall needs of the Federal and State governments. In addition, the Federation memorandum suggested that certain revenues [over and above state taxes] be assigned by the Singapore Government to enable Singapore to meet her obligations to its own local expenditure plus its contributions to the pan-Malaysian services. This, in short, amounted to a demand by the Federation government that Singapore's surplus revenue, that is the whole of the balance between revenues collected in Singapore (on both national and state taxes) and Singapore's state expenditure (in both state and Federal departments) be handed over to the Federal government.[25]

Not surprisingly, the Singapore Government objected strongly to the Malayan proposals. It argued that the demand that Singapore bore a 21.2 per cent share of the pan-Malaysian services was too high, and such a calculation should take into consideration not only Singapore's capacity to pay, but factors such as representation in the Central Parliament and population. Furthermore, the Singapore Government pointed out that the

Federation's calculations of Federal expenditure such as defence was based on projections up to 1970. As the Malayan proposal meant that all of Singapore's revenue surpluses would be taken away, thus depriving the island of the much needed revenue for its own development funds, the Singapore Government strongly objected to the proposals. On the issue of the surplus revenue, the Singapore Government pointed out that an agreement had already been reached on 1 March 1963 that the national taxes collected in Singapore would go neither to the Singapore nor the Federal consolidated fund but to an account to be opened in the Singapore branch of the Central Bank. The money must thus be physically based in Singapore and no disbursement would be made from the amount until the two governments had agreed on the percentage of Singapore's contribution to the central government for Federal services.

On 2 April 1963, after rejecting the Federation's proposals, the Singapore Government submitted an alternative proposal to the IGC. The Singapore scheme proposed that Singapore's contribution to pan-Malaysian services should be based on actual expenditure and not on projected expenditure. Furthermore, it suggested that the capital expenditure on defence and security should be financed partly from revenue and partly from loans. And finally, the amount that Singapore would contribute in addition to that for pan-Malaysian services should be determined by its representation in the Federal parliament, the size of its population and the extent of its economic growth.[26] This last determinant was referred to as the "prosperity index", which would generate a ratio determining the amount Singapore should contribute to common Malaysian expenditure, after paying the full cost of direct Federal services in Singapore. This percentage would increase in accordance with the growth of industry in Singapore, as determined by the annual census of production.[27]

The Federation, however, argued that, based on its calculations, the Singapore formula produced much less than the cost of providing defence and security exclusively for Singapore. Not unexpectedly, it rejected the Singapore proposal. It objected strongly to Singapore's suggestion to use the expenditure approach in its estimates. Razak and Tan then met Lee informally and informed him that Singapore's approach had to be abandoned if there were to be further progress in the negotiations. They pointed out to Lee that proposals would lead to accounting difficulties and may lead to acrimonious conflicts each year between the Federal and Singapore governments over the quantum to be contributed annually. Furthermore, the Federal Government was not about to have their financial accounts scrutinized each year by a state government.[28]

On 11 April, the Malayans forwarded an amended version of their earlier proposals. This time round, two concessions were made. First, instead of the earlier suggestion that Singapore surrendered its entire surplus revenue to the Federal Government, it was proposed that the Federation and Singapore should share its surplus revenue on a fifty-fifty basis after Federal and state services had been paid for. Based on the calculations on 1961 revenue figures, Singapore's surplus, which amounted to M$47 million, should be divided down the middle with each government being entitled to M$23.5 million each. This would then be added to the Federal expenditure that Singapore would be obliged to give to the government in Kuala Lumpur. Having thus determined the amounts from the surplus revenue that would go to the Federal and state governments respectively, the ratio thus arrived at would then be used as the fixed formula for future apportionment. On the above figures, the Federal Government would then be able to claim from Singapore M$143.6 million for Federal expenditure, including a 50 per cent share of the revenue surplus in Singapore, whereas Singapore would be left with M$114.8 million for its own use. This then amounted to an apportionment of 55.5 per cent of the revenue for the Federal government, while Singapore could claim 44.5 per cent.[29] The other concession made in the 11 April proposal by the Federation government was that the defence and internal security contribution by Singapore was reduced from S$93.6 million to S$75 million a year.

At the IGC plenary session during which the Malayan proposal was discussed, the Singapore Government conceded that Singapore's contribution need not be pegged too rigidly to actual Federal expenditure incurred. But it still was unable to arrive at a mutually acceptable amount of Singapore's contribution to the Federal Government. Lee at first rejected the proposal as it amounted to the same demands that were made on

Singapore at the beginning of negotiations. The Singapore Government was prepared to accept a figure of M$115 million for Federal expenditure, which would include defence, internal security, and other central expenditure. This represented a considerably lower amount than the Malayan estimate of M$143.6. Lee further pointed out that it was not sound to base the calculations of the Singapore surplus on base year 1961, as in that year, Singapore had an abnormally high surplus. This has subsequently been reduced, and Lee pointed out that by 1964, there might well be a deficit in Singapore's budget. He argued that it would not be fair to expect the Singapore Government to continue to pay similar amounts to the Federal Government if there was a deficit in the Singapore budget. The Malayan proposals were clearly unacceptable from the Singapore point of view. Furthermore it was pointed out that the Malayan proposals failed to take into account the capital development expenditure on the state subjects, which needed to be financed, at least partly, from the state revenue. The Singapore position was that the assumption behind the 50/50 apportioning of the revenue/expenditure balance was technically faulty. That then still left the problem of how much Singapore should contribute to the Federal Government, with a gap of near M$30 million between the Singapore and Federal estimates.

The Singapore Government argued that it had no difficulty agreeing to the apportionment of national taxes collected in Singapore for Singapore's contribution to the Central government, provided that a forecast can accurately be made to determine the cost of pan-Malaysian services from 1964 onwards. However, as Lee pointed out, the talks had run into difficulties because of the Federation Government's determination to use the "1961 surplus as the yardstick of prosperity". The Singapore Government agreed that prosperity in Malaysia should be shared all round, but had difficulty accepting this particular formula as proposed by the Federation ministers. Singapore's argument was that it was the future prosperity of Singapore, after it has become a part of Malaysia, and not its past prosperity, when it stood alone, that should be shared.

Failing to reach an agreement, both sides decided to dig in their heels, and discussions continued through April 1963 without much progress. The

Federal Government maintained that their proposal of 11 April was their final offer, and Singapore had declined to put forward any form of counter-proposals that would bridge the gap. Acrimonious press statements made by their respective governments further fuelled the intransigence of both sides at the negotiating table. The deadlock in the financial negotiations was soon complicated by personality clashes between the negotiators.[30] Lee, meticulous and shrewd with a sharp and legalistic mind, met his match in Razak, a fellow lawyer with an eye for detail. In the negotiations, Razak, who saw himself as the last Malayan leader to try to get along with Lee, came up against a determined opponent whom he found sometimes impossible to deal with. The Malayan Deputy Prime Minister remarked on one occasion that

> While it was possible to negotiate with Goh Keng Swee, Lee Kuan Yew was impossible. ....If Lee was not prepared to negotiate an agreement, the Federation would have to wait until Singapore produced a leader who would.[31]

But it was Malayan Finance Minister Tan Siew Sin who was especially harsh in his criticisms of Lee and the Singapore position. During the negotiations, Razak and Tan had agreed that the former would take charge of the political side of the negotiations while the latter, as Finance Minister, would focus on the financial and economic side.[32] However, as the negotiations became increasingly heated, political rivalry came to the fore. Both Tan Siew Sin and Lee Kuan Yew had been political rivals, especially with the MCA's foray into the Singapore political scene in May 1963.[33] The *Straits Times* had reported a remark by Tan, who was also President of the MCA, that his party offered Singapore's only hope for future stability and progress.[34] This was seen as an outright attack on the PAP, and the visit of two MCA senators soon after, ostensibly to recruit the support of the business community in Singapore, was seen as unwelcome encroachment and did not help relations between the two political parties. There was clearly no love lost between Lee and the MCA leader, especially when Tan, as Federal Finance Minister, was determined to stand firm with regard to Federal concessions to

Singapore. Lee felt that Tan was out to cut him down to size, but he was not about to let the Finance Minister "squat on us".[35] Tan, for his part, felt that Lee was simply impossible, and at a meeting at the Colonial Office in May 1963, remarked that "the only obstacle [in the way of an agreement] was Lee, and questioned whether it was necessary for him to be 'there' ".[36] He further remarked that "Lee was not amenable to reason [and] since he did not want to come to an agreement…complete surrender or brute force were the only two things which Lee understood".[37] Selkirk reported back to London a typical acrimonious exchange between the two politicians

> [Lee] did not think that he got very far with the Common Market negotiations and that there was a lot more to be done. With Goh by his side he had tough arguments with Razak, Ismail and Tan and had quite deliberately taken out the knuckle-dusters and given Tan hell. He had taunted Tan by saying that if Tan thought he could run Singapore he should come down and run a[sic] election here. In his view Tan had shrivelled. He had then extracted limited agreement under pressure saying that he had to get back to have dinner with me.[38]

The bitter and difficult personal relations between the ministers on both sides betrayed the "mutual distrust" they had for each other and, according to Selkirk and Tory, indicated that merger was a sham since it was viewed "by both sides …as no more than a 'marriage of convenience' ".[39]

In mid-April Lee indicated that the Singapore Government was prepared to make an additional contribution to the Federation, provided that agreement could be reached on common market arrangements, and the tying of the two issues was to feature in the final negotiations in London in July 1963.

Common Market Negotiations

From its inception in 1959, the PAP government in Singapore had been calling for common market arrangements with Malaya, but until the Tunku's announcement in May 1961 of a possible merger between the two territories, no progress had been made on that front. The reasons behind the government's call for a common market were quite obvious and understandable. As the PAP government saw it, with the relative decline in entrepôt trade, a total lack of natural resources, a rapidly growing population and the accompanying problem of rising unemployment, Singapore needed to rapidly embark on an industrialization programme as the main strategy of economic development for the island state. Soon after it took office, the PAP government established an Economic Development Board, set up largely on the initiative of Singapore Finance Minister Goh Keng Swee. Its main task was to attract overseas capital to invest in Singapore, and to aid this objective, the government did all it could to create an environment which would make Singapore an attractive place for foreign investments, including the development of land in Jurong, in the western part of the island, for industrial purposes and tax incentives.

However, the government was aware that in order to have its whole development rationale feasible, a basic condition had first to be met: increased industrialization and investment were of little use unless an expanding market was made available to absorb the goods produced in Singapore. The small island state, with its miniscule domestic market, was simply unable to generate enough demand for the goods produced. The way out of this problem lay in the creation of a common market with Singapore's nearest neighbour. By creating a common market with the Federation of Malaya, Singapore would be able to sell its goods to the larger population up north. The basis of a common market already existed, given the close proximity of the two territories, the existing use of a common currency, and common practices in banking and commercial operations in Singapore and the Federation. The Singapore Government therefore aimed to establish a situation "in which her industries [would] benefit from a protected Malaysian market, while at the same time she [hoped] to retain most of her advantages of a free port...in short Singapore [hoped] she might be able to have her cake (of protected infant industries and access to Malaysian market) and eat it (by retaining the entrepôt business)".[40]

The sense of urgency with which the Singapore Government regarded the creation of a common market as vital for its economic survival was not shared by the Malayan Government. While the Federation Government recognized that a common market would offer benefits to all components of Malaysia, it feared that the lowering of its tariff walls to Singapore would generate undue competition from Singapore, where, despite a higher per capita income, the cost of labour was significantly lower than the Federation. The Federation was cool to the idea of common market because "it was feared that virtually all industry would tend to gravitate to Singapore" and it also "objected to Singapore having the best of both worlds".[41] Federation ministers and officials were concerned that "a common market will inevitably mean the industrial development of Singapore at the expense of the rest of Malaysia".[42] If Singapore were allowed to retain her free port status, continued to import its raw materials on a tariff free basis and then gain duty free access to Malaysia for its goods, it would enjoy a tremendous cost advantage over Malayan industries which were importing resources that were subjected to Malayan tariffs.[43] Federation ministers like Lim Swee Aun, Minister for Commerce and Industry, and his permanent secretary, Raja Mohar, who were alive to the implications of the common market thus viewed it with great trepidation.[44]

Notwithstanding the importance of the common market arrangements to the Singapore Government, the issue was not raised earlier, and surfaced only during the IGC negotiations in 1963. Interestingly, common market provisions had not been included in the Heads of Agreement signed between Lee and Tunku in 1961. According to the political secretary to the Minister for Culture in Singapore, this was so because the decision had been taken to consult the International Bank on the issue.[45] It was agreed then by the Governments of Malaya and Singapore to invite the Bank "to examine and report on the feasibility of closer economic co-operation between the Federation and Singapore, taking into consideration the special difficulties confronting the proposed Common Market arrangements arising from the free port status of Singapore".[46] On 5 October 1962, it was announced that the Federation decided to seek advice from the International Bank for Reconstruction and Development (IBRD) on problems of closer economic relations within Malaysia, and a mission, headed by distinguished French economists, Professor Jacques Rueff, to study the feasibility of a common market for the Malaysia area.

Before the arrival of the International Bank mission in Malaysia, Goh Keng Swee had been meeting with Federation officials to discuss a future common market. On 6 January 1963, Goh spoke of a proposed common market on much the same terms as he had advocated before the 1959 elections.[47] He suggested that a common market should be established that would permit the free movement of goods between Singapore and the Federation without the imposition of duties either way. Under this arrangement, goods manufactured outside Singapore and Malaya would be subject to duties, but raw materials should continue to enter Singapore free of duties.[48] The Federation government did not explicitly object to the setting up of a common market, but at the same time displayed little urgency in the matter, and throughout the talks the Federation refused any commitment on their part to set up a common market within any set time.

The Singapore Government thus tried to force the issue by linking settlement on the financial arrangements after merger to the successful setting up of a common market. The case for the setting up of a common market was strengthened by a report on the economic aspects of Malaysia conducted by a mission under the chairmanship of Professor Rueff. The Rueff Mission had indeed been timely for the Singapore case. The Report on the economic aspects of Malaysia was submitted to the governments of Singapore and the Federation of Malaya in the first week of July 1963. Rueff visited the Malaysian territories for ten days in October and November 1962, but the mission's real work was carried out by a team of international experts who carried out their study in the Malaysian territories from 7 February to 16 April 1963.[49]

On 14 April 1963, Rueff wrote to Lee and Razak, putting forward two alternative suggestions "about the machinery which should be set up to determine protective tariffs and arrangements for revenue tariffs for Singapore to ensure equality of conditions within a reasonable period". He indicated that the Report would recommend the creation of a Malaysian Tariff Board, whose jurisdiction would be limited to protective tariffs. The Board would comprise a chairman and two deputy-chairmen to be appointed by the Federal Government. Within the first five years of the Board's existence, the appointment of the President would require the concurrence of Singapore, which would also nominate one of the deputy-chairman. In addition to the chairman and deputy-chairmen, the Board would include four other members chosen by the President from a panel of people nominated by institutions representing economic interests.[50]

The first alternative suggested by Rueff was that for the first five years, the decision of the Board regarding protective tariffs would be binding for Malaysia (including Singapore), subject to the concurrence of the Federal and Singapore governments. If this concurrence were not obtained, the case would be reviewed after one year, when the concurrence of the Singapore Government would no longer be required. After the first five years, the Board would restrict itself to an advisory role. There would be a gradual extension of the Malaysia revenue tariffs to Singapore, which would begin five years after Malaysia Day, and be completed within 12–15 years from Malaysia Day.[51] The second alternative was for the Tariff Board to play an advisory role from the outset, but if the Federal government accepted its proposals, they would be binding for Singapore except for a possible one-year delay. There would be no commitment to apply the Malaysia revenue tariffs in Singapore, but the position would be reviewed after five years by an independent body, and if it was found that the revenue tariffs should be extended to Singapore, compensation might be paid by Singapore to the Federal government from the sixth year in order that Singapore producers should not enjoy undue advantage over producers in other parts of Malaysia.[52]

It appeared that the Federation government might not accept the first alternative of having a Board with mandatory powers, which Singapore, as a matter of tactics, might adopt knowing that the Malayans would reject it, and then propose the second alternative which Singapore could appear to accept reluctantly.[53] The Malayans suspected that it was only on receipt of this letter that Lee realized that he had a better card to play on the common market than on financial settlement, and had raised the stakes by making his statements to the press, and then linking agreement on financial arrangement with the common market.[54]

Lee was now putting forth the proposal that a Malaysian common market agreement be written in the constitution in return for a percentage of Singapore's revenue of national taxes instead of an annual lump sum as contribution for federal services in Singapore, and he was to pursue this carrot and stick technique through to the final negotiations in London in July 1963. The Malayans, however, fearing competition from Singapore industry and the political repercussions of Singapore's prosperity, were most reluctant to accept the principle of a Common Market as a condition of Malaysia. In London, Razak and Tan Siew Sin maintained that there was no need to link a common market to the Malaysia agreement as there were enough safeguards already in place in the White Paper.[55] It was plausible that the Federation was trying to delay the establishment of a Common Market until after Malaysia has been formed, believing that as the larger partner in the Federation, it would be able to force eventual Singapore acceptance of Federation proposals.[56] The British, perhaps mindful of the Malayan tactic, pointed out that "Singapore had some cause for concern lest the Federation should put the screws on [them] after Malaysia in the form of discriminatory tariffs".[57] It, therefore, recommended to the Malayan ministers that "some understanding be reached about the way the Common Market arrangements would operate".[58]

On 29 May 1963, following a meeting between Lee Kuan Yew and Goh Keng Swee for Singapore and Tun Abdul Razak and Tan Siew Sin, representing Malaya, an announcement was made that the two governments had arrived at an in-principle agreement for the introduction of a common market once Malaysia was established.[59] Speaking at the Singapore Assembly on 7 June 1963, Goh reported that while there was little difficulty in reaching an agreement with the Federal Government for an arrangement in which there was a common external tariff for both Singapore and Malaya, upon the establishment of Malaysia, such arrangements threatened Singapore's entrepôt trade, and this was clearly unacceptable to the Singapore Government. The Singapore Government had therefore proposed a modified common market arrangement, which would provide for goods manufactured within Malaysia to move freely within its territories, but that protective tariffs should be instituted to protect them from foreign competition. However, tariffs applied elsewhere in the Malaysia territories on goods not manufactured in the territories should not be applied on goods entering Singapore. This, he explained, would not affect the bulk of Singapore's trade, which was on tropical produce, and thus would limit dislocation on the country's entrepôt trade.[60]

The London Talks

The issues of Singapore's contribution to the Federal government, common market and other related issues were left standing in the way of a successful conclusion of the merger process. As the target date of Malaysia drew closer, the British Government, concerned that failure to agree on the financial arrangements and common market threatened to jeopardize the successful achievement of Malaysia, called the delegates from the Federation and Singapore to London for a series of negotiations aimed at resolving the impasse. As direct negotiations between the two governments seemed to offer no prospects of resolving the question of the common market, as well as the apportionment of the Federal revenues, these were discussed again, with the assistance of British ministers at a series of meetings in London between 29 June and 7 July 1963. During the week both delegates met in London in a desperate attempt to arrive at an agreement. The battle-lines had already been drawn. As far as the Malayan ministers were concerned, they were most concerned that Singapore would agree to a $50 million grant to be used for the development of the Borneo Territories, a demand which Lee had likened to an "entrance fee" for Singapore's admission into Malaysia.[61] The Federation had agreed in principle to the establishment of a common market, but preferred to wait until after Malaysia Day to work out the details. The final unresolved issue, which the Malayans felt was the least important of the three, concerned the percentage of Singapore's contribution of state taxes to go to the central government. Preliminary discussions had pared down the difference to about one per cent, or the equivalent of $35 million, which was regarded as an issue that was not insurmountable.

The Singapore Government, on the other hand, had placed greatest importance to the settlement of the common market arrangement before the Malaysia Agreement was sealed. Lee had argued that this was the very basis on which the future prosperity of Singapore within Malaysia depended, and it was important that the detailed arrangements for a Common Market be included in the Malaysian constitution.[62] The rest of the financial arrangements, namely Singapore's contribution to the Borneo Development fund, and its share of the Federal expenditure would depend on how the Common Market issue was resolved.

Throughout the negotiations, which Lee had described as a process of "attrition", both sides bargained hard and gave in little. During the talks, Duncan Sandys, Secretary of State for Commonwealth Affairs, played the role of the "third man", acting as mediator to smooth over differences between the Singapore and Malayan delegations. He held separate talks with Lee and Goh on the one hand, and Razak and Tan on the other to explore how rigid their respective positions were. He finally succeeded in wearing down the Singapore and Federation negotiating teams by the tactic, as Lee remembers, of conducting long, drawn out meetings without food or water.[63] Although the tactic finally resulted in the compromises that made the Malaysia Agreement possible, it did not, however, fundamentally alter the differing mindsets of the two opposing sides.

Agreement on Common Market and Financial Arrangements

The two pressing financial issues that had reached some sort of a deadlock in May 1963 were first, the proportion of Singapore's revenue which should go to the Federal government, and second, the disposal of Singapore's surplus revenues. Singapore had agreed to make up by paying more to the centre if an agreement was reached on common market arrangements. In relation to Singapore's surplus, the Malayan Government was keen to secure more revenue to meet the development funds for the Borneo territories. Singapore sought to meet this interest by offering to make available a loan of M$150 million to the Borneo territories. The Malayan Government, however, preferred a grant of M$50 million to be made to the Borneo territories by Singapore, instead of a loan.

The resolution of these financial issues was achieved after a series of meetings in London, in which the Secretary for Common Relations, Duncan

Sandys, played a significant role. On 5 July, he was able to make both sides come to an agreement on the financial issues. On the financial side, Singapore agreed to pay 40 per cent of its national income from taxes — the equivalent of 27 per cent of its total revenue — to the Federal government as Singapore's share of pan-Malaysian expenses. It was agreed that this amount would be reviewed by an independent body one year after the establishment of Malaysia, and every two years thereafter. As a compromise, Singapore agreed to grant a fifteen-year loan of M$100 million to the Borneo Territories as development expenditure on liberal repayment terms. The loan would carry no interest demands for the first five years and thereafter bearing interests at current Malaysian market rates, and a second loan for fifteen years of M$50 million which would carry normal Malaysian rates of interests.[64] In a rider that was to create subsequent confusion, Singapore was granted the right to supply 50 per cent of the labour for the projects undertaken using loan funds.[65]

Where the common market was concerned, the terms of the agreement were embodied in Annex J of the Malaysia Agreement. In broad terms, the Annex provided for a common market to apply progressively throughout Malaysia, as protective and revenue duties are harmonized, for "all goods and products produced or manufactured in significant quantities in Malaysia".[66] Certain safeguards were instituted in the arrangement to secure the Malayan agreement. For instance, the exemption from the common market arrangements of goods with their principal terminals outside Malaysia meant that in the case of items such as tin and rubber, the Federation would continue to levy taxes before the goods cross to Singapore for sale abroad.[67] Furthermore, Singapore's position as a possible site for the manufacture of materials imported at a cheaper rate by being free of duty was curtailed in Article 1(3) of the Agreement, which provided that the common market provisions "shall not be construed to prevent the imposition…of any special tax on producers in a low-tariff state which would offset the cost inequalities arising from differential import duties".[68] Only where existing protective duties were uniform would there be no trade restrictions on the passage throughout Malaysia of goods imported into one of the territories.[69] With the above provisions, the Malayans were thus assured that the common market would not stifle the continued collection of revenue taxes by the Federation of Malaya on its major import items, and would also prevent undesirable competition between industries within the common market.

For Singapore, the gradual implementation of the market — over 12 years — would ensure the least possible disruption of the Singapore entrepôt. Singapore would thus be able to prevent the imposition of further duties up to 1975, upon payment of compensation to the Federal government for the loss of revenue, if they would seriously damage the entrepôt trade. This arrangement would allay some of the Singapore Government's concerns as to the political effects of increases in indirect taxes, which the Federal government could impose after the establishment of Malaysia.[70]

To advise the Malaysian Government on the establishment of the common market, the annex provided for the creation of a Tariff Advisory Board. The agreement obliged the Malayan Government "to establish by law before Malaysia Day a Tariff Advisory Board to advise the Federal Government...on the establishment of the common market".[71] The provisions for the Board exceeded the recommendations that were made by the Rueff Report. While the Report had originally recommended that the Tariff Board should have responsibility for making recommendations on protective duties only, the responsibility of the Board, as spelt out in the annex, included protective as well as revenue duties.[72] The Tariff Board would have the responsibility of reviewing the revenue duties in Singapore and Malaysia, and should make recommendations regarding the amendment of such duties.[73] In addition, paragraph 4(1) of the agreement spelt out the need for the Federal Government "to pay due regard to any representations made by the Singapore Government" in formulating its policy relating to the harmonization of revenue duties.[74] Singapore's interests would be safeguarded in the sense that within the first five years, the appointment of the Board's chairman would require the concurrence of the Singapore Government, and one of its three deputy chairmen would also have to be nominated by the Singapore Government.[75]

The inclusion of the common market arrangements in the Malaysia Agreement represented something of a success for Lee Kuan Yew and the

Singapore Government. However, it was clear that the provisions of Annex J in the Malaysia Agreement also represented a political compromise between the governments of Singapore and the Federation. While Singapore had achieved its objectives of securing a form of common market within Malaysia, its own capacity to compete in the market would certainly not be unrestrained as it had hoped and fought for in its earlier proposals. Unlike the Rueff Report which went into considerable detail on the ways in which Singapore could protect its entrepôt trade, the provisions of Annex J did not spell out the detailed measures as well as the criteria which would be used in deciding the application of protection duties.[76] All that it provided for was an agreement that

> Until 31st December 1968, no revenue duty shall, except at the request or with the consent of the Singapore Government, be imposed in Singapore by the Federal Government in respect of any class of goods or products not chargeable with such a duty on 1st July 1963. Such consent shall not be withheld except on the grounds that the duty would significantly prejudice the entrepot trade of Singapore.[77]

The Malayan parliament passed the Tariff Advisory Board Act before Malaysia Day. However, it failed to make clear that harmonization of the revenue duties to be applied in Singapore following the Tariff Board's report, due before 1965, did not imply immediate implementation of the revenue duties. The Annex provided that the Singapore Government could offset application of the revenue duties up to the final establishment of the common market in 1975, if it paid the cost of the revenue which would otherwise be raised. The issue was raised with the Federal government and the British a fortnight before merger, and it was successfully resolved in Singapore's favour.

The financial arrangements were on the whole advantageous for Singapore. They permitted Singapore a fair amount of freedom in control of its future development. With this financial control, Singapore could at least have the opportunity to maintain its individual approach to social services and to continue with such programmes as government housing schemes. However, it was still subjected to the Federation Government occasional review.

Perhaps more than any other issue involved in the negotiations leading to merger between Singapore and the Federation, financial and economic arrangements generated the most intense and emotional bargaining between representatives of the two territories. It was as much a contest of beliefs and issues, as of political wills and personalities. On the one hand, the Federation ministers felt strongly against giving Singapore, and in particularly Lee Kuan Yew, too much leeway and economic autonomy, preferring strong central control of all issues economic and financial, at Kuala Lumpur. Singapore's position, on the other hand, reflected its deep-seated concern to preserve and establish a sound economic future for the island state, despite its being part of a larger entity. The Singapore representatives were concerned that these arrangements that would safeguard Singapore's economic future within Malaysia had to be formalized, so as to prevent any subsequent erosion of Singapore's position. Both parties were also aware that they were playing to a packed public gallery and neither could be seen to be selling out on vital interests. As the British noted, "the Singapore Government are [sic] deriving excellent domestic political value from this controversy. Almost every time Tan [Siew Sin] opens his mouth he gives support to the impression that Singapore Ministers are fighting a battle for the economic future of Singapore against financial interests in Kuala Lumpur".[78]

Selkirk also noted that if Lee conceded too easily to the Federation position over financial negotiations, "he would appear simply to be a stooge of the Tengku (sic)".[79] Lee told Selkirk that he could not compromise on common market issues for political reasons, "even if he were to want to for other reasons, which he does not".[80] Politically, there were few options for Lee other than to dig in his heels, and he was therefore determined to "wage a war of nerves until the last minute" in the financial negotiations.[81] If he had given in on allowing Kuala Lumpur to have their hands on Singapore's taxes, it would have been a major blow to his political credibility.[82] Lee was also building up the momentum for possible general elections before 31 August 1963, the proposed Malaysia Day.[83] By standing up to Tan Siew Sin and playing the patriotic card, "Goh and Lee reckon that Tan [was] effectively sealing the doom of the Alliance in such elections".[84] Woolcott also observed that the run-up to the signing of the Malaysia Agreement represented Lee's "last real opportunity to demonstrate that he [was] not 'selling out' Singapore to the Federation as the Barisan [claimed]".[85] Thus, Lee had to be seen by the public to be driving a very hard bargain with the Federation over the terms of the merger in order to undercut the political appeal of rival political parties like the Barisan Sosialis and the Singapore People's Alliance. Under the circumstances, it was perhaps clever political tactics on the part of the Singapore Government to have all aspects of the negotiations reported in full in the local press, so that the public could be kept in full view of the stance taken by the respective parties at the negotiating table. Selkirk attributed this to Lee's political style, that he did not wish to be "belittled", and fought for and obtained satisfactory financial and commercial arrangements for Singapore.[86]

The compromise that was arrived at in July 1963 was just that — a compromise reached perhaps under pressure of the need to have an agreement hammered out before the declaration of Malaysia. The Malaysia Agreement did not represent the final resolution of the fundamental differences between both Singapore and the Federation. Instead, it reflected a compromise based on the lowest common denominator of concurrence between both parties. The compromise did not remove the problems. For the time-being these were pushed aside so that the process could move forward, but these disagreements were to subsequently contribute to the deterioration of the Singapore-Kuala Lumpur relationship following merger.

NOTES

1 Han Fook Kwang, Warren Fernandez, Sumiko Tan, *Lee Kuan Yew: The Man and His Ideas* (Singapore: Singapore Press Holdings and Times Editions, 1998), p. 73.
2 Telegram no. 290, Acting UK Commissioner (Singapore) to Secretary of State for the Colonies, 29 April 1963, DO 169/220.
3 *Straits Times*, 29 April 1963.
4 Telegram from Acting United Kingdom Commissioner (Singapore) to Secretary of State for the Colonies, 22 November 1962, CO 1030/1067.

5 *Memorandum Setting out the Heads of Agreement for a Merger between the Federation of Malaya and Singapore* (Singapore: L. K. Heng, Government Printer, 1961), Cmnd 33.
6 Memorandum No. 599, Flanagan to Secretary, Department of External Affairs, 8 March 1963, A1838/333 no. 3006/10/4 Part 2.
7 *Straits Times*, 11 June 1963.
8 Ibid., 2 March 1963.
9 Ibid., 5 March 1963.
10 Colonial Office, Annex A to Brief 4, "Financial Arrangements between Singapore and Malaya", 9 May 1963, DO 169/326.
11 Ibid.
12 *Straits Times*, 5 March 1963.
13 Singapore's expenditure on social services during the period between 1958 and 1962 had run at 40 per cent of public investment, while in the same period, in the Federation, the expenditure had varied between 25 and 33 per cent. *Report on the economic aspects of Malaysia. By a mission of the International Bank for Reconstruction and Development; under the chairmanship of Jacques Rueff* (Singapore: Government Printing Office, 1963), p. 3, hereafter referred as *The Rueff Report*.
14 Memorandum No. 599, Flanagan to Secretary, Department of External Affairs, 8 March 1963, A1838/333 no. 3006/10/4 Part 2.
15 Colonial Office, Annex A to Brief 4, "Financial Arrangements between Singapore and Malaya", 9 May 1963, DO 169/326.
16 Ibid.
17 Telegram no. 30, T. K. Critchley to Secretary of State, External Affairs, 24 May 1963, A1838/333 no. 3006/10/4 Part 2.
18 Memorandum No. 1124, R.A. Woolcott, to Secretary, Department of External Affairs, 14 May 1963, A1838/333 no. 3004/12/11/2.
19 Despatch no. 5, G. W. Tory to Secretary of State for Commonwealth Relations, 31 October 1963, DO 169/115.
20 Ibid.
21 Acting UK Commissioner in Singapore to Secretary of State for Colonies, 29 April 1963, DO 169/220
22 *Straits Times*, 11 June 1963.
23 *Singapore Legislative Assembly Debates*, 5 April 1963, Cols. 33–34; and 10 June 1963, Cols. 613 and 614.
24 *Straits Times*, 11 June 1963.
25 Ibid., 11 June 1963.
26 Ibid., 13 April 1963.
27 Ibid., 11 June 1963.

28   Ibid.

29   See Colonial Office, Annex A to Brief 4, "Brief of Financial Arrangements between Singapore and Malaya", 9 May 1963, DO 169/326.

30   Telegram no. 27, T. K. Critchley to Secretary of Department of External Affairs, 8 May 1963, A1838/333 no. 3006/10/4 Part 2.

31   Memorandum No. 32, T. K. Critchely to Secretary, Department of External Affairs, 7 June 1963, A1838/333 no. 3006/10/4 Part 3.

32   Oral History Interview with Tun Tan Siew Sin, conducted on 29 March 1986 in Kuala Lumpur, Reel 1, National Archives of Singapore.

33   John Drysdale, *Singapore: Struggle For Success* (Singapore: Times Books International, 1984), pp. 328–32.

34   *Straits Times*, 23 May 1963.

35   Lee Kuan Yew, *The Singapore Story: Memoirs of Lee Kuan Yew* (Singapore: Federal Publications, 2000), p. 477.

36   "Note of Meeting" held at the Colonial Office, 11 May 1963, DO 169/325.

37   Ibid.

38   Record of a conversation between Selkirk and Lee Kuan Yew, 30 May 1963, FO 1091/104.

39   Memorandum No. 1124, R.A. Woolcott to Secretary, Department of External Affairs, 14 May 1963, A1838/333 no. 3004/12/11/2.

40   Memorandum No. 185, Lance Joseph to Secretary, Department of External Affairs, 22 January 1963, A1838/333 no. 3006/10/4 Part 2.

41   Memorandum No. 797, W.K. Flanagan to Secretary, Department of External Affairs, 26 March 1963, A1838/333 no. 3006/10/4 Part 2.

42   Memorandum No. 560, Woolcott to Secretary, Department of External Affairs, 12 June 1963. See also "Note of Meeting" held at the Colonial Office, 11 May 1963, DO 169/325.

43   See Milton Osborne, *Singapore and Malaysia* (New York: Cornell University, 1964), p. 57.

44   Memorandum No. 560, Woolcott to Secretary, Department of External Affairs, 12 June 1963.

45   *Straits Times*, 2 July 1963.

46   The terms of reference of the Rueff Mission were later extended to include the other Malaysian territories, including Labuan, North Borneo, Sarawak and Penang. The Mission was also expected to "recommend concrete steps …to effect such economic co-ordination, and to recommend administrative arrangements for co-ordinating and integrating development planning". As such the mission's brief went beyond a feasibility study, but was to prepare a blueprint for a common market. See *The Rueff Report*, pp. vi and vii.

47 *Straits Times*, 7 January 1963.

48 Ibid.

49 *The Rueff Report*, p. vii.

50 Ibid.

51 See Colonial Office's comments on *The Rueff Report*, 10 May 1963, DO 169/326.

52 Ibid.

53 Telegram no. 290, Acting UK Commissioner (Singapore) to Secretary of State for the Colonies, 29 April 1963. DO 169/220.

54 Note of Meeting between Lord Lansdowne (Minister of State for Colonial Affairs) and Malayan Representatives, Tun Razak and Tan Siew Sin, at the Colonial Office, 11 May 1963, DO 169/325.

55 Ibid.

56 *Straits Times*, 1 May 1963.

57 Note of Meeting between Lansdowne and Malayan Representatives, Tun Razak and Tan Siew Sin, at the Colonial Office, 11 May 1963 DO 169/325.

58 Ibid.

59 *Straits Times*, 30 May 1963.

60 *Singapore Legislative Assembly Debates*, 7 June 1963.

61 Lee pointed out that "Singapore was too poor to play Santa Claus and give away $50 million as its entrance fee to join Malaysia". Lee, *The Singapore Story*, p. 478.

62 *Straits Times*, 26 June 1963

63 Lee, *The Singapore Story*, p. 480.

64 *Straits Times*, 9 July 1963.

65 This was one of the issues in which Lee evidently got Tunku's approval at the last moment at the back of an envelope that it was mandatory that 50 per cent of labour had to come from Singapore. In the details announced earlier, on 6 July 1963, it appeared that the terms of the loan stipulated that Singapore workers would be employed in Borneo only if it was not possible for labour to be obtained there. See *Straits Times*, 24 July 1963.

66 United Kingdom Command Paper 2094, 1963. Malaysia Agreement, Annex J, 1(1).

67 Ibid.

68 Ibid. 1(3) (a).

69 Ibid. 1(2).

70 Ibid. 3(3), p. 229.

71 *Malaysia Agreement*, Annex J, 2(1).

72 See *The Rueff Report*, p. 49; and *Malaysia Agreement*, Annex J, 4(4), p. 230.

73 *Malaysia Agreement*, Annex J, 4(4).

74 Ibid., Annex J, 4(1)

75 Ibid., Annex J, 2(2).

76 *The Rueff Report*, pp. 57 and 74.

77 *Malaysia Agreement*, Annex J, 4(3), p. 230.

78 Telegram no. 290, Acting High Commissioner (Singapore) to Secretary of State for the Colonies, 29 April 1963, DO 169/220.

79 Memorandum No. 1124, R.A. Woolcott to Secretary, Department of External Affairs, 14 May 1963, CRS A1838/333 no. 3004/12/11/2.

80 Selkirk's conversation with Woolcott over his talks with Lee Kuan Yew in Telegram no. 276, Woolcott to Secretary, Department of External Affairs, 11 May 1963, A1838/333 no. 3006/10/4 Part 2.

81 Critchley to Secretary Department of External Affairs, 12 June 1963, A1838/333, no. 3006/10/4.

82 Drysdale pointed out that Lee would be finished politically if he allowed Kuala Lumpur to take over collection of taxes in Singapore. See Drysdale, *Singapore*, p. 322.

83 See "Singapore Political Affairs", 26 July 1961 to 4 October 1963, DO 169/19.

84 Telegram no. 290, Acting High Commissioner (Singapore) to Secretary of State for the Colonies, 29 April 1963, DO 169/220.

85 Telegram no. 19, Woolcott to Secretary, Department of External Affairs, 15 June 1963, A1838/333 no. 3006/10/4 Part 3.

86 Woolcott to the Secretary, Department of External Affairs, 14 May 1963, A1838/333, no. 3004/12/11, Part 2, Commissioner-General Meeting, 8 July 1963.

CHAPTER SIX

The Borneo Territories and Brunei

The focus in the preceding chapters has been on the complicated negotiations leading to an Ulster-type merger between Singapore and Malaya. The story of Malaysia would be incomplete without an analysis of how that crucial piece of the jigsaw, the Borneo Territories, was eventually put in place for the realization of the Malaysia Plan. At the outset, the Malayan Prime Minister had made it clear that Singapore would be incorporated into the Federation only on condition that the Borneo Territories were brought in first. Indeed, his grudging attitude towards merger with Singapore stood in striking contrast to his almost unbridled enthusiasm for the Borneo Territories to be brought into the Federation. However, despite Malayan interests and British intentions — British officials generally agreed that the political future of the Borneo Territories lay in an association with a larger Federation — the amalgamation of the Borneo Territories with the Federation of Malaya and Singapore was not going to be a straightforward affair. Colonial officers were concerned that the vast disparity in social and political development between the Borneo Territories on the one hand and Singapore and Malaya on the other would make any form of federation of these territories untenable. Yet, the British Government was determined to press ahead with the association of the Borneo Territories with the Federation of Malaya, without which the latter would not accept merger with Singapore. If Malaya could not bring the Borneo Territories into the Federation, merger with Singapore would be jettisoned. Without merger, the Government in Singapore would fall, and this would result in the loss of the use of the base, a worst case scenario for the British. This chapter explains why the proposed federation of the Borneo Territories with Malaya and Singapore was not as plain-sailing as the British and Malayans had hoped, as well as the circumstances, events and tactics employed by the British and Malayans that eventually secured the entry of North Borneo and Sarawak into the Federation.

British Plans for the Borneo Territories

In contemplating the political future of the Borneo Territories, political backwardness of the two territories had been of primary concern. While the Colonial Office spoke of eventual self-government for the people of the territories when the time was ripe, governors on the ground argued that both Borneo and Sarawak were far from ready for political advancement (the view in 1960 was it would be between 15 to 20 years before self-government was a feasible option), and that both these territories were contented with colonial rule and would like to remain as Crown Colonies, allowed to develop gradually under British protection from the expansionist designs of neighbouring countries.[1] The Borneo Territories, the governors felt, were especially vulnerable because of their racial make-up and proximity to neighbours like China, Indonesia and the Philippines. If the British moved out, it was likely that both North Borneo and Sarawak would not survive as viable states on their own and the political vacuum would inevitably invite intervention for these neighbouring powers.[2] The option of federating of territories there to form a larger, and therefore more viable state, had been discussed in several conferences in North Borneo, but no conclusive consensus had emerged that this would be a workable solution because of the different stages of social and economic development between North Borneo and Sarawak. Since the late 1950s, cooperation and co-ordination between the administrations of both territories had been effected and talks of free trade areas and custom unions had been circulating. However, advancement in concrete terms had been slow because of fears by North Borneo that a closer association could lead to subjugation and "contamination" by its more advanced neighbour.[3] Even if the two would agree to come together, the British were not entirely convinced that they would form a viable federation, especially if Brunei would not come in. Throughout the 1950s, Brunei deliberately distanced itself from any suggestion of joining in a federation with North Borneo and Sarawak. In 1958, the idea of forming a federation of the three north Borneo territories had been shelved. The ultimate option, it seemed at that time to the British, was for the territories to be part of an association of Malaya, Brunei and possibly Singapore. However, the disparities between the Borneo Territories and the Federation of Malaya were simply too great to effect such a federation at that stage, and colonial officers witnessing the problems and imminent collapse of the Central African Federation cautioned that the combination of self-governing and non-self governing units within a constitutional framework was simply not workable.[4] The preferred approach, advocated most strongly by the local governors, was for a gradual, evolutionary progress towards constitutional association of the territories. While the British would facilitate the eventual association of the Borneo Territories with the Malayan Federation, while being careful not to "force Borneo opinion", the governors of North Borneo and Sarawak preferred that the Tunku took on a policy of "benevolent neutrality" until the conditions were ready.[5]

Colonial officials in the territories did not protest the concept of Malaysia as much as they did the timing of the enterprise. However, the Malaysian Plan had to be rushed forward because of the Singapore situation — the Tunku would not agree to a merger with Singapore unless the British were committed to allowing the Borneo Territories to join the Federation first — and reservations from the colonial office notwithstanding, the British Prime Minister was anxious that they be seen doing all they can to meet the Tunku's demands, while at the same time assuring the people in the territories that the British were committed to charting the best course for their future. In October 1961 Macmillan suggested to the Tunku that an announcement to be issued by the British Government welcoming the Tunku's proposals for Greater Malaysia should include an assurance to consult the wishes of the peoples on any commitment affecting their future. The Tunku, however, was not keen to have that sentence included in the public announcement, not wishing to "over-emphasise the need for consultation with the people of the Borneo Territories who, he believed, were not sufficiently advanced in their political outlook to give an unbiased opinion of their own as they are very much under the influence of the British colonial administrators".[6] This would be a recurring theme in the relationship between the Malayans and the British between 1961 and 1963, when the interests of the Malayans often came at odds with the British where the Borneo Territories were concerned. There were suspicions on the part of the Malays that the British were working harder to secure the merger with Singapore than to facilitate the incorporation of the Borneo Territories, especially Brunei, into the Malaysian Federation.

Initial Responses

The Tunku's announcement on May 1961 created a stir in the Borneo Territories, and groups emerged to articulate their concerns about the future, especially about the possibility of the incorporation of their territories into Malaya. In the absence of elections, viewpoints that were expressed came largely from unofficial members of the executive and legislative councils and community leaders, the first reactions of which were largely negative.[7] Sarawak had, by 1960, established an executive council and a legislative council, both of which had members which were chosen by a process of indirect elections. The executive and legislative councils in North Borneo had no elected members as political parties did not exist in 1960. Views on Malaysia were encouraged by the governors of Sarawak and North Borneo and the High Commissioner of Brunei who expressed concerns that the territories were simply not quite ready for such a major political initiative. William Goode, Governor of North Borneo, articulated the fears faced by the people on the ground when he advised that "the quicker you try to do it, the more difficult it would be for the Borneo Territories because they feel they lag behind Singapore and the Federation politically".[8] The critical issue, it seemed, was one of proper timing and development. Both the governors of Sarawak and North Borneo felt that it made more sense for the territories to federate among themselves first, before looking towards

Malaya and Singapore. That the interests of the Borneo Territories were advocated on behalf of its people by paternalistic colonial officials was the surest indication that the region was not in a state of political readiness to negotiate the complicated process of forming an association with the Malayan Federation.

In Sarawak, the newly formed political parties, the Chinese-dominated Sarawak United People's Party (SUPP), founded by Hokkien businessmen on June 1959,[9] and the Party Negara Sarawak (PANAS), a party of Malay aristocrats formed in April 1960, and led by Datu Bandar Abang Haji Mustapha, a former official Malaya Affairs adviser to the government, reacted cautiously to the Tunku's announcement by suggesting that such a federation would take time to materialize, and that the concept of Malaysia should only follow self government in the Borneo Territories, and a form of Borneo federation first.[10] As a Malay party, PANAS welcomed establishing closer political and economic co-operation between Malaya, but argued that the three territories should merge as one unit and not as three separate entities.[11] This view was shared by Stephen Yong, Secretary-General of the SUPP, who added that merger should only be considered when Sarawak had attained "a large measure of self-government and independence (sic)".[12] North Borneo's first political party was still in embryonic stage in 1961, but its most prominent local leader, Donald Stephens, the Eurasian Roman Catholic proprietor and editor of the *Sabah Times* and chairman of the Kadazan Society , objected to the Malaysia Plan, on the grounds that North Borneo was not politically ready for it, and that joining Malaya at this stage would simply mean switching their status as "British colonies" to become "Malayan colonies", in which North Borneo would be handed over to the Tunku's control.[13] The largely cautious reactions to the first mention of the Malaysia Plan stemmed from the primary concern that diversity of political culture and disparity in economic development between North Borneo and Sarawak on the one hand, and Singapore and Malaya on the other was simply too great for the territories to be incorporated as equal partners in the federation. Underlying this was the general fear that without strong local political institutions, the territories would be in danger of being politically subjugated by the government in Kuala Lumpur once Malaysia came about.[14] The leaders in Sarawak and North Borneo wanted merger on their own terms, and were not about to be pressured into an arrangement that would profit others at their expense.[15] The leader of the newly formed Sarawak National Party (SNAP), a predominantly Dayak political party, Stephen Ningkan, asserted that his party opposed Sarawak's joining of Malaya, which he saw as a "foreign power".[16] In any case, political developments in Sarawak were at a very nascent stage, and the primary preoccupation among the emerging parties was for political progress towards self-government and eventual independence. The proposal for a merger with Malaya, which has become a distinct possibility with the Tunku's announcement in May 1961, presented the fledgling political community in the Borneo Territories with an unfamiliar scenario, and they responded in almost parochial terms, along communal lines.

Communal-based parties emerged in the wake of the Tunku's proposal, each seeking to protect their interests of the communities they represented. There was no sense of an emerging nation as such, and parties split along ethnic, class and communal lines. The young Malay intelligentsia in Sarawak, impatient with the approach of conservative leadership of PANAS, broke away to form the Barisan Rakyat Jati Sarawak (BARJASA) to oppose the former's pro-Malaysia stance, which it believed was adopted to safeguard the traditional position of the conservative aristocratic class. New parties representing the majority Iban population, such as the Sarawak National Party (SNAP),[17] founded on 10 April 1961 and Party Pesaka anak Sarawak (PESAKA),[18] formed by a breakaway group from PANAS, opposed the Malaysia Plan which they believed would perpetuate inter-ethnic inequalities in the Borneo Territories and would therefore be detrimental to the interests of the indigenous people. These parties advocated instead for complete independence.[19] The SUPP's reaction to Malaysia was rather ambivalent. Its business and professional leadership was not prepared to dismiss the Malaysia option outright as they saw immense economic benefits in joining a larger federation. Its left-leaning members, however, opposed Malaysia vehemently as a neo-colonial plan. Concerned that the party was being infiltrated by communists,[20] the British encouraged the establishment of a rival Chinese party, the Sarawak Chinese Association (SCA), an affiliate of the Malayan Chinese Association (MCA), to compete for Chinese support in Sarawak.[21] The SCA's predictable pro-Malaya platform of independence for Sarawak through Malaysia prompted the leftist members of the SUPP to label them as "colonial stooges".

The Malaysian cause was not helped by the Tunku's visit to Borneo in July 1960, during which, it was reported, "he quite misjudged the temper of the Territories, spoke as if all non-Chinese in Borneo were Malays, and took an overbearing and uncompromising stance which alarmed opinion in North Borneo and Sarawak and may well have convinced both the Sultan and his people in Brunei that they should stay out of the Federation."[22] Still, the Malayan Prime Minister could not comprehend why the people of the Borneo Territories would not be happy to join with the Federation. He believed that there was a natural affinity between the Borneo Territories and Malaya, and that the former stood a greater chance of achieving rapid political and economic development within Malaysia. He could not understand why the British were not doing more to "organise their agreement".[23] Still, not wishing to generate adverse reactions from the Borneo Territories to his proposal, the Tunku refrained from further references to his idea of federating the Borneo Territories with Malaya when he sensed that the main political parties in Sarawak and Brunei, and the opinion of local leaders in North Borneo, were responding in a lukewarm manner to his May announcement. The Tunku had also realized that his earlier desire to incorporate the Borneo Territories on exactly the same footing as the existing states in the Federation was a major stumbling block. In October 1961, speaking on Malaysia in the Malayan Parliament, he had come to accept that he was prepared to concede to the Borneo Territories special powers on immigration, customs, Borneanization and control of state franchise rights.[24] The Tunku, however, continued to work on the British, seeking to secure their agreement to relinquish sovereignty of the Borneo Territories for the formation of Malaysia. Not wishing to appear to be conspiring with the Malayans to foist a decision without proper consultation in the territories concerned, the British hesitated. However, if they were thought to be rendering less than full-hearted support for the Malaysia project, then it would be difficult for them to persuade the Tunku to agree to a merger with Singapore. In June 1961, Alex Waddell and William Goode, the governors of Sarawak and North Borneo respectively met with Selkirk, who had become High Commissioner of Singapore, to discuss the possibility of political emancipation of the Borneo Territories through the formation of Malaysia.[25] An agreement was reached and tacit approval was indicated when British Prime Minister Harold Macmillan gave a guarded endorsement to the proposal in the House of Commons on 20 June 1961.[26] While British officials in Southeast Asia were now prepared to support the idea that "Greater Malaysia offer[ed] the best future for the Borneo Territories", they were convinced that in order to secure acceptance of federation in Borneo, a number of concessions would have to be given by the Malayans. This would include a large measure of self-government, especially for local control over immigration, education, language, control of revenues, citizenship and the retention of existing British staff for a transitional period. It was on this last point that the British and Malayans were to face major disagreements.

Marketing the Malaysia Plan

The initial reactions from various political parties in Sarawak, North Borneo and Brunei ranged from the ambivalent to the negative. The larger parties had come out in opposition to the Malaysia Plan, arguing for constitution advancement towards political independence instead of merger with the Malayan Federation. Indeed, a united front, comprising Ong Kee Hui, Chairman of the SUPP, Donald Stephens, then about to form the first party of North Borneo, the United National Kadazan Organisation (UNKO) and A.M. Azahari, President of the Party Ra'ayat of Brunei, was inaugurated on 9 July 1961, declaring that "any plan in accordance with the pronouncements made by [the Tunku] would be totally unacceptable to the people of the three territories".[27] The state of affairs required the British to steer political opinion towards their ultimate objective. Selkirk had remarked to Macleod that "…even though we are prepared to cede sovereignty over the Borneo Territories … we should clearly have to try to ensure that the result was the one that we and the Tunku wanted".[28] In a separate missive to the Commonwealth Relations Office, he reiterated his belief that" incorporation [of the Borneo Territories] into Greater Malaysia [was] to their best advantage" and that he was "anxious to press ahead as fast as possible".[29] The British administration in Sarawak realized it needed a "skilled selling job ... to get [Malaysia] off the ground".[30]

In August 1961, a British-sponsored regional meeting of the Commonwealth Parliamentary Association in Singapore attended by legislative members led to the establishment of a Malaysia Solidarity Consultative Committee (MSCC), comprising representatives from Malaya, Singapore, North Borneo, Sarawak and Brunei, to generate discussion on the feasibility of the Malaysia Plan. The MSCC was supposed to be a consultative body, but it was perhaps a measure of its true purpose when one of its terms of reference included the fostering of activities to provide for and expedite the realization of Malaysia.[31] The MSCC was obviously an exercise in overcoming apprehensions and fears on the part of the political leaders of the Borneo Territories by the British as well as the Malayan and Singapore delegates. In four meetings that were held in Jesselton, Kuching, Kuala Lumpur and Singapore, delegates from the Federation took opportunities to answer questions from representatives of the Borneo Territories. Most of these questions concerned timing of implementation of the Malaysia Plan, economic and security benefits of Malaysia, and safeguards for the territories. While the Sarawak delegates cautioned against haste lest it led to a hardening of opposition to the Malaysia Plan, the Malayans continued to argue the benefits of the Plan.[32] The Tunku raised the bogey of the communist threat and argued that combined with the Federation of Malaya, the Borneo Territories had a better chance of protecting themselves against the communist threat, which was spreading from China to Southeast Asia.[33] He assured that the Federation sought no territorial gain in Borneo, and that Malaya, which had all the resources it needed, had no wish to exploit the colony. He promised that the territories would join the Federation as constituent states, their separate existence and entrenched rights safeguarded by the Federation constitution. He also agreed that the Borneo territories should be able to exclude immigration of Chinese from Singapore, and that he would consider any other matters which Sarawak and North Borneo might want to have under their control as states.[34] The assurances from the Malayan Prime Minister and other delegates had a positive effect on the Borneo leaders and resonated with Malay leaders from both territories. Lee Kuan Yew, too, played a keen role in persuading the leaders in the Borneo Territories to push forth the Malaysia Plan, and was the chief advocate for the signing of the Memorandum of Malaysia following the conclusion of the fourth MSCC meeting.[35]

Alongside high-level meetings among the leaders of the five territories, visits to Malaya were organized for the people of the Borneo Territories. These visits were sponsored by the Malayan Government and aimed to project a favourable image of Malaya's development, especially of its record in looking after the welfare and development of its rural population. The objective was simple: Malaya was projected as a progressive state which had the wherewithal to assist its constituent parts to a higher level of social and economic development. The same could be done for the Borneo people once their territories were integrated into the Federation. Participants of these tours to Malaya often returned with optimistic reports of the feasibility of an association with the Federation of Malaya.[36]

By early 1962, the efforts of the Malayans and the British began to pay off and most of the Borneo delegations were almost sold on the desirability of joining the Federation, persuaded perhaps by assurances that resources would be available for economic and social developments in Malaysia, and that the special position of the indigenous people in the Borneo Territories would enjoy constitutional safeguards in the new state. For twenty-one months, from July 1961 to March 1963, the Borneo leaders saw their position change from rejection to acceptance. The Tunku's arguments may have been persuasive, but the fact that the Philippines claim was seen as a very unpleasant alternative to Malaysia was a contributing factor. The change in mood towards the Malaysian Plan might also have been prompted by the joint declaration between Britain and Malaya in November 1961 on the formation of Malaysia. Political leaders in North Borneo and Sarawak were left in no doubt that the Malaysia die had been cast, and that the best way forward was to secure the best safeguards for each of their territories in the federation that they would have to join, willy nilly, in the near future. In

January 1962 the local government of Sarawak, encouraged by the British, issued a White Paper outlining the perceived advantage of joining Malaysia. The fundamental premise behind the paper was that it would be "very difficult and very expensive" for Sarawak, with its small population, to "stand alone as an independent territory".[37] Joining a larger federation of Malaysia was the only practicable and feasible way for Sarawak to gain political and economic development, for not only would membership of Malaysia save the under-developed polity from being "devoured" by the communists, the larger free-trade area and market that Malaysia promised would rapidly increase the rate of domestic economic development.[38] The White Paper left little choice for its people:

> This opportunity ... [of] joining Malaysia [was] unlikely to recur and [an independent] Sarawak [would] be left with no alternative than a perilous existence as a small, defenceless country in a large predatory world.[39]

The British had adroitly steered the Borneo Territories into the desired path towards Malaysia. The stage was thus set for the work of the Cobbold Commission, tasked to ascertain the wishes of the Borneo people for joining the Malaysian Federation. The findings of this independent Commission of Enquiry would legitimize a decision by the British to withdraw from Sarawak without first granting self-government, a commitment they had made at the time of Cession and embodied in the nine Cardinal Principles of the English Rajahs.[40]

The Cobbold Commission

Following the Anglo-Malayan Agreement of November 1961, an independent Commission of Enquiry was established to "ascertain the views of the peoples of North Borneo and Sarawak ... and in the light of their assessment of these views, make recommendations".[41] At the outset, the expectations of the Malayans and the British on the functions and roles of the Commission had been at odds. From the British point of view, the agreement from the

Anglo-Malayan talks of November 1961 was for the establishment of a commission of enquiry that would survey the wishes and opinions of the people of the Borneo Territories on the Malaysia Plan. The Tunku, on the other hand, had earlier intimated to Macmillan in their meeting in June 1961 the idea of forming an independent commission to work out the constitutional details by which the Borneo Territories would join the Malayan Federation. He was not expecting the commission to actually investigate whether the people in the territories were interested to join Malaya.[42] Although the tasks of the commission had been settled, the Tunku, who did not want the findings of the Commission to dash his hopes of incorporating the Borneo Territories, was especially anxious that the Commission be constituted "correctly". He was concerned that a "wrong commission" might recommend matters which the Malayan leaders would find impossible to accept, and thereby causing the whole question of Malaysia to fall to pieces.[43] Disagreements between the British and the Malayans surfaced immediately over the chairmanship of the Commission. Following extended arguments between Macmillan and the Tunku on who would be a suitable chairman for the Commission, a compromise was finally agreed in the person of Lord Cobbold, former governor of the Bank of England. Having a neutral person who had no knowledge of North Borneo and Sarawak was seen as an attempt to ensure objectivity in the deliberations of the Commission, but Lord Cobbold's inexperience and lack of knowledge was a major handicap for such an important enterprise. The five member Commission was eventually appointed on 16 January 1962, comprising three British and two Malayan members. The other two British members, Anthony Abell, former Governor of Sarawak, and David Watterston, former Chief Secretary of the Federation of Malaya, brought with them immense knowledge of the Borneo Territories, while Malaya was represented by two political heavyweights, Wong Pow Nee, former Chief Minister of Penang and Ghazali Shafie, permanent secretary of the Malayan Ministry of Foreign Affairs and trusted aide of the Malayan Prime Minister. The Commission's work lasted from February to April 1962. The work and findings of the Cobbold Commission have been covered and analysed extensively in many other accounts, and it is not the intention here to reiterate those, but to focus on the conduct of the Commission in so far as it throws light on the priorities of the Tunku and the political dynamics between the Malayans and British during this critical episode which would define the political future of the Borneo Territories. That this Commission was an Anglo-Malayan exercise was immediately obvious from the fact that it did not include a single Bornean representative.

The work of the Commission was complicated by the tensions between the Malayan representatives and the local British officials whom the former felt were instigating local opinion against joining Malaya. The governors of North Borneo and Sarawak complained to their superiors in London that the consultation process was a "farce" as they were expected to present the advantages of the Malaysia Plan to the local population when no constitutional details had yet been settled.[44] The representatives kept their respective governments informed of their activities,[45] and a process of external consultations meant that deliberations and the eventual recommendations extended beyond the confines of the Commission. Not surprisingly, the deliberations revealed major differences between the views of the British and Malayan representatives. The Commission's revelations that there were deep doubts and fears in the territories at the prospects of Malayan rule based on a widespread dislike and distrust of Malays unsettled the Tunku. He had all along felt that there was great affinity between the Malays and the indigenous populations of the Borneo Territories. He reacted by accusing the British of insincerity towards Malaysia. The Tunku's accusations that the British official in the Borneo Territories were influencing the local people against the idea of Malaysia were reported in the local newspapers.[46] He alleged that these officers were taking an "apathetic attitude" and had a "bitter attitude" towards Malaysia. The Tunku argued that the discerning leaders could see the value of Malaysia, especially as protection against a growing communist threat, and that it was the British business interests that were acting in opposition to Malaya.[47] He warned that the British Government had agreed to the formation of Malaysia, and he was not going to let the attitude of the local officials jeopardize the project by allowing them "to influence the natives, like the Malays and Dayaks".[48]

The British members of the Commission felt strongly, however, that constitutional safeguards had to be put in for the Borneo people to allay suspicions and fears, especially in Sarawak, that the British were prepared to allow the territories to be handed over to the Malays without adequate consideration for the interests of the local populations. Cobbold had indicated to the Colonial Secretary in March 1962 that the bulk of the population in Sarawak, apart from the Malays who were happy to join Malaya, and the "younger nationalists and/or communist Chinese" who wanted independence, "would prefer to see continuation of British rule".[49] He had been warned that "what [was] said by hospitably entertained delegations in Kuala Lumpur [was] no safe indication of opinion in the territories ... and some of the spokesmen have little claim to be regarded as representative leaders".[50] He felt that the majority could be brought around to accept the Malaysia Plan if they believed that they would be entering into a partnership with and not being "gobbled up" by Malaya. But he believed the chances were slim, especially with Kuala Lumpur sending unmistakeable signals to London that the Tunku was not prepared to budge on the terms on which the Borneo Territories would join Malaysia. He took pains to emphasize to Macmillan, in a personal and confidential note to him following the Commission Report, that it would not "be wise, or generally acceptable in the territories, to fill vacancies by appointment of officers from Malaya and Singapore ....and that it would be necessary that in the next few years the highest posts (those of Governor and Chief Secretary or their equivalents) should be held by expatriate officers ... who should retain their authority over domestic affairs".[51] He added that he had omitted this from the official report "in order to meet strong representations ... by the Malayan members".[52]

The two sets of representatives were thus split on the contentious issue of the transitional period following the formation of Malaysia. The British members were anxious that an extended interim period of between three to seven years be provided so that a proper handing over period could be effected which would soften the shock of such a major political change. During this period, the Federation Government would be responsible only for external affairs, defence and anti-subversive aspects of internal security, while the British Government would continue to be responsible for the government of the two territories in all other aspects.[53] This extended transitional arrangement, which would see the continuance of British civil servants and governors for a period of time after the formation of Malaysia, was deemed especially critical for the constitutionally and politically backward Borneo Territories.[54] This was unacceptable to the Malayans, and the Tunku was fervently against the idea, arguing that "having British Governors in Malaysia after the transfer of sovereignty for a period ... would open [him] to very severe attack and criticism from [his] own people and ...provide the Communists ... the ... opportunity to create dissension .... [His] standing in the eyes of the people would suffer a severe setback".[55] The Tunku was thus adamant that "the British Governors should be replaced and with their replacement there should be some form of responsible government, however rudimentary".[56] Only then would he be able to say to his critics that the creation of Malaysia had brought about an element of "liberation" and constitutional advancement towards independence from Britain.

Just before the release of the Commission findings, the Tunku, who had been made aware of the views of the British members, instructed the Malayan delegates to withdraw from the Commission if the British members insisted on including "in the final report a recommendation that there should be a division of responsibility between London and Kuala Lumpur during a transitional period, and hence dual sovereignty, after the formal creation of the new federation". As the Malayan members of the delegation protested against retaining a British governor, even in the initial stages of the formation of Malaysia, these recommendations were excluded from the report "to lessen the difficulties of negotiations later on".[57] The Tunku's vehement objections of the recommendations of the Cobbold Commission were accompanied by a veiled threat to call off the entire Malaysia Plan.[58] This alarmed the British Prime Minister and the Commonwealth Secretary, both of whom were anxious that the Malaysia Plan not be de-railed by reactions in the Borneo Territories. The Prime Minister clearly had other concerns. When William Goode, the governor of North Borneo, protested against the suppression of some of the findings just because the Tunku had found them "disagreeable", the British Prime Minister reacted with some irritation, asking if the governor had realized that the British Government was more concerned about their "weakness in Singapore" and the "urgent need to hand over the security problem there".[59] Malaysia had to happen, and he was prepared to pacify the Tunku by suggesting that he was ready to press the Commission to exclude "certain conflicting views from the report".[60] The Tunku was invited to London for further talks, and was assured that the "real negotiations [would] be between [the British] and [the Tunku] and not inside the Commission".[61] British Prime Minister Macmillan expeditiously wrote to the Tunku, assuring him that "the British government [had] not the slightest desire to maintain its authority during the transitional period over the Borneo Territories" and that it was in no way bound by the recommendations of the Commission or any of its members.[62] The British cabinet subsequently endorsed Macmillan's stand and urged that negotiations should be urgently pursued to bring about Malaysia as early as practicably possible.

The British Government was clearly prepared to go the extra mile to secure the entry of the North Borneo Territories into Malaysia.[63] The published findings of the Cobbold Commission showed that opinions in the Borneo Territories were indeed divided on the question of joining Malaysia. Although many people were still hesitant about the prospects, others had come round to the view that Malaysia was already a *fait accompli*, and that the more practical response was to secure the best possible deal for the territories following merger. Although the Commission pointed out that about twenty per cent of the people in Sarawak and somewhat less in North Borneo were opposed to federation on any terms, unless preceded by independence and self-government, and that a further third of the populations would accept it only if sufficient safeguards were in place — the Tunku translated this, in a speech on 9 August, that 80 per cent had agreed to the concept of Malaysia.[64]

The Work of the Inter-Governmental (Lansdowne) Committee

Following the release of the Cobbold Report and the London talks in July 1962, by which the British had assumed that all parties concerned (including

Brunei) had agreed to the formation of Malaysia, an official announcement was made that the new federation would be established by 31 August 1963. This had all but made Malaysia a done deal, with Brunei's participation possibly the only unsettled issue. The announcement, however, assumed that all the details of the federation, especially the terms and safeguards which the Territories deemed to be essential, would be expeditiously and happily settled by the various components of the federation. As shown in the earlier chapters, this was certainly not the case in the negotiations between Singapore and Malaya, for the tricky details of financial arrangements and common market were to be argued over until literally the eve of the signing of the agreement.

The situation in the Borneo Territories was not dissimilar. The work of negotiations between the member states on the constitutional arrangements for North Borneo's and Sarawak's entry into Malaysia was left to an inter-governmental committee, chaired by the Marquess of Lansdowne, British Minister of State for Colonial Affairs. Tun Abdul Razak, Deputy Prime Minister of Malaya, was appointed Vice-Chairman of the Committee.[65] The rest of the committee comprised representatives from North Borneo and Sarawak. The IGC was to "consider the precise form in which the territories of North Borneo and Sarawak [would] take their places as constituent states of the new Federation and the form of necessary safeguards of their interests".[66] The British had agreed that there was no need to take the unnecessarily complicated step of developing an entirely new constitution for Malaysia, and that the existing Malayan constitution, which had provisions for the admission of new states in the form of schedules, would be used as a basis for the new Malaysian Federation.[67] The British were happy for the new Federation to be recognized in international law "as an expanded form of the existing Federation of Malaya...with a new name".[68] In this way, the Borneo Territories would simply be grafted onto the existing state of Malaya.

While it seemed that the IGC's work entailed the details of the merger, the tasks were not as straightforward as it seemed. Having only four months to work out the many details of the merger was only part of the problem. The tight time frame given to the IGC was necessitated by the deteriorating political situation in Singapore, which required a quick conclusion of the Malaysia deal. The larger challenge was the task of reconciling the conflicting views and interests of the many parties concerned. Indeed, British officials who understood the complicated conditions on the ground had reservations if the IGC could perform such an insurmountable task.[69] The Chairman of the Committee, Lord Lansdowne, lamented the rush with which his committee had to conduct its work, arguing that time was needed for the Borneo people to understand the issues thoroughly.[70] He feared that the entire enterprise had the look of a Malayan "takeover" and felt that it was important to persuade and convince the people and the territories that this was not the case.[71]

Throughout the negotiations, which had been anything but plain-sailing, the Malayan leaders in Kuala Lumpur were seen as the mastermind behind the deliberations in the committee, directing their delegates who merely acted as their mouthpieces.[72] Lansdowne had observed that the Malayan members of his committee were given no latitude to negotiate and stuck closely to the briefs, and if they had not been given a definite brief from Kuala Lumpur would reserve their positions.[73] The indecisiveness of the Malayan delegation, Lansdowne commented, had delayed the work of the IGC.[74] The British felt that the Tunku could not appreciate that there were real difficulties that existed in the Territories where merger negotiations were concerned. Razak had taken a number of Malay officials on a tour of the Borneo Territories in August 1962, and one member of the entourage, Dato Abdul Aziz bin Haji Abdul Majid, permanent secretary of the Prime Minister's Department, told William Goode that "whereas in London he had thought the Governors' attitude obstructive, he now realised they had only been representing the true views of the people".[75]

In North Borneo, the leading representatives of the main political parties, UNKO, USNO, the Democratic and United Parties, and UNPMO came together for a meeting and drafted a fourteen point programme of minimum safeguards which they demanded be met before North Borneo joined Malaysia. The list was subsequently enlarged to twenty points, and represented the basis for negotiations for the North Borneo representatives on the IGC. These "Twenty Points", which generated support from Sarawak, went beyond what the Malayans had been prepared to concede when the agreement was earlier reached in London. It covered, *inter alia*, religion, language, education, immigration, citizenship, special position of the indigenous races, local control of finance, development and tariff, localization of the state civil service, transitional arrangements and representation in the federal parliament. The penultimate point proposed that North Borneo be renamed Sabah, the ancient name of the locality. In essence, the Borneans wanted assurance that Malayan priorities, such as the official status of Islam as national religion, use of Malay, and the possible imposition of Malay control over the state civil service, would not be foisted on the state when it became part of Malaysia. Autonomy in the form of immigration restriction, local control of financial resources for development, education and legislative power was also deemed crucial conditions for Borneo's entry into Malaysia. Finally, there was the demand for the ultimate safeguard that no constitutional change affecting the state should be undertaken except with the concurrence of the people and government of the state. As an added guarantee, sufficient representation in the federal parliament was required. On 12 September, the North Borneo Legislative Assembly passed unanimously a resolution supporting the principle of Malaysia, "provided that the terms of participation and the constitutional arrangements [would] safeguard the special interests of North Borneo".[76]

The Council Negri in Sarawak had on 26 September 1962 passed a similar resolution welcoming Malaysia in principle, on the understanding that the special interests of the people of Sarawak would be safeguarded. The political parties in Sarawak had accepted the inevitability of Malaysia, and were advocating safeguards along the lines of the Twenty Points, especially amongst the Sea Dayaks and Ibans, who feared domination by the Malays. Some of the groups who had earlier been opposed to merger had come to see the economic value of Malaysia, especially in the promise of development aid by the Malayans. The moderate Chinese of the SUPP were prepared to support Malaysia, although the left-leaning members remained entirely opposed to the idea. On 23 October, the five other political parties in Sarawak formed a united front to support Malaysia.

The key safeguards demanded by the Sarawak and North Borneo delegations revolved around the matters of religion, language and the special position of the indigenous people. The pagan indigenous of Sarawak and North Borneo wanted freedom of religious worship, education and propagation, a guarantee the Malayan delegation readily promised, and an agreement was secured for an amendment to the Malayan Constitution that would oblige the government to grant the Sarawak government proportionate amounts of financial aid for social welfare purposes. No amendment was, however, made to Article 3(1) of the Malayan Constitution that stated that Islam would remain the national religion of Malaysia. Concessions were made for language and education, and while the Malayans wanted Malay to be the national language of Malaysia, agreed that English would be used for Sarawak and North Borneo for a transitional period of ten years after Malaysia Day and thereafter, until the Parliament provided otherwise. Similar concessions were made for education, which was regarded as a state subject.

To assure the people from Sarawak and North Borneo that their interests would be adequately protected in the new Federation, the Tunku agreed to give North Borneo and Sarawak forty seats in the Malayan Parliament as a "special concession" and that the Federal Parliament would be enlarged to 159 seats from 104.[77] The announcement to this effect by the Tunku when he visited Sarawak and North Borneo in the second half of November 1962 helped consolidate popular support for merger in both territories, although it caused a great deal of embarrassment to the Singapore Government.

Finance proved to be one of the trickiest issues in the negotiations. The Borneo Territories were concerned about the continuation of financial grants from the British Colonial Development and Welfare Funds after the formation of Malaysia. This was deemed critical for the development expenditure of the underdeveloped economies of the territories. The political parties of North Borneo and Sarawak queried if the Malayan Government would have the capability to allocate large sums required for their massive development programmes if Malaya itself was dependent on British financial aid. There was also concern that generous treatment being accorded to the Borneo Territories might create resentment among existing states.[78] Lansdowne had admitted that the financial position of the Federation was not entirely healthy and despite a heavy reduction in their own development expenditure the government might face a large drop in federal reserves by the end of 1965. The Malayans would therefore need to look to the British for continued financial assistance in the development programmes of North Borneo and Sarawak.[79] After extensive negotiations, it was agreed that the Federal government would assume control over taxation in the Borneo Territories, and the levels of taxes would be gradually raised to federal levels. The Malayan Government also promised an additional $300 million development fund for the territories, in addition to the British grant of 1.5 million sterling pounds a year.[80]

As deliberations entered the last fortnight before Christmas, Secretary of State Duncan Sandys took a personal hand in pushing the negotiations along. He was determined to conclude the deliberations before Christmas and "brought the whole of his authority ... ruthlessly pushing from point to point, even until the hitherto obdurate Malayan delegates began to wilt". Eventually, both sides found themselves yielding points "more from exhaustion than from conviction".[81]

The details of the IGC negotiations were completed in December 1962, and the report was published at the end of February 1963. The outcome had been a series of compromises. While the Borneo Territories secured concessions on religion, education, language and representations in the Federal Parliament, and got their way on the critical issue of immigration control, they could not secure Malayan approval for transitional arrangements that would have kept the British in the territories for an extended period. In exchange for special treatment in terms of developmental and indigenous interests, the British territories traded their status as a component of a five entity confederation. The Borneo Territories had little option once the decision had been taken by the British and Malayans to form Malaysia. In four weeks, the details had to be settled, and the Borneo Territories saw in the IGC their last chance to ensure that safeguards could be secured in the federation they were to join.[82] From as early as 1961, Lord Selkirk and the governors of the Borneo Territories had suggested that certain provisions needed to be adopted to secure the agreement of the people of the territories in joining Malaysia. These included guarantees for a large measure of internal government, including control over immigration, language, land development and the retention of all local revenues, and some form of British guarantee that the territories could opt out of the Federation after a period if the marriage did not work. The British knew even then that some compromises were needed, and that the Malayans would find the last option particularly unacceptable. The Malayans had secured the deal by agreeing to key constitutional safeguards in the form of seats in the Federal Parliament, and the deal was further sweetened by promise of substantial provisions of social and economic aid for development of the territories.[83]

Just as the IGC had sewn up the deal for North Borneo and Sarawak, the final piece for the completion of the Greater Malaysia Plan came no closer to finding its way into the Federation. In the preceding months, the Sultan of Brunei had maintained a polite but firm distance from overt commitment to joining the Malaysian Federation. He had turned down the offer by the Cobbold Commission to conduct a similar exercise in Brunei, offering instead to organize his own fact-finding committee, which never materialized. Just as arrangements were being settled between the Federation and the Borneo Territories, which would have placed pressure on the Sultan to eventually bring his Brunei on board as well, an anti-Malaysia revolt broke out in the kingdom.

Effects of the Brunei Revolt on the Sultan's Views on Joining Malaysia

In December 1962, an armed rebellion broke out in Brunei, led by A.M. Azahari, charismatic leader of the Parti Rakyat Brunei (PRB), Brunei's first mass-based party, established in 1956. The party was committed to end colonialism in Brunei, and advocated political progress towards parliamentary democracy. As a champion of Bornean nationalism and unity, Azahari had long been a keen advocate of a Bornean Federation of the type promoted by the British in the late 1950s, although the federation he envisioned would not be a colonial scheme but an achievement of the nationalistic ambitions of the Borneo people.[84] Azahari's political appeal extended beyond Brunei and his ideas found support from political parties in Sarawak and North Borneo, but he was also a parochial Bruneian nationalist who dreamt of resurrecting the historical glory of the Brunei empire in North Borneo. In 1961, following the Tunku's announcement, however, Azahari and the PRB had dedicated themselves to stirring up anti-Malaysia feelings in Brunei. The idea of Malaysia was diametrically opposed to his vision of a Borneo Federation, in which Brunei would constitute its political core. Malaysia would mean the political subjugation of Brunei as a small member state of a large federation and the suppression of Bruneian nationalism by Malayan nationalism. If Malaysia were realized, Azahari's hopes of positioning himself as an anti-colonial, nationalist leader would be dashed. In a written response to the Tunku's proposition, the PRB accused him of being a colonialist and a tool of "one of the big powers". The Tunku was also branded a racialist for trying to unite the Malays of the three Borneo Territories.[85] The PRB's stand against Malaysia seemed to have struck a chord with the people in Brunei. In the 1962 elections to the district councils, the question of Malaysia became the key issue and the elections were seen as a referendum on Malaysia. The result was an overwhelming endorsement of the PRB, which captured all the four district councils, indicating that Malaysia had not been well received in Brunei.

The rebellion broke out on the morning on 8 December 1962, spread through Brunei and affected the towns of Weston and Spitang in North Borneo and the districts of Limbang and Lawas of Sarawak. The fighting was carried out by the PRB's underground military arm, the North Borneo National Army (Tentera Nasional Kalimantan Utara), comprising mainly Brunei Malay youths who functioned as irregular troops supporting a core group trained in jungle camps in Indonesian Borneo.[86] The Sultan denounced the rebellion, despite Azahari's claims that the revolution had the support of the Sultan,[87] and immediately sought British military aid to suppress the revolt. The British reacted quickly, and within a week, the poorly-led and ill-equipped rebellion was suppressed by British troops. Alas for Azahari, who had hoped that the rebellion would spread quickly through the Borneo Territories and anti-Malaysia elements would join his ranks, political parties in Sarawak and North Borneo which had hitherto supported his anti-Malaysia stand chose to keep a safe distance, asserting that their opposition would be conducted through constitutional, and not violent, means.

Azahari's self-proclamation as "prime minister of Kalimantan Utara" did not go down well with his former allies, who saw in the revolt an act of self-aggrandisement of a Brunei nationalist. His deals with the Philippines Government and later the Indonesians suggested he might sell-out the territories to these two powers. Almost without exception, all political parties in the Borneo Territories distanced themselves from the rebellion, with many condemning the actions of Azahari and his conspirators.[88]

What was the impact of the Brunei Revolt on the Sultan's eventual decision to stay out of Malaysia? It has been suggested that the impact of the incident on the Sultan's outlook was minimal, and it was the dispute and disagreement over the issues of precedence and finance that sealed the Sultan's decision not to join Malaysia. The Revolt, these views argue, shook the Sultan and made him keener than ever to join Malaysia as a safeguard against the radical and unconstitutional politics as advocated by the Azahari, leader of the PRB and perpetrator of the Revolt.[89] Recent scholarship has suggested otherwise. Stockwell, for instance, has argued that the revolt proved to be a defining moment in the Sultan's attitude towards Malaysia; it may have reinforced the Sultan's earlier reluctance to join Malaysia, and it was from that point onwards that the Sultan's mind on Malaysia had been made up.[90]

Contrary to conventional accounts that Sultan Omar Ali Saifuddin III, who ascended to the throne in 1950, had long been enthusiastic about the Malaysia proposal and that he only withdrew at the last stages when negotiations broke down in July 1963, the Sultan's reactions at various stages of the Malaysia Plan discussions suggested that he had consistently been wary of the idea since it was first mooted in the 1950s. The idea of a sub-federation of the North Borneo Territories was flatly rejected by him in 1958, and the Colonial Office decided against pursuing the idea in view of his opposition. A federation of the Borneo Territories would disadvantage Brunei as its small Malay population would be submerged by the larger mix of communities in the other territories, especially if closer association meant opening the floodgates to non-Malay immigrants.[91] If the union of the three states were formed, Brunei Malays were not likely to get a major stake in democratically elected government, in view of their small numbers, and his own status as ruler might be threatened. There was the additional concern that closer association would play into the hands of the radical PRB, which was advocating for a unified Borneo federation. Also, it was apparent to the Sultan that a federation of the Borneo states would require Brunei's surplus oil revenue for its development expenditure.[92] This was the main issue — the use of oil revenues for the benefit of Sarawak and North Borneo — that had kept the Brunei Sultan aloof from all talk of merger of the North Borneo Territories in the 1950s.

It had also been suggested that the Sultan was especially keen on a merger with the Malayan federation because of the affinity of the ruling Malay races of Brunei and Malaya. Indeed, his decision to replace British civil service officials with Malay civil servants from Malaya soon after the launch of the 1959 Constitution and the granting of generous development loans to Malaya were seen as evidence of his proclivity for closer relations with the Federation.[93] The signals were seen to be so positive that the British High Commissioner, Dennis White, believed that a separate Brunei-Malaya merger was a distinct possibility,[94] and that Omar was keen to join the Sultan's Club in Malaya. However, the Sultan denied any knowledge of or interests in a merger with Malaya when news reached him that the Tunku had broached the possibility to Bruneian students in London in June 1960.[95] The Sultan was not prepared to have open discussions with his Malayan counterpart on a merger, and while he was not probably entirely averse to the idea of having close ties with Malaya, the idea of a merger was probably not on his agenda.

The relationship between Brunei and Malaya, while generally cordial, was also marked by degrees of distrust and differences. On the question of Malaysia, the Sultan "blew hot and cold", welcoming the idea in principle, "yet avoided definite commitment to it".[96] A personal visit by Selkirk to Brunei in July 1961 failed to elicit any form of commitment from the Sultan, and when two of the Tunku's close advisors, Sardon bin Jubir and Osman Talib, met the Sultan in the same month to gauge his response to the Malaysia proposal, the latter simply refused to discuss the subject.[97] It was also telling that in the MSCC deliberations, the delegations sent from Brunei were mainly observers, not participants. Attempts at building sound bilateral relations through the seconded Malayan officers to the Brunei bureaucracy often had the opposite effect of antagonizing local officers and politicians who saw the sending of Malayans to fill posts in Brunei as an act of aggression on the part of the Malayan Prime Minister.[98] The Malayan-Brunei relationship reached a nadir following the mass resignation of seconded Malayan officers in the middle of 1961.[99] Tensions eventually boiled over resulting in an assault case of a Malayan officer by some Bruneians in January 1962.[100] The conditions leading to the unfortunate event and the Tunku's clumsy intervention created suspicions in the Sultan's mind on the relationship with Malaya, and when he was asked to make some preliminary comments on the Tunku's Malaysia proposal, the Sultan flatly refused, citing the excuse that it was inappropriate for him to express such views of external relations when this was constitutionally under the purview of the British.[101] The Tunku tried to salvage the situation by paying a personal visit to Brunei, ostensibly to investigate the assault case. The sub-text of his visit, which was underscored by the Tunku's threat to withdraw his Malay officers from Brunei, was to place an ultimatum for the Sultan to accept Malaysia. Instead of "selling the idea of Malaysia", the Tunku only succeeded in further alienating the Sultan from his Malaysia Plan.[102] All attempts to draw expressions of interest from the Sultan to the Malaysia Plan met with silent intransigence. On the few occasions that the Sultan had discussions with Lord Cobbold, he was reported to be secretive about the conduct of his own inquiry in Brunei and did not offer the chairman of the Commission any views on Brunei's own reactions to the Malaysia Plan.[103]

The Sultan's reluctance to contemplate any form of merger either with Sarawak and North Borneo on the one hand, and with Malaya, on the other, was perhaps understandable as the benefits of such mergers were not immediately evident to him. Brunei had been a protectorate since 1888, and with a conclusion of a new treaty in September 1959 attained internal self-government while the defence, internal security and external relations remained in British hands. This arrangement suited the Sultan well, as he would enjoy full control over the internal administration of his kingdom while the United Kingdom's responsibilities for its security would reduce the vulnerabilities of the small state. There was little incentive for the Sultan to surrender his separate status and the identity of Brunei through membership of a larger political framework. Worst, any merger would certainly result in a dilution of his political power, as well as control over its oil wealth, which would have to be surrendered to federal control once Brunei joined the Malaysian Federation.[104] The Sultan had dismissed all serious considerations of merger because he believed he had all to lose and little to gain through such political arrangements. British and Malayan estimations of the Sultan's interests and intentions had clearly been off the mark. The British had believed that the Sultan would be keen to be part of a Greater Malaysia as it promised security and defence of the small kingdom, but this did not seem to bother the Sultan as he was quite pleased to leave the security of his kingdom to the British. The desire for being a member of the Sultans' Club in Malaya and the prospects of being the next Agong, a carrot which the Malayans evidently dangled in front of the Sultan for him to join the Federation, did not appeal to him as this promise of ceremonial position without power meant little to the Sultan who was enjoying absolute power in his own kingdom, as provided for in the 1959 Constitution. The Sultan's interests in preserving his political power was evident from the fact that he had constantly delayed the introduction of the democratic process in Brunei on the grounds that the rudiments necessary for democratization were not present in Brunei.[105] Although Sultan Omar had instituted limited political change in his kingdom in response to an ostensibly growing political consciousness among the population, he and his aristocrats were not quite prepared to widen the base of power-sharing. The Sultan's tardiness in opening up the political process in Brunei was one of the contributing factors that precipitated the PRB's decision to instigate an armed uprising. On the matter of Malaysia, the Sultan was shrewd enough to realize that the British and Tunku were keen on the Malaysia Plan because it suited their respective needs and interests. But these were of no interest to the people of Brunei, least of all to the Sultan and his aristocrats.

The rebellion and its aftermath could have reinforced the Sultan's belief that there was indeed no necessity for him to surrender his kingdom to a Greater Malaysian Federation. To begin with, the British handling of the revolt convinced the Sultan that the British were not about to compromise the security of the kingdom. The swift and decisive manner in which the

Revolt was pacified by British-led Gurkha troops was a sure indication that Brunei's security would be well taken care of by the British, and there was no need for other forms of security promised by Malaysia.[106] While the Sultan's faith in the reliability of the British was enhanced, his trust in the Tunku was, conversely, eroded. The initial reaction of the Tunku upon receiving news of the impending outbreak was to withdraw his Malayan officials who had been seconded to Brunei. The Tunku had argued that it would be the responsibility of the British to settle the problem of the administrative vacuum as a consequence.[107] Although the British eventually persuaded the Malayan premier to retain the officials in Brunei, and Malayan troops were eventually despatched to the troubled spots following the outbreak of the revolt, the earlier actions of the Tunku had left a bitter after-taste where the Sultan was concerned.[108]

The Revolt, which was quickly squashed by British military actions, not only convinced the Sultan of the security of his position (in so far as the British were not about to see him deposed in an unconstitutional manner) but it also showed clearly too that claims of popular opposition to the Sultan, as personified by Azahari, were probably grossly over-stated. The Revolt did not seem to enjoy widespread support on the ground as earlier thought, and was roundly condemned by political leaders in the neighbouring Borneo Territories. Most political parties, even erstwhile allies, began dissociating themselves from Azahari and the PRB.[109] As things turned out, following the Revolt, the Sultan's position became stronger than ever for his greatest political rival in Brunei had been totally defeated and discredited.[110] There was little incentive, at that point in time, for the Sultan to seek the security embrace of Malaysia.

The Sultan's position was further strengthened by the evocation of emergency powers that allowed him to outlaw the PRB, suspend the constitution and all political processes in the country. He used the occasion of the Revolt to prohibit the functioning of political parties from December 1962. The political authority of the Sultan was therefore substantially enhanced, and had almost become absolute, in the wake of the Revolt.

The 1962 Revolt removed the last significant challenge to the political authority of the Sultan in Brunei. Thereafter, the political process towards democratization took a back seat as the Sultan sought to consolidate his hold over the kingdom. He knew he could secure the support of the British should there be subsequent threats to the security of his throne, or of the country. The decisive action on the part of the British in quelling the revolt had convinced him of that. With his power and authority intact, there was even less incentive for the Sultan to acquiesce to the Tunku's determined overtures for the amalgamation of Brunei into a greater Malaysian Federation. However, the Sultan knew that the British were keen to "decolonise" in Southeast Asia, and saw the only plausible future for small states like Brunei within a larger federation that would be firmly committed to the Commonwealth. Despite the urgings from the British and Malayans, the Sultan maintained his desire to keep to status quo, insisting that Brunei would be better off remaining a protectorate than as a member of Malaysia.

This political position did not, however, generate much enthusiasm in London.[111] The British had been persuaded by the Revolt that Brunei had little option but to join Malaysia and threatened to cultivate the support of some of the detained PRB leaders in order to pressure the Sultan to participate in the Malaysia proposal.[112] They had hoped that the repercussions of the Revolt, which should be portrayed as an act of treason against a self-governing state, would persuade the Sultan of his vulnerability and thus the urgency of joining Malaysia. The Malayan leaders and the British High Commissioner in Brunei agreed that the occasion was opportune, "when the population was reeling and the Sultan shocked and distressed" to nudge Brunei into Malaysia.[113] The Sultan, who should be grateful for Malayan and British assistance in saving his country, would certainly be ready to move in that direction now. With the proscription of the PRB, which had been a vehement opponent of the Malaysia Plan, the Tunku decided to leverage on the circumstances and wrote to the Sultan in December 1962, urging him to use his authority and declare his decision to join Malaysia, now that Azahari and the PKB were out of the way.[114] The Tunku was keen to persuade the Sultan to commit himself at this opportune time, and believed that the rich but defenceless Brunei would find in Malaysia a source of protection.[115] The signals that were sent to the Sultan were unmistakable: the only way forward, as far as the British were concerned, was for Brunei to join Malaysia. In order not to exhaust the goodwill of the British, the Sultan decided to go along with the proposed negotiations for Malaysia, and publicly indicating that he was open to the idea of joining Malaysia, openly supporting the British view that Malaysia provided "the best solution to Brunei's problems".[116] However, that the Sultan turned down the offer of the Cobbold Commission extending its work to his territories was perhaps indicative of his true position on the Malaysia question. His subsequent decision to hold a local commission of inquiry in Brunei, with the purported intention of seeking the views of Bruneians on the idea of joining Malaysia and his reluctance to publish the outcomes of his findings showed his true intentions: a demonstration of willingness not to foreclose the Malaysia idea, but the ultimate decision on whether to join the Federation or not, would be his, and not others, to make.

As it turned out, although the Sultan went through the motion of conferring with the Tunku on constitutional and financial matters relating to the Brunei's entry into Malaysia, his mind seemed to have been made up. The Tunku was anxious not to lose Brunei, regarding it as an attractive fit by way of royal connections and financial promise. The Sultan, on the other hand, was never convinced that joining Malaysia would serve his and his people's interests, seeing no reason to "flout the strong anti-Malaysia feelings revealed by the uprising".[117] In the upshot, on account of disagreements over financial arrangements and the question of precedence in the hierarchy of rulers in the Federation, the Sultan decided not to sign the Malaysia Agreement on 9 July. The British eventually came to the conclusion that the Sultan never intended to go through with the merger. In a confidential note to a parliamentary brief, the point was made that "the Sultan never intended to sign the Agreement and would have found some pretext even if his demands ... had been fully met".[118]

The Borneo Territories' entry into Malaysia in 1963 marked the culmination of a hasty process of de-colonization in Sarawak and North Borneo. Neither colony was considered ready for self-government in 1961, when the Tunku first broached his idea of a "Greater Malaysia", yet within a space of twenty four months, the British were happy to transfer sovereignty of those two territories to the Malaysian Government, thereby ending more than a century of colonial rule in North Borneo. In order to secure Singapore's merger with the Federation, the British did their best to facilitate the realization of the Malaysia Plan, despite reservations that they were doing the Borneo Territories no favours by "rail-roading" them into a situation for which they were not sufficiently prepared. Eventually, however, the colonies were handed to the Malayans to ensure that the Tunku would do what the British were most interested in achieving: Singapore's merger with the Federation. The Tunku prodded the British on, anxious to secure the Borneo Territories before Singapore was thrust upon Malaya. In his calculations, the ethnic factor proved to be a major consideration. He seemed to have held the conviction, which he also often expressed for the benefit of his Malay supporters, that the Malays and most of the non-Chinese peoples in the Borneo Territories would be more inclined to support Malay rather than Chinese opinions in political matters. That this belief did not seem to match the reality on the ground baffled him. His advisors believed that the fault lay not with the Prime Minister's vision, but with "hard core die-hard colonialists who were living in the past".[119]

In any case, the Consultative Committee meetings, Cobbold Commission enquiry and the work of the IGC all sought to achieve the effect that the British were acting in the best interests of the people of North Borneo and Sarawak, and that Malaysia was an arrangement that did not contradict British obligations to the Borneo people. The period leading to Malaysia witnessed a political awakening in Sarawak and North Borneo, with political parties, organized mainly along ethnic lines, emerging to articulate their respective visions of the political future of the territories. These nascent sub-nationalisms that emerged in a large unstable political framework, compounded by the haste with which Malaysia was formed, were to subsequently cause complications in Malaysia's nation-building efforts.[120] That Brunei, which would have been financially the most attractive prize for the Tunku, stayed out of Malaysia was seen as something of a lost opportunity for Malaysia. The prize may have eluded the Tunku, but his trusted aide, Ghazali Shafie, judged that Brunei's omission had been a blessing in disguise, arguing that "with undemocratic Brunei in, Malaysia could never claim to be based on parliamentary democracy".[121]

The manner in which the Borneo Territories were incorporated into the Federation revealed the Tunku's intentions behind his idea of a Greater

Malaysia. He was interested in building a wider Malay-based Federation that would incorporate the Borneo Territories, in particular Sarawak and Brunei, because these "territories have the same types of culture and racial origin as the Malayans".[122] This longer-term political ambition took on a sense of urgency when Malaya had to give serious consideration to a merger with Singapore. Under pressure to take in Singapore, the Tunku did all he could to ensure that the Borneo territories would come on board as well. Thus, while the Malayans engaged in hard bargaining with their Singapore counterparts, they were eager to make the passage of the Borneo Territories into Malaysia as uncomplicated as possible. However, on a couple of critical areas — citizenship rights and representation in the Federal parliament — the terms of Singapore's entry into Malaysia were seen to be less satisfactory than those that were accorded to the Borneo territories. The differences in approach adopted by the Malayans with regard to merger with Singapore on the one hand, and the incorporation of the Borneo Territories on the other were indicative of the Tunku's actual design. As he explained in his speech to the Malayan Parliament on 16 October 1961:[123]

> ... the States of the Borneo territories and the States of the Federation of Malaya [will] join together as a Federation of Malaysia, and Singapore [will be joined] in partnership on a footing something like that which exists between the United Kingdom and Northern Ireland. An association of such a nature would recognise the Federation of Malaysia with Singapore as partners in one identity.

What was meant by a common identity was never fully explained, but clearly, Greater Malaysia was conceived as a federation of Malaya and Borneo territories primarily, in which Singapore would not be an integral part.

NOTES

1 William Goode to Ian Macleod, "North Borneo: Review of Affairs", 30 December 1960, CO 1030/1153.

2 Memorandum by MacLeod for the Cabinet Colonial Policy Committee,

"Possibility of an Association of the British Borneo Territories with the Federation of Malaya and Singapore', 15 July 1960, CAB 134/1559, CPC (60) 17.

3 Selkirk to MacLeod, "Closer association of the Borneo Territories", 2 May 1961, CO 1030/1079 no. 2.

4 "Report by Joint Intelligence Committee (Far East) for the British Defence Co-ordinating Committee (Far East)", 17 March 1961, DO 169/18 no. 11.

5 Memorandum by MacLeod, 15 July 1960, CAB 134/1559.

6 "Greater Malaysia", Tory to Sandys, forwarding a personal message from Tunku Abdul Rahman to Macmillan, 7 October 1961, PREM 11/3422.

7 James. P. Ongkili, *The Borneo Response to Malaysia, 1961–1963* (Singapore: D. Moore, 1967), p. 22.

8 *Straits Times*, 29 June 1961, p. 1.

9 See Chin Ung-Ho, *Chinese Politics in Sarawak: A Study of the Sarawak United Peoples Party* (New York: Oxford University Press, 1996).

10 *Sarawak Tribune*, 27 June 1961.

11 *Sarawak by the Week*, No. 22/61, p. 6.

12 Ibid.

13 Open letter from Donald Stephens to Tunku, *North Borneo News and Sabah Times*, 7 July 1961.

14 Ongkili, *The Borneo Response to Malaysia*, pp. 34–38.

15 Willard A. Hanna, *The Formation of Malaysia: New Factor in World Politics* (New York: American Field Staff, 1964), p. 20.

16 *Straits Times*, 6 July 1961, p. 16.

17 Nelson Liap Kudu, *Sarawak National Party: Its History, Organisation and Leadership* (Kuching: Sarawak Press Sdn. Bhd., 1973), p. 1.

18 Michael Leigh, *The Rising Moon. Political Change in Sarawak* (Sydney: Sydney University Press; Portland, Or: International Scholarly Book Services, 1974), pp. 36–38.

19 *Sarawak Tribune*, 31 May 1961 and 24 June 1961.

20 See John Chin, *Sarawak Chinese* (Kuala Lumpur: Oxford University Press, 1981), pp. 44–45.

21 C.A. Lockard, "Leadership and Power within the Chinese Community in Sarawak: A Historical Survey", *Journal of Southeast Asian Studies* 11, no. 2 (Sept, 1971): 212–16.

22 FCO Research Department Memorandum, "The Origins and Formation of Malaysia", 10 July 1970, FCO 51/154, in Anthony J. Stockwell, ed., *Malaysia. British Documents on the End of Empire*, Series B, Vol. 8 (London: Stationery Office, 2004), pp. 600–01.

23 Memorandum submitted by Colonial Office, 2 October 1961, CAB 134/1949.

24 FCO Research Department Memorandum, "The Origins and Formation of Malaysia", 10 July 1970, FCO 51/154 in Stockwell, ed., *Malaysia*, p. 604.

25 John Bastin, *Malaysia: Selected Readings* (Nedeln, KTO Press, 1979), p. 398.

26 Harold MacMillan, *Memoirs: Volume VI, At the End of the Day, 1961–1963* (London: Macmillan Press, 1973), p. 247.

27 *Straits Times*, 10 July 1961.

28 Selkirk to Macleod, 16 September 1961, PREM 11/3418.

29 Selkirk to Commonwealth Relations Office, 10 November 1961, DO 169/123.

30 Humphry Berkeley to Sandys, 23 January 1962, DO 169/214.

31 Minutes of MSCC Meeting in Jesselton, 24 August 1961, CO 947/8.

32 MSCC Communique, 19 December 1961, CO 947/8.

33 "Report by Datu Mustapha on Recent Visit to Federation", 17 August 1961, in Goode Papers — MSS.Ind.Ocn.s.323, Box 2, File 1.

34 Ibid.

35 Selkirk to Sandys, 10 February 1962, DO 169/214; and Minutes of MSCC Meeting, 2 February 1962, CO 947/11.

36 *Sarawak by the Week*, No. 34/61, p. 24

37 HMSO, *Malaysia and Sarawak* (Kuching: Government Printing Office, 1962), p. 1.

38 Ibid.

39 Ibid., p. 4.

40 Cited in Chin, *Chinese Politics*, p. 311.

41 *Federation of Malaysia: Joint Statement by the Governments of the United Kingdom and of the Federation of Malaya* (London: Her Majesty's Stationery Office, 1961), Cmd. 1563, p. 3.

42 See Matthew Jones, *Conflict and Confrontation in Southeast Asia, 1961–1965: Britain, the United States and the Creation of Malaysia* (Cambridge; New York: Cambridge University Press, 2001), p. 80.

43 Ongkili, *The Borneo Response to Malaysia*, p. 124.

44 Jones, *Conflict and Confrontation in South East Asia*, pp. 80–81.

45 Goode to Sandys, 17 June 1962, CO 1030/1017; see also Shafie, *Ghazali Shafie's Memoir*, pp. 213, 227–28.

46 *Straits Times*, 11 March 1962.

47 Ibid.

48 Ibid.

49 Jones, *Conflict and Confrontation in South East Asia*, p. 83.

50 Martin to Lord Perth, 31 January 1962, in Goode Papers, Box 2, File 1.

51 Cobbold to Macmillan, 21 June 1962, CO 1030/1028, no. 1.

52 Ibid.

53 Memorandum by Anthony Abell and David Watherstone relating to

arrangements for a transitional period to Lord Cobbold, 21 June 1962, CO 1030/1028 no. 4.

54 *Report of the Commission of Enquiry, North Borneo and Sarawak, 1962* (London: Her Majesty's Stationery Office, 1962), Cmd 1794, pp. 26, 75, 87, hereafter referred to as *The Cobbold Commission*.

55 Tunku to Sandys, 25 July 1962, CO 1030/1024.

56 Memorandum by G. Tory, enlarging on the implications of Malaysia for the Tunku's political position, "The Tunku and Malaysia", 28 June 1962, DO 169/214 no. 95.

57 Cobbold to Macmillan, 21 June 1962.

58 Tunku to Macmillan, "The Tunku's rejection of the Cobbold Report", 4 July 1962, PREM 11/3867.

59 Jones, *Conflict and Confrontation in South East Asia*, p. 85.

60 Martin to Zuluetta, "Suggested talking points for PM's meeting with the Tunku on 16 July 1962", 11 July 1962, CO 1030/1024.

61 Ibid.

62 Sandys to Tory, enclosing Macmillan's reply to Tunku's message of 4 July 1962, PREM 11/3867.

63 Telegram no. 641, Commonwealth Relations Office to Tory, 4 July 1962, CO 1030/1024.

64 FCO Research Department Memorandum, "The Origins and Formation of Malaysia", 10 July 1970, FCO 51/154 in Stockwell, ed., *Malaysia*, p. 614.

65 *Malaysia — Report of the Inter-Governmental Committee, 1962*, Cmnd. 1954 (London: HMSO, 1963).

66 Golds to Pickard, 29 October 1962, CO/1036.

67 Federation of Malaya Paper for Constitutional Committee, IGC30/2/FM/3, *IGC Report*, p. 9, CO 1030/1054.

68 Golds to Harris, 12 October 1962, CO 1030/1045.

69 *North Borneo News and Sabah Times*, 13 September 1962.

70 Tory to Commonwealth Relations Office, 3 September 1962, CO 1030/1038.

71 Lansdowne to Sandys, 10 September 1962, CO 1030/1038; and attached memorandum from Private Secretary to SOS for the Colonies to Wallace, 11 September 1962, CO 1030/1039.

72 Selkirk to Lansdowne, 6 October 1962, CO 1030/1039.

73 Waddell to Sandys, 14 November 1962, CO 1030/1032.

74 Ibid.

75 FCO Research Department Memorandum, "The Origins and Formation of Malaysia", 10 July 1970, FCO 51/154 in Stockwell, ed., *Malaysia*, p. 624.

76 Ibid., p. 625.

77 *Straits Times*, 17 November 1962; IGC Report, p. 14.
78 IGC Sarawak Paper No. 6, IGC 40/2/S/2, 12 October 1962, p. 1, CO 1030/1053.
79 "Malaysia: Progress Report by Lansdowne", 6 December 1962, p. 1, CO 1030/1052.
80 *The Cobbold Commission*, pp. 19–20.
81 Turner, "From the Depths of My Memory", Brit.Emp.S.454, Rhodes House Library, University of Oxford.
82 Jakeway to Sandys, 5 October 1962, CO 1030/1036.
83 James P. Ongkili, *Nation-Building in Malaysia, 1946–74* (Singapore: Oxford University Press, 1985), pp. 168–69.
84 D. S. Ranjit Singh, *Brunei 1839–1983: The Problems of Political Survival* (Singapore; New York: Oxford University Press, 1984), p. 151.
85 Ibid., p. 159.
86 Ibid., p. 173.
87 *Straits Times*, 10 December 1962.
88 Singh, *Brunei*, p. 175.
89 Ongkili, *The Borneo Response to Malaysia*, p. 109. See also Singh, *Brunei 1893–1983*, p. 70; Graham E. Saunders, *A History of Brunei* (Kuala Lumpur; Singapore: Oxford University Press, 1994), p. 153; and Sopiee, *From Malayan Union to Singapore Separation*, p. 175.
90 Anthony J. Stockwell, "Britain and Brunei, 1945–1963: Imperial Retreat and Royal Ascendancy", *Modern Asian Studies* 38, no. 4 (2004): 787.
91 Ibid., p. 789.
92 Ibid.
93 White to Maudling, 15 January 1962, CO 1030/1447.
94 White to Wallace, Head of Far Eastern Department, 28 April 1960.
95 Record of Interview between White and MacLeod on "Brunei/Malaya Relationships", 12 July 1960, CO 1030/937.
96 Stockwell, "Britain and Brunei, 1945–1963", p. 791.
97 White to Selkirk, 27 September 1961, CO 1030/1447.
98 Stockwell, "Britain and Brunei, 1945–1963", p. 796.
99 White to Melville, 24 July 1961, CO 1030/1447.
100 White to Maudling, 15 January 1961, CO 1030/1447.
101 White to Macleod, 8 August 1961, CO 1030/1447.
102 White to Maudling, 15 January 1961, CO 1030/1447.
103 White to Wallace, 13 March 1962, CO 1030/1012.
104 Telegram from Kuala Lumpur to Commonwealth Relations Office, 11 October 1962, CO 1030/1036.
105 Tunku to Sandys, 15 June 1961, DO 169/25.

106 Commonwealth Relations Office to all Commonwealth Relations Office Posts, 9 December 1962, CO 1030/1068.

107 Kuala Lumpur to Commonwealth Relations Office, 8 December 1962, CO 1030/1068.

108 Sandys to Waddell, 9 December 1962, CO 1030/1068.

109 Maudling to Tory, 9 December 1962, CO 1030/1068.

110 Commonwealth Relations Office to Kuala Lumpur, 13 December 1962, CO 1030/1072.

111 Singapore to Foreign Office, 18 December 1962, CO 1030/1074.

112 FO to certain HM representatives, 14 December 1962, CO 1030/1073.

113 Ibid.

114 Kuala Lumpur to Commonwealth Relations Office, 15 December 1962, CO 1030/1073.

115 Martin to Wallace, 5 December 1962, CO 1030/1074.

116 Record of questions and answers on Malaysia during Ian MacLeod's visit to the United States, June 1963, DO 169/327.

117 Stockwell, "Britain and Brunei, 1945–1963", p. 813.

118 Ibid., p. 814.

119 Shafie, *Ghazali Shafie's Memoir*, pp. 197–98, 242.

120 R.S. Milne and K. J. Ratnam, *Malaysia — New States in a New Nation: Political Development of Sarawak and Sabah in Malaysia* (London: Frank Cass, 1974), pp. 6–7.

121 Shafie, *Ghazali Shafie's Memoir*, p. 300.

122 Cited in ibid., p. 120.

123 Cited in ibid., pp. 118–19.

Conclusion

On 9 July 1963, the agreement for the establishment of Malaysia was signed by the United Kingdom, Malaya, North Borneo, Sarawak and Singapore. The agreement envisaged that all legislative and related activities leading to the formal constitution of Malaysia would be completed by the end of July or early August, and Malaysia Day could be declared on 31 August 1963. As things turned out, Malaysia's birthday was delayed and the new state came into existence on 16 September 1963, after a last gasp bid by the Indonesians to abort its birth. Both Indonesia and the Philippines had opposed the concept of Malaysia from the outset, and when it appeared that the British and Malayans were pushing ahead with the formation of "Greater Malaysia" despite the unresolved Philippines' claim to North Borneo, the Brunei Revolt and the Indonesian declaration of *Konfrontasi* (Confrontation),[1] the United Nations was summoned in a last ditch attempt to stop Malaysia. The Tunku had earlier attempted to mollify his unhappy neighbours by suggesting, in a summit in Manila early August 1963, the formation of a super-federation known as "Mal-phil-indo", incorporating Malaysia, Philippines and Indonesia. The latter two were not entirely assuaged, and demanded that the United Nations' Secretary-General, U Thant, send a team to Sarawak and North Borneo to ascertain whether it was the wishes of the people there to join Malaysia. This last minute intervention by the United Nations meant that the date originally proposed for the establishment of Malaysia — 31 August 1963 — would have to be postponed. The fact-finding mission merely delayed the inevitable. A few days after the Manila Agreement, the legislative council in North Borneo voted unanimously that the colony would declare independence under the new name of Sabah, irrespective of the findings of the UN mission. A similar statement was issued by Sarawak, declaring that "Malaysia shall be born on 31 August, no matter what happens". Singapore too decided to declare its independence unilaterally on 31 August 1963, in accordance with the Malaysia schedule agreed a year earlier. In any case, the UN Mission subsequently confirmed that the overwhelming majority of people in both Sarawak and Sabah were prepared to join the Federation of Malaysia.

Malaysia was inaugurated amidst a number of major and minor challenges. Externally, it was exposed to the taunts and hostility of anti-Malaysia forces, most notably from Indonesia and various communist organizations, prompted probably by Moscow and Peking that regarded the new state as nothing more than a perpetuation of imperialism and twentieth century neo-colonialism. The Indonesians had rejected the United Nation's findings, and the Malayan ambassador in Jakarta was informed by the Indonesian Foreign Minister a day after U Thant's report was published that "there would be no recognition of Malaysia".[2] Such reactions to Malaysia, whose legitimacy and independence as a post-colonial state many of its critics doubted, were perhaps not unexpected, especially when the British "Grand Design" appeared to have served as the blue-print for this new state. While anti-(neo) colonialism may have served as a convenient and popular rhetoric with which to attack Malaysia, personalities and political rivalries played a part as well. The Indonesians had their own axes to grind with Malaysia, which they saw as a rival to their own vision of a *Melayu Raya* (Greater Malay Nation), a greater Malay world of which Indonesia would constitute its cultural and political centre, the antecedents of which, the Indonesians claimed, were evident in the pre-colonial empires of Srivijaya and Majapahit. *Konfrontasi*, with its motto "Crush Malaysia", put paid to all hopes of the "Malphilindo" accord and pitched the Tunku and Sukarno as rivals for leadership of the Malay world. That the creation of Malaysia had engendered a common land boundary in Borneo between Indonesia and Malaysia created a territorial dimension in this strained relationship.

Then, there was the unresolved contest from the Philippines on the ownership of the Borneo Territories. The Philippines had raised a formal claim to North Borneo in its capacity as the successor to the Sultan of Sulu, who had originally ceded part of his territory to the Chartered Company.

According to the Philippines claim, the original cession had been a lease and not an outright grant. Although it did not appear probable that the Philippines intended to annex North Borneo, the unsettled claims, to which the British and Malayan governments refused to give any recognition, became grist to the mill of strained relations between the Philippines and the Malayan Federation. While the Philippines did not join the Indonesians in active opposition to Malaysia, Manila issued a press statement on 15 September deferring "action on the question of the recognition of the proposed Federation of Malaysia".[3]

The virulent opposition to Malaysia from the anti-imperialists, nationalists and communists stemmed from their belief that Greater Malaysia was the realization of the British Grand Design, a well-executed neo-colonial plot carried out by Whitehall in cahoots with its colonial sympathizers in Malaya and Singapore. But as the recent works of historians like Anthony Stockwell and Matthew Jones have shown, and which I have tried to reinforce in the preceding chapters, although ministers in London and colonial officials in the region played a major role in the construction of Malaysia, the British were not the primary architects. The Grand Design was in many ways a misnomer as the British did not have a single, uncontested policy for post-war Southeast Asia. Even if there was one, the British were in no position to impose the pace and substance of the scheme, but relied instead on "painstaking negotiations to reconcile the diverse objectives of the participating territories" through discussions, identifying interests, assessing opinions, brokering compromises, and eventually cobbling together "an uneasy agreement on the constitution of the prospective state".[4] The negotiations and processes to the Malaysia agreement demonstrated this very clearly.

Yet, the more fundamental challenge for the new state was an internal one — whether the framework of Greater Malaysia would be "able to support the nation of the future".[5] The Malaysia that came into being on 16 September was a federation of different parts; a remarkable act of political consolidation. The political, economic and ethnic differences that the new state had to pull together and accommodate posed fundamental challenges to its aspirations to turn the federation into a nation-state. There was as yet no nation in the Malaysian Federation in 1963. Singapore, the Borneo Territories and Malaya had been assembled in a constitutional arrangement that was hastily put together. Underlying the association was the Tunku's desire for a Malaysia that would secure the ethnic and, therefore, political dominance of the Malays. Greater Malaysia would be the structure on which he would build a Malaysian nation predicated on the political primacy of the Malays and indigenous races. This fitted well with British plans to leave their erstwhile dependencies, in particular Singapore, to the secure, anti-communist hands of the Malayan Prime Minister. While the British were content with the construction of the Malaysian state, the building of the Malaysian nation would have to be taken care of by the leaders of the new state. Malaysia, with the Federation of Malaya as its core, was framed as a Malay nation-state in legal, constitutional terms. However, as the new state had to accommodate a number of dissimilar interests, special political and constitutional arrangements were put in place so that the Malay dominant *ethnie* could be preserved, while guarantees were given at the same time to ethnic communities in Singapore, Sarawak and Sabah, to ensure that their rights would be protected at the same time.[6] This was the manner in which Singapore and the Borneo Territories were brought into the Federation, as an annex to Malaysia with a large measure of autonomy, rather than an integral part. The requirement to resolve the tension between the political need to maintain an ethnic Malay basis for the new state and the new reality of an expanded multi-ethnic state that Malaysia came to represent would challenge the leadership from 1963 onwards.

The Singapore case took on a more extreme form, and the Ulster arrangement that had been arrived at between Lee Kuan Yew and the Tunku, proved problematic because of the uncertain and ambiguous position of Singapore in the body-politic of Malaysia. All along, the Tunku had indeed referred to Singapore as a "problem child", and that he was more amenable to securing a relationship that was more akin to an "association" rather than a full-fledged "merger".[7] If he had to take Singapore into the Federation, he would do so on a contract "under which the island state would leave the peninsula alone (in political terms)".[8] He thus insisted that there would not be any complete merger with Singapore, but that the latter would join the Federation as a largely autonomous state with rights to determine its own internal affairs, except in matters of defence, external affairs and internal security. In return for that special status, Singapore would have to accept a proportionately smaller representation in the central parliament than it could claim on a population basis. While the citizenship agreement acknowledged common status for all under the Federation, Singapore citizens were not allowed to vote or participate in Federal elections. In his scheme, Singapore could prosper as the "New York of Malaysia", but it was important that its Chinese population stay out of politics in the peninsula. By joining Malaysia, Singapore would enjoy economic security and freedom from outside interference, but this must not come at a price for the people of the Federation. The Tunku had to ensure that the peninsula be insulated from the pernicious politics of the island-state. The final price that the Tunku exacted from Singapore just on the eve of merger was the launching of Operation "Cold Store" in February 1963, a security swoop ordered by the joint Security Council of Singapore, Malaya and Britain which resulted in the detention of some 130 communist sympathizers, which included political, trade union and student leaders. In December 1962, a similar security action was taken in Malaya, when about 50 suspected communists were rounded up by the Malayan Special Branch. These actions were undertaken to pre-empt communist front organizations from linking up with conspirators aiming to disrupt the formation of Malaysia, and were regarded by British and Malayan ministers as "crucial in securing Malayan acquiescence in the creation of [the] Malaysian Federation".[9] While Cold Store thwarted any attempt to "stir violence or disorder in the closing stages of the development of Malaysia", it dealt a severe blow to the Barisan Sosialis in Singapore as several of its leaders were arrested. This eased the political tension for Lee Kuan Yew and enabled him to see through the final stages of negotiations with the Federation.[10]

Lee was initially quite prepared to accept the Tunku's terms for merger as such an arrangement would also work for the benefit of Singapore. A degree of local autonomy, particularly in the areas of education and labour, would ensure Singapore would develop the island-state on its own terms. However, while the broad outlines were agreed upon, the details were to cause consternation to both parties on how best to fit the Singapore annex to the main Malaysian structure. While the political objective of merger may have been achieved in 1963, Lee realized that the job, as far as he was concerned, was far from completed. Unless he was able to secure for Singapore the economic and political benefits that he had earlier promised a merger with the Federation would bring, he would be subjected to tremendous pressures from his political rivals in Singapore who had fought hard against joining Malaysia. When the Agreement was signed, the PAP government knew that Singapore was already at a disadvantaged position in a number of ways. Their bitter opponents in the Legislative Assembly had continued their criticisms of the citizenship arrangement that they argued would make Singapore citizens second-class in the new Federation. Their criticisms carried extra bite when the Malaya-Singapore merger terms were compared to the much better deal under which the Borneo Territories were brought into the Federation. The agreement over financial arrangements and the Common Market were a series of compromises whose advantage to Singapore were not immediately obvious. For Lee, at least, the battles for merger did not end with the signing of the Malaysia Agreement or of the formal establishment of Malaysia in September 1963; against the explicit wishes of the Tunku for Singapore to stay out of Federal politics, Lee knew that unless he was able to exercise influence in Kuala Lumpur, he would be doubly defeated, both in the Federation and in Singapore politics.

While Lee Kuan Yew strenuously argued that Singapore would be a loyal and integral part of the Federation, he was concerned, at the same time, that his government should be in a position to exercise its political will in the Federal politics. Here, he had to push the boundaries as the political space that the Federation was prepared to accord the PAP was never made clear. As he recalls in his memoirs, "the more control the government in KL exercised over [Singapore's finances] the more it must expect Singapore to participate in the politics of Malaysia in order to influence its policies towards Singapore .... This was a fundamental problem that was never resolved before or after Singapore joined Malaysia."[11] Without a PAP voice in the Federal Cabinet, and with the merger agreement failing to specify the political latitude that the Federal Government was prepared to accord Lee

Kuan Yew and the PAP government in Malaysia, Lee had to test the boundaries and push the envelope as far as he could.

Consequently, the ambiguity of the agreements contributed to and was aggravated by a series of political quarrels between Singapore and Kuala Lumpur between 1963 and 1965. The decision by the Alliance and PAP to contest elections in Singapore and the Federation respectively soured the relationship between the two. The Alliance's decision to contest the 1963 elections in Singapore (where it performed dismally) convinced Lee that Kuala Lumpur was not likely to leave Singapore to its own devices. The MCA would try to win the Chinese over, just as UMNO felt that it had the right to champion the rights of Singapore's Malay community. For his part, Lee felt that the PAP needed to participate in Federal politics to ensure that Singapore's interests were not jeopardized, hence the decision to participate in the Federal elections in 1964. This was to mark the beginning of the end. The degree of distrust between the Singapore and the Alliance leaders widened into an unbridgeable gulf.

Lee's advocacy for a "democratic Malaysian Malaysia", possibly his attempt to overcome the restrictions of the limited citizenship rights for Singapore and to create an integrated, all-Malaysia political arena for all Malaysians, was the proverbial straw that broke the camel's back. PAP leaders had decided that perhaps the only way to fight extremist Malay politicking was to promote a national identity that would not be based on race. Communal politics simply made it harder for Chinese majority Singapore to be brought back into the main political ground, and at the rate things were going, Singapore would be politically marginalized, a tolerated but inconvenient appendage that had no place in the Malaysian mainstream. The PAP went into discussions with the non-Malay parties in Malaya, Sarawak and Sabah and the result was the formation of the Malaysian Solidarity Convention (MSC) in May 1965. The MSC was reminiscent of the MSCC which in 1962 had played a significant role in selling the idea of Greater Malaysia to the political parties of the Borneo Territories. In the context of heightened communal politics in Malaysia in 1965, UMNO found itself facing the possibility of a non-Malay majority in Malaysia. Instead of the non-Chinese majorities in Sarawak and Sabah acting as a counterweight to the Chinese in Singapore, there was now, under the instigation of the PAP, the possibility of a big non-Malay bloc challenging Malay hegemony in Malaysia. The Malaysian Solidarity Convention declared:

> A Malaysian Malaysia means that the nation and state is not identified with the supremacy, well-being and the interests of any one particular community or race. A Malaysian Malaysia is the antithesis of a Malay Malaysia, a Chinese Malaysia, a Dayak Malaysia, an Indian Malaysia or a Kadazan Malaysia. The special and legitimate rights of different communities must be secured and promoted within the framework of the collective rights, interests and responsibilities of all races. The people of Malaysia did not vote for a Malaysia assuring hegemony to one community. Still less would they be prepared to fight for the preservation of so meaningless a Malaysia.

At the first MSC rally held in Singapore, the leaders of Malaya, Sabah and Sarawak parties that were throwing in their lot with the PAP's "Malaysian Malaysia" call signalled their dissatisfaction with Malay hegemony. This was what the UMNO leadership had been most fearful of, and the MSC's clarion call to challenge the status quo brought tensions between the Malays and non-Malays to boiling point. Perhaps this was Lee's attempt to create an alternative political force to the Alliance, but his questioning of the sacrosanct rights of the *bumiputra* (indigenous) Malay population in the peninsula had put the PAP in open confrontation with the Malaysian Government.

The adversarial manoeuvring between Singapore and Kuala Lumpur during the Malaysia years could be traced to the compromises that were arrived at in July 1963, when both parties were under pressure to have an agreement hammered out before the declaration of Malaysia. It quickly became apparent that these arrangements did not in themselves obviate the possibility of future difficulties, and the seeds of dissension sown by the disagreements between the two governments, engendered fundamentally by their different political perspectives, were to sprout into major crises during the short-lived merger between Singapore and the Federation. In this regard, the causes of separation could be traced to the proceedings leading to merger. Malaysia thus proved, in some ways, to be a short-lived victory for Lee Kuan Yew and his PAP government. While the PAP's political position in Singapore had been entrenched as a result of its successes in the battles for merger, the Singapore Government under Lee Kuan Yew was forced, in August 1965, to re-examine its political beliefs and priorities and to re-build a new Singapore without the Malaysian hinterland.

The manner of and haste with which the Borneo Territories were incorporated into Malaysia in 1963 was one of the major reasons for the tenuous relationship between Kuala Lumpur and the capitals of East Malaysia. That the states did not join the Federation on the same basis of the existing states of Malaya but required special safeguards to maintain their distinctiveness laid the seeds of divisiveness and hindered the promotion of Malaysian nationalism. The divergence between peninsular and East Malaysia had its roots in the period leading to Malaysia, when the North Borneo Territories were rushed into a "shot-gun" marriage with minimal preparation and an inadequate process of consultation which led the people in the Borneo Territories to accept Malaysia because of the belief that the deal had already been decided.

The circumstances of Malaysia's origins and formations placed formidable challenges to the new state. Within two years of its formation, the federation lost one of its components when Singapore, which was the object of the British initiative in the first place, left Malaysia in rather unhappy circumstances in 1965 although the communist threat that drove London into action in the first place did not eventually materialize. The Tunku secured his Borneo Territories, while Brunei, which he believed had the greatest affinity with Malaya remained outside Malaysia. Britain had hoped that a federation of its dependencies in the form of Greater Malaysia would lessen its defence commitment in the region, but instead, it ended up having to deal with *Konfrontasi* from the Indonesians. And finally, despite all that had to be done to safeguard the Singapore bases, the British decided to pull out of their bases less than eight years after the formation of Malaysia, an end which the Grand Design did not originally envisage.

NOTES

1. In January 1963, Indonesian Foreign Minister, Dr Subandrio announced that Indonesia would pursue a policy of "Confrontation" against Malaysia, to protest against its being used as a tool of colonialism and imperialism. Although no action plans were spelt out that that time, Confrontation involved the breaking of diplomatic ties, infiltration of Indonesian military personnel into Sarawak and Sabah, and isolated military activities of raids and sabotage. The tension lasted from 1963 to 1966.

2. FCO Research Department Memorandum, "The Origins and Formation of Malaysia", 10 July 1970, FCO 51/154, in Anthony J. Stockwell, ed., *Malaysia. British Documents on the End of Empire*, Series B, Vol. 8 (London: Stationery Office, 2004), pp. 658–59.

3. Ibid., p. 659.

4. Anthony J. Stockwell, "Forging Malaysia and Singapore: Colonialism, Decolonisation and Nation-building", in Wang Gungwu, ed., *Nation Building: Five Southeast Asian Histories* (Singapore: Institute of Southeast Asian Studies, 2005), p. 207.

5. Ibid., p. 210.

6. Cheah Boon Kheng, "Ethnicity in the Making of Malaysia", in Wang, ed., *Nation Building*, p. 103.

7. Cited in Lee Kuan Yew, *The Singapore Story*, p. 404.

8. Dennis Bloodworth, *The Tiger and the Trojan Horse*, p. 289.

9. See Matthew Jones, "Creating Malaysia: Singapore Security, the Borneo Territories, and the Contours of British Policy, 1961–63", *Journal of Imperial and Commonwealth History* 28, no. 2 (2000): 85–109.

10. See Ooi Kee Beng, *The Reluctant Politician: Tun Dr Ismail and His Time* (Singapore: Institute of Southeast Asian Studies, 2006), p. 142; and Lee Kuan Yew, *The Singapore Story*, pp. 472–83.

11. Lee, *The Singapore Story*, p. 477.

Bibliography

UNPUBLISHED SOURCES
United Kingdom (Public Record Office, London)
CAB 134
Cabinet Office — Cabinet Minutes, Committee Papers, Other Papers.

PREM 11
Prime Minister's Office. Correspondence and Papers. 1951–64.

CO 1030
British Colonial Office — Original correspondence of the Far East Department relating to the Federation of Malaya and Singapore, 1954–1967.

DO 169
Commonwealth Relations Office. Far East and Pacific Department: Registered Files, 1960–1964.

FO 1091
File of the Office of the Commissioner General for the United Kingdom of Southeast Asia, 1955–1962.

DEFE 4/137
Chief of Staff Committee, Minutes.

FCO 51/154
Foreign Office. Research Files-South and Southeast Asia.

Rhodes House Library, Oxford University
Goode Papers

Australia (Australian Archives)
A 1838 Department of Foreign Affairs and Trade: Correspondence files, 1948–1989.

PUBLISHED OFFICIAL SOURCES

Dewan Ra'yat (Parliamentary Debates) Vol. 3, 1961.

Federation of Malaysia: Joint Statement by the Governments of the United Kingdom and of the Federation of Malaya. Command 1563 of 1961. London: Her Majesty's Stationery Office, 1961.

Lee Kuan Yew. *The Battle for Merger.* Singapore: Government Printing Office, 1961.

———. *Prime Minister's Speeches, Press Conferences, Interviews, Statements, etc.* Singapore: Prime Minister's Office, 1962–63.

Malaya. *Report of the Commission of Enquiry, North Borneo and Sarawak, 1962 (Cobbold Commision),* Command 1794. London: Her Majesty's Stationery Office, 1962.

Malaysia — Report of the Inter-Governmental Committee, 1962, Command 1954. London: HMSO, 1963.

Malaysia and Sarawak. Kuching: Government Printing Office, 1962.

Memorandum Setting out the Heads of Agreement for a Merger between the Federation of Malaya and Singapore, Command 33. Singapore: L. K. Heng, Government printer, 1961.

Ministry of Culture. *A Year of Decision.* Singapore: Government Printing Office, 1961.

Report of the Singapore Constitutional Conference held in London in March and April, 1957. Presented by the Secretary of State for the Colonies to Parliament by command of Her Majesty April 1957, Command 147. London: Her Majesty's Stationery Office, 1957.

Report of the Superintendent of the Singapore Referendum on the Results of the Referendum held on 1st September 1962, Command 18. Singapore: Singapore Government Printers, 1962.

Report on the Economic Aspects of Malaysia by a Mission of the International Bank for Reconstruction and Development; Under the Chairmanship of Jacques Rueff. Singapore: Government Printing Office, 1963.

Sarawak by the Week (various). Kuching: Government Information Service.

Select Committee on the Singapore National Referendum Bill: Official Report. Singapore: Government Printing Office, 1962.

Singapore Legislative Assembly Debates (1961–1963).

Tunku Abdul Rahman. *Looking Back — Monday Musings and Memories.* Kuala Lumpur: Pustaka Antara, 1977.

NEWSPAPER AND PERIODICALS

Far Eastern Economic Review
North Borneo News & Sabah Times
Sarawak Tribune
The Echo

Straits Times
Sunday Standard
Sunday Times

Party Publications
Petir (People's Action Party)
Barisan Sosialis. *Letter to the Secretary-General, United Nations, from Lee Siew Choh.* Singapore: Barisan Sosialis, 1963.

BOOKS
Bastin, John. *Malaysia: Selected Readings.* Nedeln: KTO Press, 1979.
Cheah Boon Kheng. *Malaysia: The Making of a Nation.* Singapore: Institute of Southeast Asia Studies, 2002.
————. "Ethnicity in the Making of Malaysia". In Wang Gungwu, ed., *Nation-building: Five Southeast Asian Histories*, pp. 91–115. Singapore: Institute of Southeast Asian Studies, 2005.
Chew Ernest C. T. and Edwin Lee, eds., *A History of Singapore.* Singapore: Oxford University Press, 1991.
Chin, John M. *Sarawak Chinese.* Kuala Lumpur: Oxford University Press, 1981.
Chin Kin Wah. *The Defence of Malaysia and Singapore: The Transformation of a Security System 1957–71.* Cambridge, New York: Cambridge University Press, 1983.
Chin Ung-Ho. *Chinese Politics in Sarawak: A Study of the Sarawak United Peoples Party.* New York: Oxford University Press, 1996.
Darby, Philip. *British Defence Policy East of Suez 1947–1968.* London: Oxford University Press, 1973.
Drysdale, John. *Singapore, Struggle for Success.* Singapore: Times Books International, 1984.
Hack, Karl. *Defence and Decolonisation in Southeast Asia: Britain, Malaysia and Singapore 1941–1968.* Richmond: Curzon, 2001.
Han Fook Kwang, Warren Fernandez, Sumiko Tan. *Lee Kuan Yew: The Man and His Ideas.* Singapore: Singapore Press Holdings and Times Editions, 1998.
Hanna, Willard A. *The Formation of Malaysia: New Factor in World Politics; An Analytical History and Assessment of the Prospects of the Newest State in Southeast Asia, based on a series of reports written for the American Universities Field Staff.* New York: American Field Staff, 1964.
Hill, Michael and Lian Kwen Fee. *The Politics of Nation Building and Citizenship in Singapore.* London; New York: Routledge, 1995.
Jayakumar, S. and Trindade, F.A. "Citizenship in Malaysia". *The Malayan Law Journal* (reprint), Singapore: Malayan Law Journal, 1964.
Jones, Matthew. *Conflict and Confrontation in Southeast Asia 1961–1965, Britain, the*

United States and the Creation of Malaysia. Cambridge; New York: Cambridge University Press, 2001.

Kudu, Nelson Liap. *Sarawak National Party: Its History, Organisation and Leadership.* Kuching: Sarawak Press Sdn. Bhd., 1973.

Lau, Albert. *A Moment of Anguish: Singapore in Malaysia and the Politics of Disengagement.* Singapore: Times Academic Press, 1998.

———. *The Malayan Union Controversy, 1942–48.* Singapore: Oxford University Press, 1990.

Lee Kuan Yew. *The Singapore Story: Memoirs of Lee Kuan Yew.* Singapore: Federal Publishing, 2000.

Leigh, Michael B. *The Rising Moon: Political Change in Sarawak.* Sydney: Sydney University Press; Portland, Or.: International Scholarly Book Services, 1974.

Harold MacMillan. *Memoirs: Volume VI, At the End of the Day, 1961–1963.* London: Macmillan Press, 1973.

Milne R. S. and K. J. Ratnam. *Malaysia — New States in a New Nation: Political Development of Sarawak and Sabah in Malaysia.* London: Frank Cass, 1974.

Saunders, Graham E. *A History of Brunei.* Kuala Lumpur; Singapore: Oxford University Press, 1994.

Sopiee, Mohamed Noordin. *From Malayan Union to Singapore Separation: Political Unification in the Malaysia Region 1945–1965.* Kuala Lumpur: Penerbit Universiti Malaya, 1974.

Ongkili, James P. *Nation-Building in Malaysia 1946–74.* Singapore: Oxford University Press, 1985.

———. *The Borneo Response to Malaysia 1961–63.* Singapore: D. Moore, 1967.

Osborne, Milton E. *Singapore and Malaysia.* Southeast Asia Program Data Paper No. 53. New York: Cornell University, 1964.

Ooi Kee Beng. *The Reluctant Politician: Tun Dr Ismail and His Time.* Singapore: Institute of Southeast Asian Studies, 2006.

Poulgrain, Greg. "The Genesis of Konfrontasi: Malaysia, Brunei and Indonesia". Adelaide: Crawford House Publishing, 1995.

Rahim, Lily Zubaidah. *The Singapore Dilemma: The Political and Educational Marginality of the Malay Community.* Kuala Lumpur: Oxford University Press, 1998.

Said Zahari. *Dark Clouds at Dawn: A Political Memoir.* Kuala Lumpur: INSAN, 2001.

Saunders, Graham. *A History of Brunei.* Kuala Lumpur: Oxford University Press, 1994.

Shafie, Ghazali, *Ghazali Shafie's Memoir on the Formation of Malaysia.* Bangi, Selangor: Penerbit Universiti Kebangsaan Malaysia, 1998.

Singh, Ranjit. *Brunei, 1839–1983: The Problems of Political Survival.* Singapore; New York: Oxford University Press, 1984.

Stockwell, Anthony J., ed. *Malaysia, British Documents on the End of Empire*. Series B; Volume 8. London: Stationery Office, 2004.

————. "Forging Malaysia and Singapore: Colonialism, Decolonisation and Nation-building". In Wang Gungwu, ed., *Nation-Building: Five Southeast Asian Histories*, pp. 191–219. Singapore: Institute of Southeast Asian Studies, 2005.

————. *British Policy and Malay Politics during the Malayan Union Experiment, 1945–48*. Singapore: Malaysian Branch of the Royal Asiatic Society, 1979.

Tarling, Nicholas. *Nations and States in Southeast Asia*. Cambridge and New York: Cambridge University Press, 1998.

Tunku Abdul Rahman. "Formation of Malaysia: The Trend Towards Merger Cannot Be Reversed". In *Looking Back: Monday Musings and Memories*, pp. 77–89. Kuala Lumpur: Pustaka Antara, 1977.

Turnbull, C. M. *A History of Singapore 1819–1988*. 2nd edition. Singapore: Oxford University Press, 1989.

Yeo Kim Wah. *Political Development in Singapore, 1950–55*. Singapore: Singapore University Press, 1973.

———— and Albert Lau. "From Colonialism to Independence, 1945–65". In *A History of Singapore*, Ernest Chew and Edwin Lee, eds., pp. 117–53. Singapore: Oxford University Press, 1991.

ARTICLES

Bradley, C. Paul. "The Formation of Malaysia". *Current History* (February 1964), pp. 89–116.

Dartford, Gerald P. "Plan for Malaysian Federation". *Current History* (November 1962), pp. 278–313.

Hanna, Willard A. "The Separation of Singapore from Malaysia". *American Universities Field Staff Report* 13, no. 21 (1965).

Jones, Matthew. "Creating Malaysia: Singapore Security, the Borneo Territories and the contours of British policy 1961–1963". *Journal of Imperial and Commonwealth History* 28, no. 2 (2000): 85–109.

Leifer, Michael. "Singapore in Malaysia: The Politics of Federation". *Journal of Southeast Asian History* 6, no. 2 (September 1965): 54–70.

Lipsker, S. "Formation of Malaysia". *Current Notes on International Affairs* 34 (October 1963), pp. 5–27.

Lockard, Craig A. "Leadership and Power Within the Chinese Community in Sarawak: A Historical Survey". *Journal of Southeast Asian Studies* 11, no. 2 (September 1971): 195–216 .

Means, Gordon. "Malaysia — A New Federation in Southeast Asia". *Pacific Affairs* 36, no. 2 (1963): 138–59.

Milne, R. S. "Malaysia: A New Federation in the Making". *Asian Survey* 3, no. 2 (February 1963): 76–82.

———. "Malaysia". *Asian Survey* 4, no. 2 (February 1964): 695–701.

———. "Singapore's Exit from Malaysia: The Consequences of Ambiguity". *Asian Survey* 6, no. 3 (March 1966): 175–84.

Ong Chit Chung. "The 1959 Singapore General Election". *Journal of Southeast Asian Studies* 6, no. 1 (1975): 61–86.

Smith, T. E. "Proposals for Malaysia". *The World Today* 18, no. 5 (May 1962).

Sopiee, Mohd. Noordin. "The Advocacy of Malaysia Before 1961". *Modern Asian Studies* 7, no. 4 (1973): 717–32.

Stockwell, Anthony J. "Colonial Planning during World War II: The Case of Malaya". *Journal of Imperial and Commonwealth History* 2, no. 3 (1974): 333–51.

———. "Malaysia: The Making of a Neo-colony". *Journal of Imperial and Commonwealth History* 26, no. 2 (May 1998): 138–56.

———. "Malaysia: The Making of a Grand Design". *Asian Affairs* 34, no. 3 (November 2003): 227–42.

———. "Britain and Brunei, 1945–1963: Imperial Retreat and Royal Ascendency". *Modern Asian Studies* 38, no. 4 (October 2004): 785–819.

Tarling, Nicholas. "Some Rather Nebulous Capacity: Lord Killearn's Appointment in Southeast Asia". *Modern Asian Studies* 20, no. 3 (July 1996): 559–600.

Tilman Robert O. "Malaysia: The Problems of Federation". *The Western Political Quarterly* 26, no. 4 (December 1963): 897–911.

White, Nicholas. "The Business and Politics of Decolonisation: The British Experience in the Twentieth Century". *Economic History Review* 53, no. 3 (August 2000): 544–64.

THESES

Tan, Sunny. "Barisan Sosialis: Years at the Front Line 1961–1966". Academic exercise submitted to the Department of History, National University of Singapore, 1997.

ORAL HISTORY INTERVIEW

Tun Tan Siew Sin, interview by the Oral History Centre on 29 March 1986 in Kuala Lumpur, National Archives of Singapore, Reel 1.

Index

1955 elections, 34
1959 Constitution, 25
1959 elections, 35
1961 announcement, 7, 9
1963 Constitutional Review Talks, 43

A

Abang Haji Mustapha, Datu Bandar,
    155
Abdul Aziz bin Haji Abdul Majid
    (Dato), 168
Abdul Rahman, Tunku, *see* Tunku
    Abdul Rahman
Abdul Razak, Tun, 55, 84, 104, 105,
    209
    Lee Kuan Yew, discussion with, 71
Abell, Anthony, 20, 162, 209
Admiralty House, 104
Alliance government
    fear regarding PMIP, 50
Amery, Julian, 19
Anglo-Malay constitutional
    discussions (1946), 32
Anglo-Malayan Agreement
    (November 1961), 161
Anglo-Malayan talks, 162
arrests without trials, 35
Attlee, Clement
    priority for liquidation of Indian
        empire, 14
Australia, 18

Azahari, A.M., 209
    leader of Party Rakyat Brunei
        (PRB), 172
    political appeal of, 172
    President of Party Ra'ayat of
        Brunei, 158
    self-proclamation as prime
        minister of Kalimantan Utara,
        174
    stirring up of anti-Malaysia feelings,
        173

B

Barisan Rakyat Jati Sarawak
    (BARJASA), 156
Barisan Sosialis (Socialist Front, BS), 7
    advocate of complete merger, 87
    citizenship issue, debate on, 103, 115
    concessions for special powers, offer
        of, 157
    objections to merger, 76
    press statement re citizenship issue,
        107
    rivalry with PAP, 7
Borneo Development Fund
    Singapore's contribution, 141
Borneo territories
    British plans for, 152–54
    Cobbold Report, 101
    constitutional safeguards, 160, 164
    distrust of Malays, 163

employment for Singapore workers
in, 149
entry into Malaysia, 180
governors' views regarding merger,
152
initial responses to Tunku's merger
announcement, 154
integration of, 6
leaders' visit to Malaya, 160
loan from Singapore, 142
manner of incorporation into
Malaysia, 197
Philippine claim, 160
Tunku's enthusiasm re merger, 151
Bourdillon, H.T., 26, 55, 209
Britain
Brunei, views on need for merger
for, 179
commitment to merger, 25
Grand Design, 190
British bases
Tunku's proposals, 69
British Colonial Development and
Welfare Funds, 170
British Nationality Acts, 81
British policies
post-war Southeast Asia, 13
Brunei
anti-Malaysia feelings, 173
British opinion on merger, 179
delegation to MSCC deliberations,
175
distancing itself from suggestions of
a federation, 153
reasons for staying out of Malaysia,
175, 176
reluctance to enter merger, 17
Brunei Revolt, 189
effects of, 172–82

impact on Sultan's decision, 174
pacified by British-led Gurkha
troops, 178
significant challenge to political
authority of Sultan, 178
bumiputra rights, 196
Byrne, K.M., 97

C
Cabinet Colonial Policy, 24
capital development expenditure, 132
Cardinal Principles of the English
Rajah, 161
Central African Federation
collapse of, 153
Central Bank, Stock Exchange, 51
Cheah Boon Kheng, 6, 116
Chew Swee Kee, 36, 209
Chinese community
Sarawak, 20
Chinese education policy
implications of merger, 87
Chinese middle school riots, 16
Chinese students
militants, 35
chronology of events, 205–207
Citizenship Arrangements for
Singapore Within the Proposed
Federation of Malaysia, 118
citizenship issue, 91–121
Barisan Sosialis' arguments, 91, 92,
97
Borneo territories, 101, 102
British unwillingness to intervene,
111
Chinese in Singapore, 102
controversy, 93–103
David Marshall, opposition of, 94
Lee Siew Choh, views of, 94

Malayan citizens, right of, 94
re-negotiations, 104–12
referendum, 112
right to vote, issue of, 94
Singapore Citizenship Ordinance, 97
Singapore White Paper proposals,
91, 92
citizenship rights
persons born in Malaya, 117, 118
civil service
quota of jobs to Malays, 106
Cobbold (Lord), 209
discussions with Sultan of Brunei,
175
personal note to Macmillan, 164
Cobbold Commission, 161–66
Brunei, turning down of offer by,
180
tension between Malayan and
British officials, 163
transitional period after formation
of Malaysia, 164
Cobbold Report, 101
Tunku's objections, 165
Cold War, 22
Colonial Office
fears concerning Singapore, 34
union of Malay states, plans for, 15
Colonial Policy Committee, 24
Commission of Enquiry, 161
common market, 123–50
agreement on, 141–46
compromise, 194
negotiations, 134–40
Commonwealth Parliamentary
Association
meeting in Singapore, 159
Commonwealth Relations Office, 29,
159

communism
Tunku's fear, 5
communist China
emergence of, 17
communists
promise of support to PAP, 43
Constitutional Review Talks (1963), 43
constitutional safeguards
Borneo territories, for, 160
Consultative Committee meetings
best interest of peoples of Borneo
territories, 181
Council of Joint Action
opposition to merger plans, 103
Critchley, T.K., 108, 128, 209
Crown Colony
establishment of Singapore as, 31

D
Datu Bandar Abang Haji Mustapha,
155, 210
decolonization
aspects of British policy, 13–28
defence framework, British, 59
Democratic and United Parties, 168

E
East Indies
Dutch's loss of empire, 13
East of Suez, 29, 32
Economic Development Board, 135
economic relations
Singapore and Malaya, 61
Eden Hall Conference, 23
education
English as medium of instruction,
80
Malay citizens in Singapore, 42

elections
  1955, 34
  1959, 35
Emergency, 96
English language
  medium of instruction in Singapore
    schools, 80
Europe
  economic fatigue, 13

F
FCO Research Department
  Memorandum, 184, 198
Federal Constitution
  Article 22, 97
Federal Constitutional Amendment
  (1962), 105
Federal Nationals, 81
Federation government
  power during transitional period
    after formation of Malaysia, 164
Federation of Malaya, 184
  compromise, 194
  danger of keeping Singapore out of,
    58
  financial arrangements
  Inter-Governmental Committee
    (IGC), 167
  political difference with Singapore,
    50
  tariffs on imported goods, 38
Federation of Malaysia: Joint
    Statement of the Governments of
    the United Kingdom and the
Federation Police Commission, 81
Federation Citizen (Singapore), 106
financial arrangements
  agreement on, 141–46
Five-Power Federation, 53

Foreign Office
  union of Malay states, plans for, 15
France
  opposition from Viet Minh forces, 14

G
Ghazali bin Shafie, 68, 105, 211
  Cobbold Commission, 162
  Lee Kuan Yew, dialogues with, 70,
    71
  memoirs, 8
  research on Ulster Constitution, 70
  view on Brunei's omission, 181
Goh Keng Swee, 37, 44, 77, 78, 98, 106,
    137, 210
  common market, emphasis on, 124
  Internal Security Council,
    discussion on, 71
Goode, William, 154, 158, 210
Grand Design, 13–28, 45
  concern with British bases, 22
  desirability of, 21
  emphasis on, 9
  formation of anti-communist super
    federation, 21
  Lee Kuan Yew's paper on, 45
  maintenance of British influence, 22
  merger as major component of, 24
  urgency for, 18
Great Britain
  withdrawal from Indian
    subcontinent, 14
Greater Malaysia, 21
  broad framework, 58
  formation of, 30
  objection by Sukarno, 22
  political attitudes towards, 29–65
  solution to satisfy all parties, 47
  specific conditions, 68

H

Hong Lim constituency
  by-election, 44
  Ong Eng Guan, 43

I

Ibans
  fear of domination by Malays, 169
Indian subcontinent
  British withdrawal from, 14
Indonesia
  declaration of independence, 14
  rejection of UN's findings, 190
industrial development programme, 38
Inter-Governmental Committee (IGC)
    on Federation/Singapore Merger,
    124, 166–72
  completion of negotiations, 171
  detailed terms of merger, working
    out of, 125
  financial arrangements and
    common market, 167
  indecisiveness of Malayan
    delegation, 168
  Singapore's alternative proposal to,
    130
  terms of reference, 167
  Twenty Points represented by North
    Borneo representatives, 168
  unresolved issues, discussion of, 126
inter-territorial conference, 23
Internal Security Council, 42, 55, 60
  Barisan Sosialis' view on, 77
  meeting between UK and Singapore
    delegation, 62
International Bank for Reconstruction
    and Development (IBRD), 136
Ismail Abdul Rahman (Dr), 52, 55, 84,
    210

J

Japanese occupation
  sponsorship of nationalist leaders, 13
Jones, Matthew, 8, 191
Jurong
  development of, 135

K

Kadazan Society
  objection to Malaysia Plan, 155
Konfrontasi, 189, 190

L

Labour Front, 33
  1955 elections, 34
Lansdowne, Marquess of, 210
  admission re financial position of
    Federation, 170
  remarks relating to IGC, 168
Lee Kuan Yew, 7, 192
  advocacy for "democratic
    Malaysian Malaysia", 195
  advocate of "independence through
    merger", 30, 37
  Borneo territories, 160
  call for resignation of Lim Yew
    Hock government, 36
  common market, emphasis on, 124
  creation of pan-Malayan outlook in
    Singapore, 42
  debate with Marshall re citizenship
    issue, 112
  Ghazali Shafie, discussion with, 71
  Internal Security Council,
    discussion on, 71
  leader of PAP, 6
  memoirs, 6, 8
  Memorandum of Malaysia, 160
  National Day Rally (1961), 48

paper on Grand Design, 45, 46, 47
paper setting out proposed basis for
    agreement, 74
proposal for Citizen of the New
    Federation (Singapore), 106
radio broadcast, 107
Tan Siew Sin, rivalry with, 133
The Singapore Story, 6
Tun Abdul Razak, discussion with,
    71
United Nations, appearance before,
    103
White Paper, publishing of, 76
Lee Siew Choh, 98, 101, 121, 210
views on citizenship issue, 94
Legislative Assembly
push for National Referendum Bill,
    113
Lennox-Boyd, Alan, 20, 210
memorandum for Cabinet Colonial
    Policy, 26
Lim Chin Siong, 39, 57, 210
Lim Swee Aun, 128, 136, 210
Lim Yew Hock, 33, 210
Chief Minister, as, 35
merger, in favour of, 33
London archives
declassification of records, 8
London Agreement on Citizenship, 106
London Talks, 140–41

M
MacDonald, Malcolm, 15, 32, 52, 210
MacLeod, Ian, 158, 187
assurances to Tunku regarding
    Cobbold Report, 166
memorandum for Cabinet Colonial
    Committee, 43
Macmillan, Harold, 70, 104, 153, 210

Malay Affairs Bureau
PAP, in, 42
Malay Education Advisory
    Committee, 42
Malay language
national language Singapore, 42
Malay nationalism
opposition of Malayan Union plan,
    16
Malaya
primary producer in rubber and tin,
    14
pursuit of Greater Malaysia, 48–59
Malayan Chinese Association (MCA),
    49, 157
Malayan citizens
special rights, 110
Malayan Constitution
Article 3 (1), 170
Malayan Indian Congress, 49
Malayan Special Branch, 193
Malayan Union
British post-war plan, 16
uproar against, 16, 96
Malayan Union Alliance, 34
Malays
ethnic dominance, securing of, 192
political primacy in Federation, 49
quota for civil service, 106
Malacca, 59
Malaysia
circumstances of origin, 197
Malaysia Day, 145
Malaysia Solidarity Consultative
    Committee (MSCC), 71
Brunei delegation, 175
establishment of, 159
third meeting, 100

Malaysian Agreement, 104, 146
Annex J, 142, 144
Article 1(3), 142
Malaysian Citizens, 95, 98, 103
Malaysian Federation
to remain indigenous majority state,
6
Malaysian Nationals, 95, 98, 103
Malaysian Plan
marketing of, 158–61
rushing forward of, 153
Malaysian Solidarity Convention
(MSC), 195, 196
establishment of, 159
Malaysian Tariff Board, 137, 138
Malphilindo, 189
Manila Agreement, 189
Marshall, David, 33, 211
debate re citizenship provisions, 111
first Chief Minister of Singapore,
34
opposition to citizenship provision,
94
resignation of, 34
Maulding, Reginald, 211
Melayu Raya, 190
Memorandum of Malaysia, 160
Memorandum Setting out Heads of
Agreement for a Merger between
the Federation of Malaya and
Singapore, 85, 147
merger
Chinese in Singapore, issue of, 48
citizenship, issue of, 83, 91–121
civil service, effect on, 80
common market, 123–50
complicated negotiation terms, 7
details discussed in London, 78
economic reasons for, 39

financial arrangements, 123–50
financial relations between
Singapore and Federation, 83
importance to Singapore, 24
Lee Kuan Yew's belief in necessity
of, 37
political attitudes, 29–65
referendum on, 72, 86, 88
security considerations, 6
special conditions, 10
Tunku's announcement (27 May), 89
Tunku's reservations, 5
Working Party, 73
militants
challenge to Lee Kuan Yew, 40
Ministry of Home Affairs
Singapore, 79
Mohar, Raja, 136
Moore, Philip, 41, 73, 75, 211
Mountbatten, Louis, 21, 211

N
National Referendum Bill, 113
nationalist leaders
Japanese sponsorship, 13
Nationals of the Federation, 108
New Zealand, 18
Ningkan, Stephen, 156
Noordin Sopiee, 52
North Borneo
crown colony, 17
demand for key safeguards, 169
Legisative Assembly, 169
renamed to Sabah, 169
North Borneo National Army (Tentera
Nasional Kalimantan Utara), 173

O
Ong Eng Guan, 43, 47, 211

Ong Kee Hui, 158
Operation Cold Store, 193
Othman Wok, 42, 211

P
Pan Malayan Islamic Party (PMIP), 30
    political support, waning, 50
Party Negara Sarawak (PANAS), 155,
    156
Party Pesaka Anak Sarawak
    (PESAKA), 156
Party Ra'ayat of Brunei (PRB), 158
Party Rakyat Brunei (PRB), 172, 178
    stirring up anti-Malaysia feelings,
        173
Penang, 59
People's Action Party (PAP), 6
    1959 elections, 36
    advocate of "independence through
        merger", 30
    left-wing
        opposition to merger, 40
    Malay Affairs Bureau, 42
    merger, push for, 36
    National Referendum Bill, push for,
        113
    policies of conciliation and
        goodwill, 42
    Sixth Anniversary Celebrations
        Souvenir, 61
    threatened resignation, 43
Philippines
    claim to North Borneo, 160, 189, 191
policy-makers
    London, 32
pro-communists
    influence of, 39
Profumo, John, 21
prosperity index, 130

R
Rajaratnam, S., 98, 212
referendum on merger, 72, 86, 88, 112–
    17
    Alternative A, 115
    Alternative C, 115
    alternatives, 114
    blank ballots, treatment of, 114
    lead up to, 115
    Select Committee, 114
regional cooperation
    creation of structure of, 15
Rendel Constitution
    adoption of, 33
Rendel Report, 60
Report of the Commission of Enquiry
    North Borneo and Sarawak, 119, 185
Report of the Singapore Constitutional
    Conference, 60
Report of the Superintendent of the
    Singapore Referendum on the
    Results of the Referendum, 121
revenue tariffs, 138
riots
    Chinese middle schools in
        Singapore, 16
Rubber Market, 51
Rueff, Jacques (Professor), 136, 137,
    211
    report, 143, 144
    suggestion, 138
    terms of reference, 148

S
Sabah, 169, 189
Samad bin Ismail, 211
Sandys, Duncan, 21, 141, 142, 171, 211
    visit to Malaya (1961), 56
Sarawak, 17

Chinese community, 20
Council Negri, 169
demand for key safeguards, 169
White Paper outlining advantages
    of joining Malaysia, 161
Sarawak Chinese Association (SCA),
    156
Sarawak National Party (SNAP), 156
Sarawak United People's Party
    (SUPP), 155, 158, 169
Scott, Robert, 20, 211
Sea Dayaks, 169
Security Council of Singapore, 193
Select Committee on the Singapore
    National Referendum Bill, 114,
    121
Selkirk (Lord), 7, 23, 44, 53, 73, 211
    meeting with governors of Borneo
        territories, 158
    recommendations, 24
    remark to Macleod, 158
    Tunku and Lee to London, 70
    view on tussle over financial
        control, 128
Senu Abdul Rahman, 53
Singapore
    autonomous powers, 106
    Borneo Development Fund,
        contribution to, 141
    Borneo territories, loan to, 142
    citizenship, issue of, 194
    coalition government, 34
    command of vital sea lanes, 14
    Chinese middle school riots, 16
    Chinese population, 16, 48
    Crown Colony, as, 31
    declaration of independence, 190
    demand for independence, 6
    duty free entry of goods, 51

economy
    dependence on provision of
        services to Malaya, 51
    education, control over, 72
    enthusiasm for merger with Malaya,
        19
    fear of it turning to communism, 5
    Federation, danger of keeping out
        of, 58
    financial control, tussle over, 125,
        133
    free port, 38
    Head of State, 42
    independence through merger, 6,
        31–48
    internal self-government, 60
    labour costs, 136
    Malay citizens, 42
    merger, independence through, 6, 24
    national language, 42
    "New York of Malaysia", as, 193
    opposition to merger in Legislative
        Assembly, 194
    pan-Malayan outlook, creation of,
        42
    police, control of, 79
    political differences with
        Federation, 50
    powers, exclusive, 74
    "problem child", considered as, 192
    representation in Central
        Parliament, 129
    riots, 35
    self government, heading towards,
        18
    separation from Malaya (1946), 16
    separation from Malaysia, 197
    smaller representation in merger, 67
    social services, expenditure of, 147

surplus revenue, treatment of, 129,
130, 131
taxes, collection of, 126, 130, 132
trade unions protests, 16
Singapore Citizen (National of the
New Federation)
Lee's proposal, 105
Singapore citizens
rights after merger, 95
voting rights, 104
Singapore Citizenship Ordinance, 97
Singapore Civil Service, 80, 81
Singapore Labour Party, 33
organizational base, 60
Singapore Legislative Assembly
debates on merger, 85, 86
Singapore People's Alliance (SPA), 36,
146
Singapore Police Force, 81
control by Federation, 82
Singapore Port and Harbour, 79
Singapore Progressive Party (SPP), 32
1955 elections, 34
Singapore White Paper on merger, 79–
88
Heads of Agreement, 93, 125
publication date, 85
Southeast Asia
domination of British businesses, 22
SPA-UMNO Alliance, 113
State Port Authority, 79
Stephens, Donald, 155, 158, 212
Stockwell, Anthony, 8, 19, 22, 191, 198
Straits Settlements, 59
Subandrio, Dr, 198
Sultan of Brunei
discussions with Cobbold, 176
impact of Brunei Revolt, 174
opposition to merger, 177

refusal to subject kingdom to
Sarawak control, 17
suspicion over relationship with
Malaya, 176
view towards integration, 20
views on joining Malaysia, 172–82
Sultan Omar Ali Saifuddin III, 174,
175
Sultan of Sulu, 190
Sukarno, 190, 212
revolutionary politics, 22

T
Tan, C. C., 32, 212
call for early tie-up between
Singapore and Federation, 33
Tan Siew Sin, 78, 82, 84, 105, 128, 133,
139, 212
Lee Kuan Yew's political rival, 133
President of MCA, 133
rejection of Singapore's proposals,
126, 127
Tariff Advisory Board, 143
Tariff Advisory Board Act, 144
taxes
apportionment of collections, 132
collection of, 126, 150
trade unions
protests, 16
The Singapore Story, 6
Toh Chin Chye, 212
Tory, Geofroy, 41, 52, 110, 212
transitional arrangement, after
formation of Malaysia, 165, 166
view on tussle over financial
control, 128
Trade Union Ordinances, 99
Tun Abdul Razak, 55, 84
Lee Kuan Yew, discussion with, 71

Tunku Abdul Rahman, 209
  1961 announcement, 7, 9, 20
  Borneo territories, concern over, 71, 163
  Brunei, attitude towards, 54
  Brunei, personal visit to, 176
  change in nomenclature, conceding to a, 107
  Chinese, fears relating to, 68, 116
  citizenship, statement on, 108, 109
  early refusal relating to merger, 35
  enthusiasm over
  essential conditions for merger, 67
  fears that Lee Kuan Yew's support dwindling, 57
  Grand Design, more receptive to, 51
  inter-racial cooperation, development of, 62
  interest in wider Malay-based Federation, 182
  leader of UMNO, 20
  memoirs, 8
  mistrust of Chinese, 68
  objections to recommendations of Cobbold Commission, 165
  policy of benevolent neutrality, 153
  promise of parliamentary seats to North Borneo and Sarawak, 170
  proposal re British bases, 69
  radical Chinese influence, fear of, 49
  reservations about merger, 5
Turnbull, Roland, 20, 212
Twenty Points, 168, 169

U
U Thant, 190, 212
Ulster-type merger, 10, 67–90

UN Mission
  Sabah and Sarawak, 190
United Malays National Organisation (UMNO), 16
  political dominance of, 50
  right wing leader of, 20
United National Kadazan Organization (UNKO), 158, 168
United Nations
  intervention by, 189
United Sabah National Organization (USNO), 168
UNPMO, 168

V
Viet Minh forces, 14

W
Waddell, Alexander, 158, 212
Watterston, David, 162
White, Dennis, 175, 212
White Paper on merger, 79–88
  British views on, 75
  citizenship agreement, 108
  consideration by Federal Government, 82
  draft sent to Philip Moore, 79
  Heads of Agreement, 104
  Lee's intentions, 76
Wong Pow Nee, 162, 212
Working Party
  details of merger, 73
  meeting in KL, 74
  terms of reference, 74
Wright, Thomas, 27, 52

Y
Yong, Stephen, 155, 212

About the Author

TAN Tai Yong is a historian at the National University of Singapore. His recent books include: *Partition and Post-Colonial South Asia — A Reader* (2007, co-edited); *The Garrison State. The Military, Government and Society in Colonial Punjab* (2005); *The Aftermath of Partition in South Asia* (2000 and 2002, co-authored with Gyanesh Kudaisya); and *Decolonisation and the Transformation of Southeast Asia* (2003, co-edited).